Memoirs
of a Book Thief

First published in English in 2019
by SelfMadeHero
139-141 Pancras Road
London NW1 1UN
www.selfmadehero.com

Written by: Alessandro Tota
Illustrated by: Pierre Van Hove
Translated from the French edition by Edward Gauvin

Publishing Director: Emma Hayley
Sales & Marketing Manager: Sam Humphrey
Editorial & Production Manager: Guillaume Rater
Layout designer: Kate McLauchlan
UK Publicist: Paul Smith
With thanks to: Nick de Somogyi

ROYAUME-UNI

This book is supported by the Institut français (Royaume-Uni)
as part of the Burgess programme.

First published in French by Futuropolis in 2015
© Futuropolis, Paris, 2015

A CIP record for this book is available from the British Library

ISBN: 978-1-910593-63-9

10 9 8 7 6 5 4 3 2 1

Printed and bound in Slovenia

Memoirs
of a Book Thief

Written by...A. TOTA
Illustrated by................................P. VAN HOVE
Translated by....................................E. GAUVIN

SELF MADE HERO

C H A P T E R 1

"WORK IS FOR SUCKERS."
LINDA C.

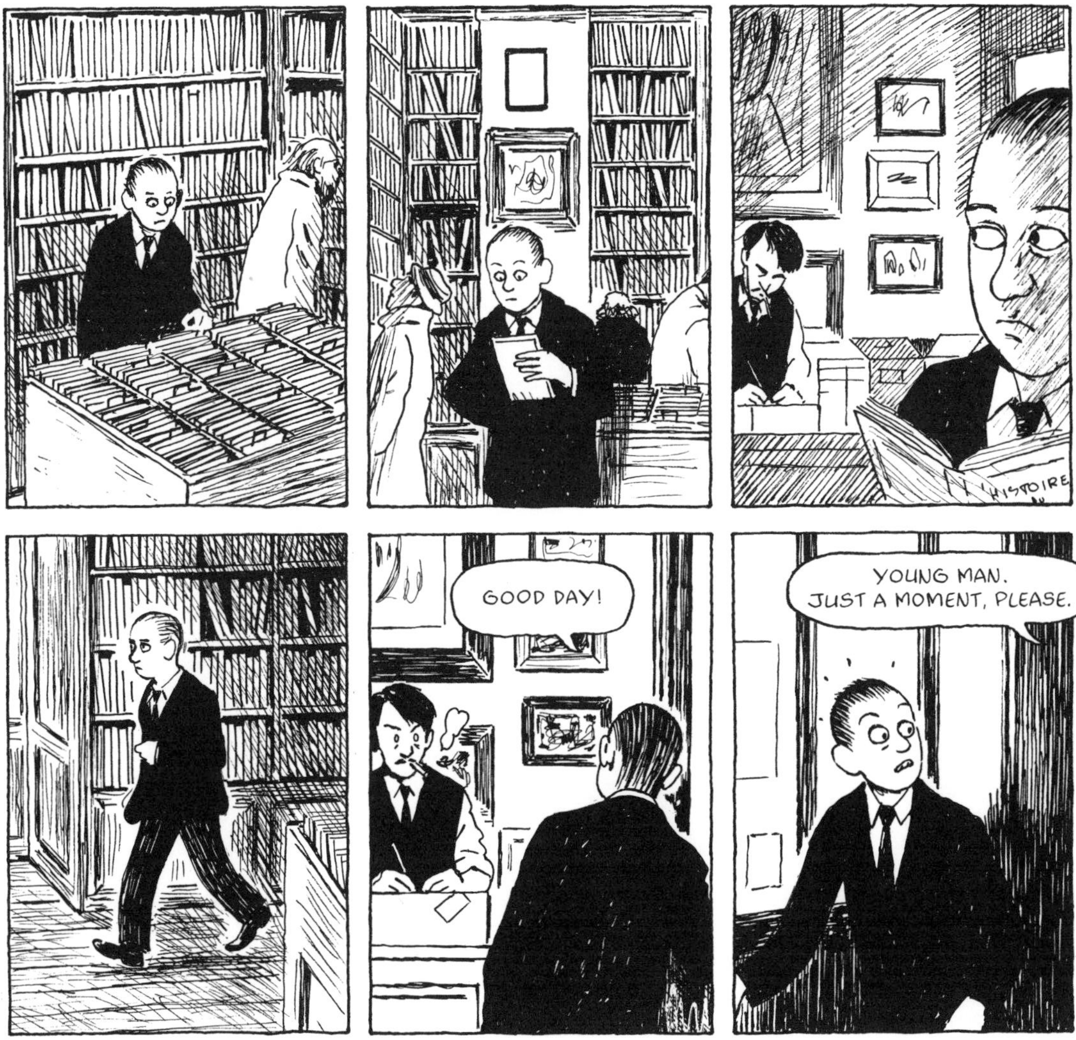
HISTOIRE
GOOD DAY!
YOUNG MAN. JUST A MOMENT, PLEASE.

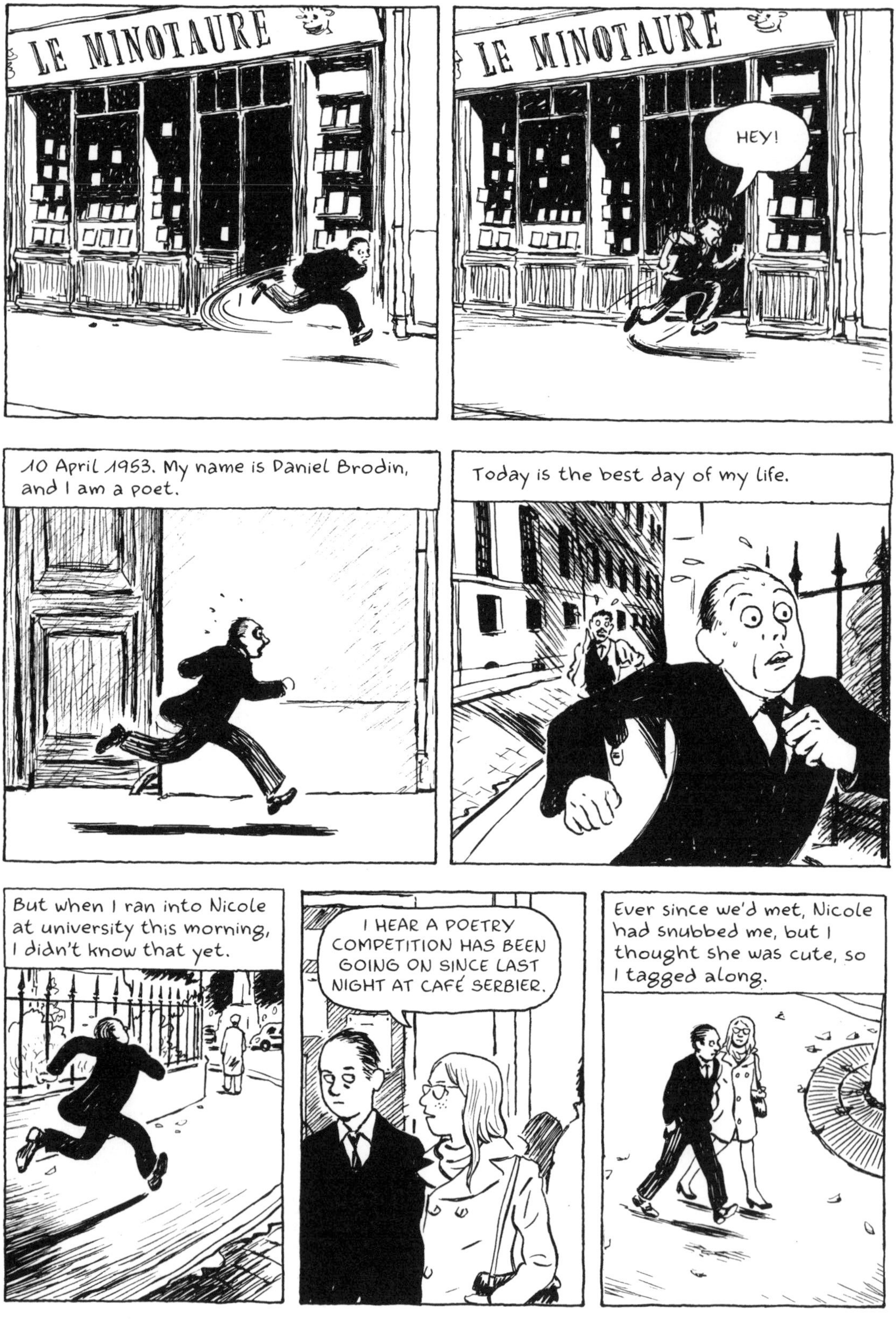
LE MINOTAURE
LE MINOTAURE
HEY!
10 April 1953. My name is Daniel Brodin, and I am a poet.
Today is the best day of my life.
But when I ran into Nicole at university this morning, I didn't know that yet.
I HEAR A POETRY COMPETITION HAS BEEN GOING ON SINCE LAST NIGHT AT CAFÉ SERBIER.
Ever since we'd met, Nicole had snubbed me, but I thought she was cute, so I tagged along.

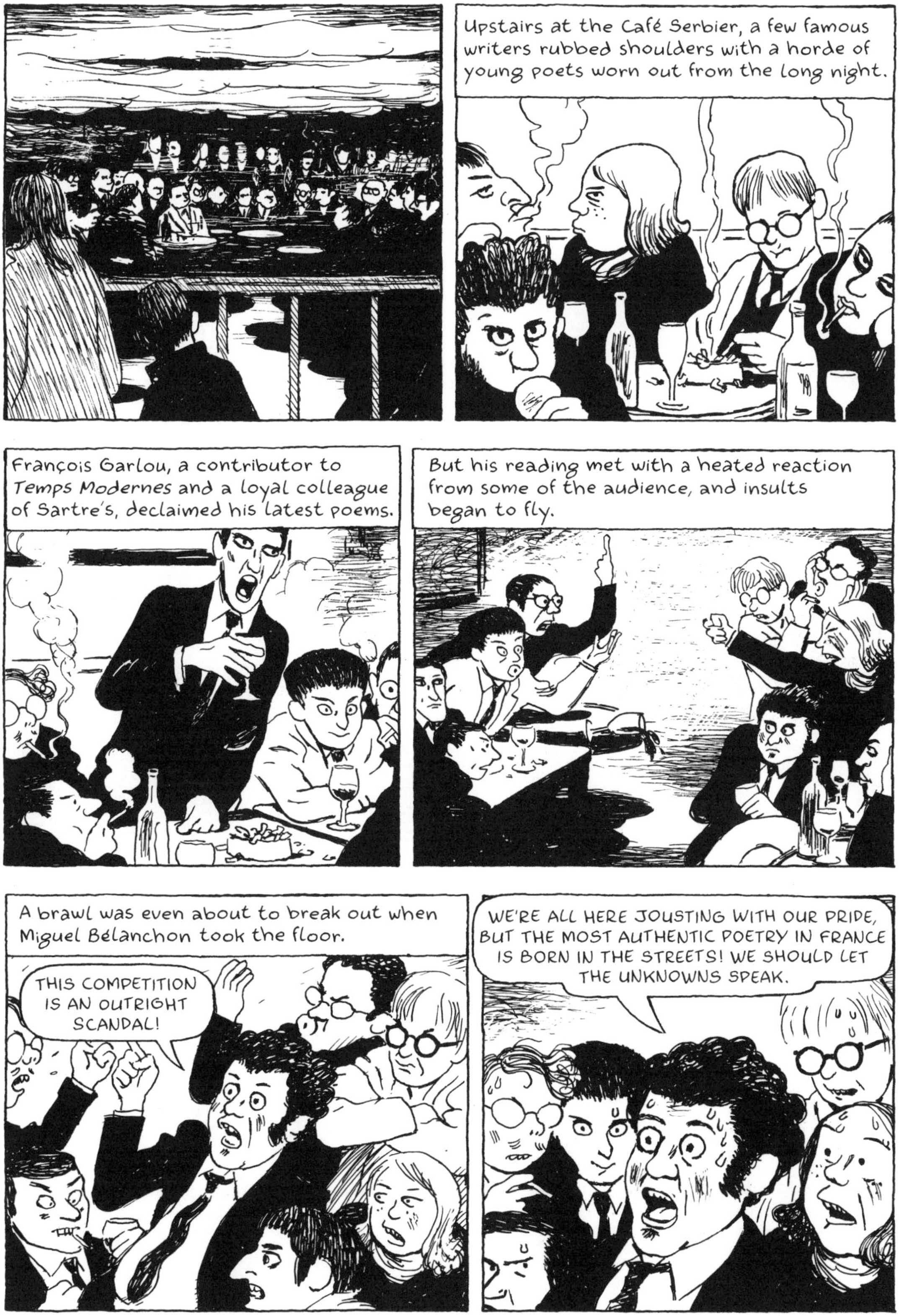
Upstairs at the Café Serbier, a few famous writers rubbed shoulders with a horde of young poets worn out from the long night.
François Garlou, a contributor to *Temps Modernes* and a loyal colleague of Sartre's, declaimed his latest poems.
But his reading met with a heated reaction from some of the audience, and insults began to fly.
A brawl was even about to break out when Miguel Bélanchon took the floor.
THIS COMPETITION IS AN OUTRIGHT SCANDAL!
WE'RE ALL HERE JOUSTING WITH OUR PRIDE, BUT THE MOST AUTHENTIC POETRY IN FRANCE IS BORN IN THE STREETS! WE SHOULD LET THE UNKNOWNS SPEAK.

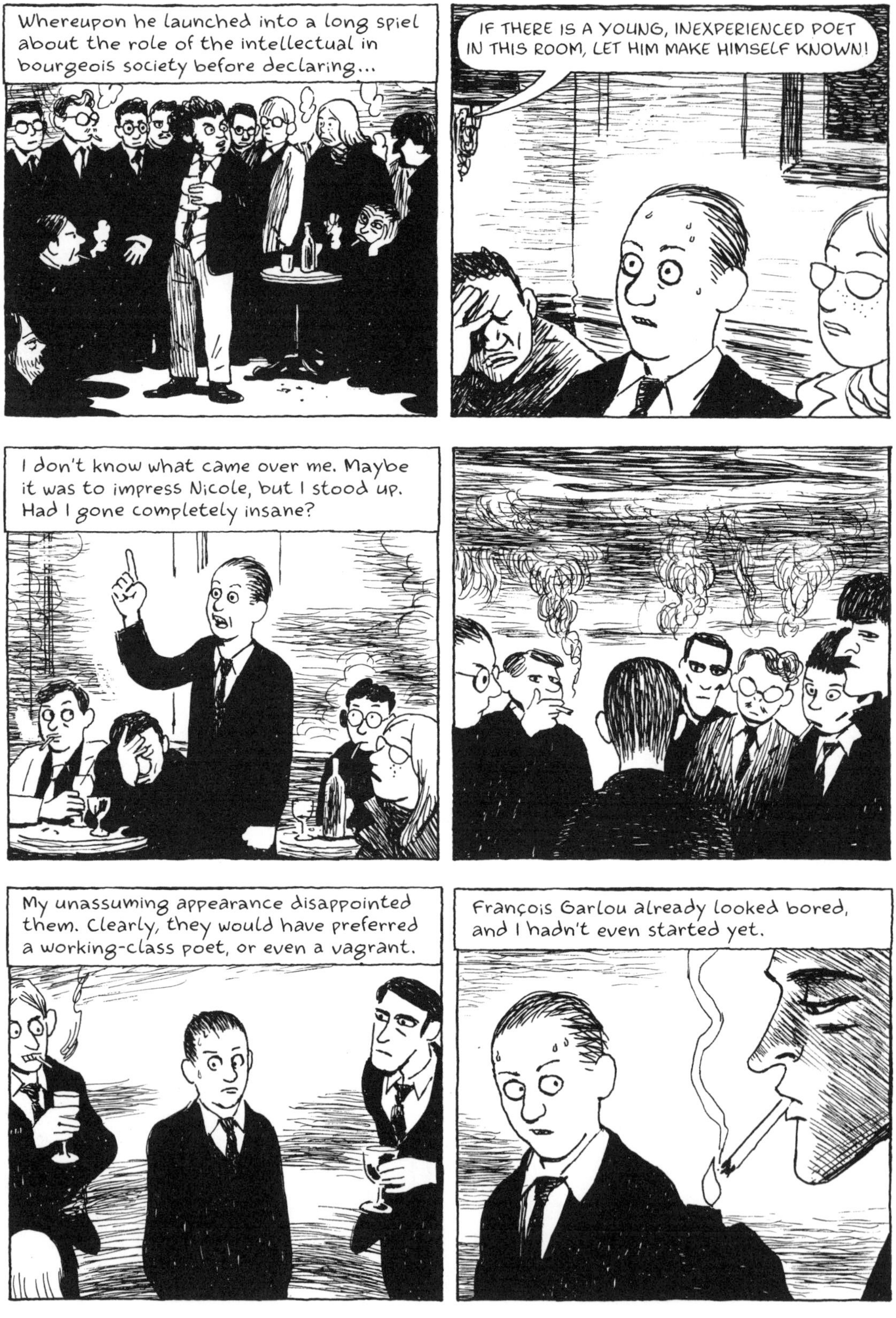
Whereupon he launched into a long spiel about the role of the intellectual in bourgeois society before declaring...
IF THERE IS A YOUNG, INEXPERIENCED POET IN THIS ROOM, LET HIM MAKE HIMSELF KNOWN!
I don't know what came over me. Maybe it was to impress Nicole, but I stood up. Had I gone completely insane?
My unassuming appearance disappointed them. Clearly, they would have preferred a working-class poet, or even a vagrant.
François Garlou already looked bored, and I hadn't even started yet.

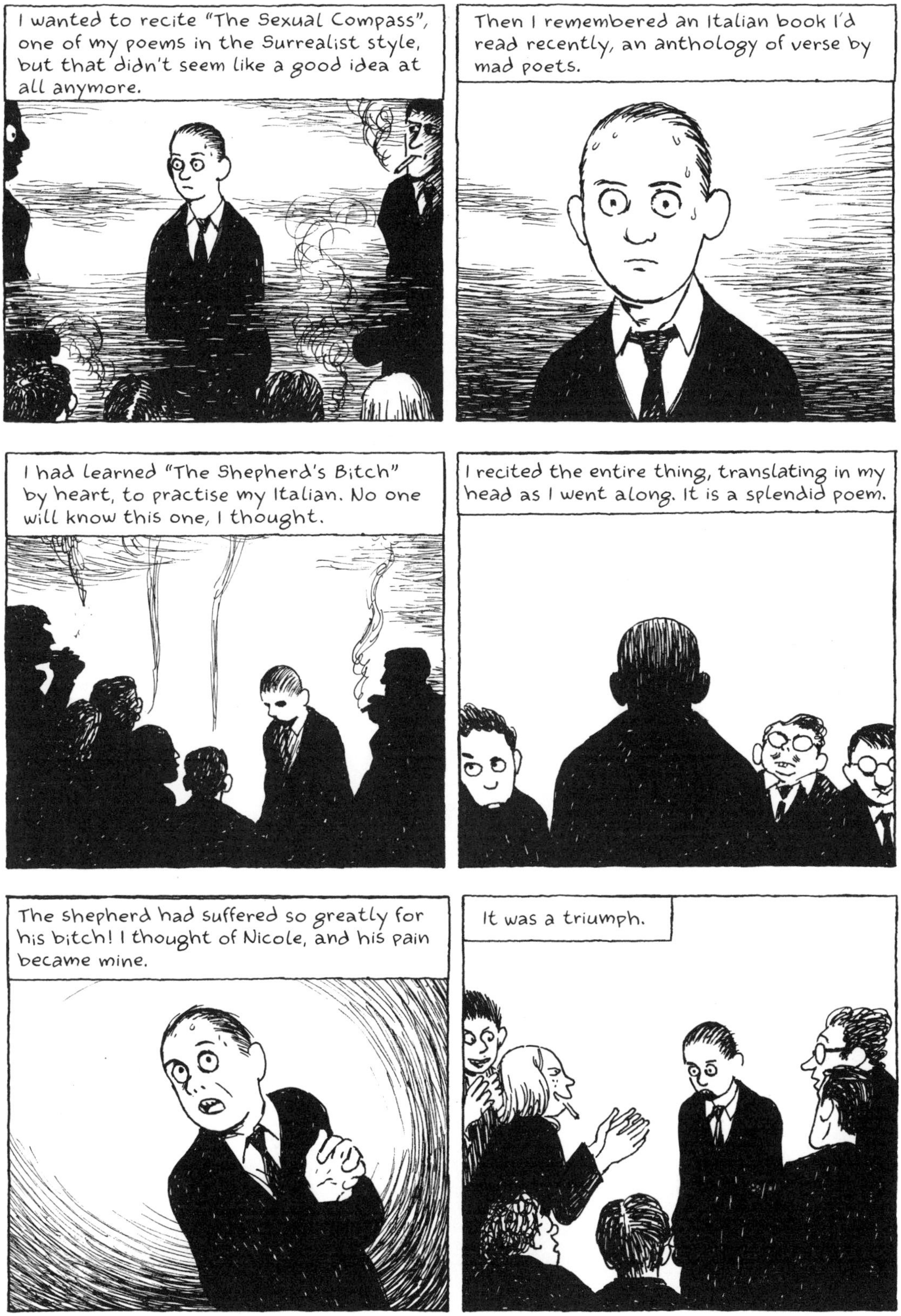
I wanted to recite "The Sexual Compass", one of my poems in the Surrealist style, but that didn't seem like a good idea at all anymore.
Then I remembered an Italian book I'd read recently, an anthology of verse by mad poets.
I had learned "The Shepherd's Bitch" by heart, to practise my Italian. No one will know this one, I thought.
I recited the entire thing, translating in my head as I went along. It is a splendid poem.
The shepherd had suffered so greatly for his bitch! I thought of Nicole, and his pain became mine.
It was a triumph.

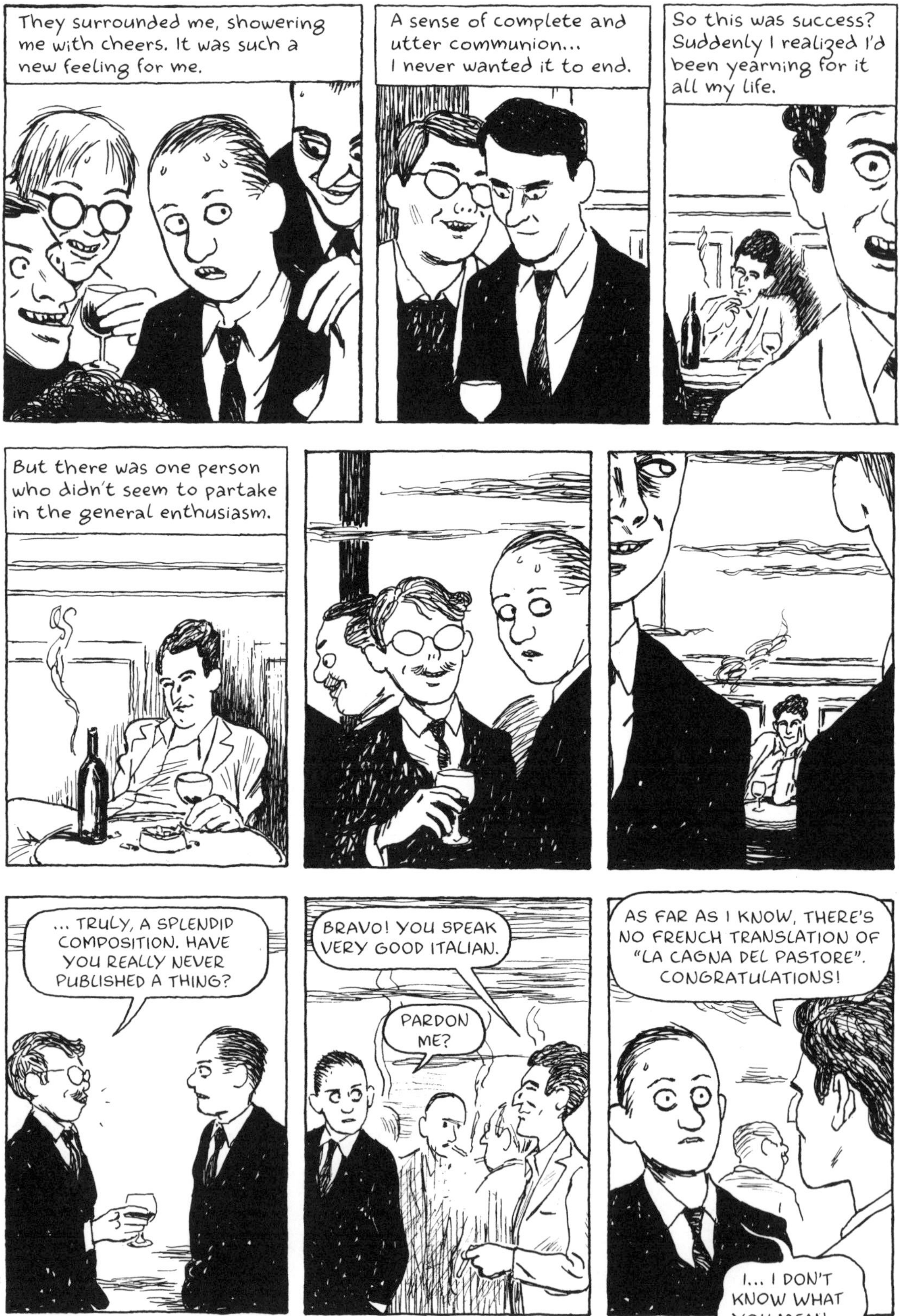

They surrounded me, showering me with cheers. It was such a new feeling for me.
A sense of complete and utter communion... I never wanted it to end.
So this was success? Suddenly I realized I'd been yearning for it all my life.
But there was one person who didn't seem to partake in the general enthusiasm.
... TRULY, A SPLENDID COMPOSITION. HAVE YOU REALLY NEVER PUBLISHED A THING?
BRAVO! YOU SPEAK VERY GOOD ITALIAN.
PARDON ME?
AS FAR AS I KNOW, THERE'S NO FRENCH TRANSLATION OF "LA CAGNA DEL PASTORE". CONGRATULATIONS!
I... I DON'T KNOW WHAT YOU MEAN...

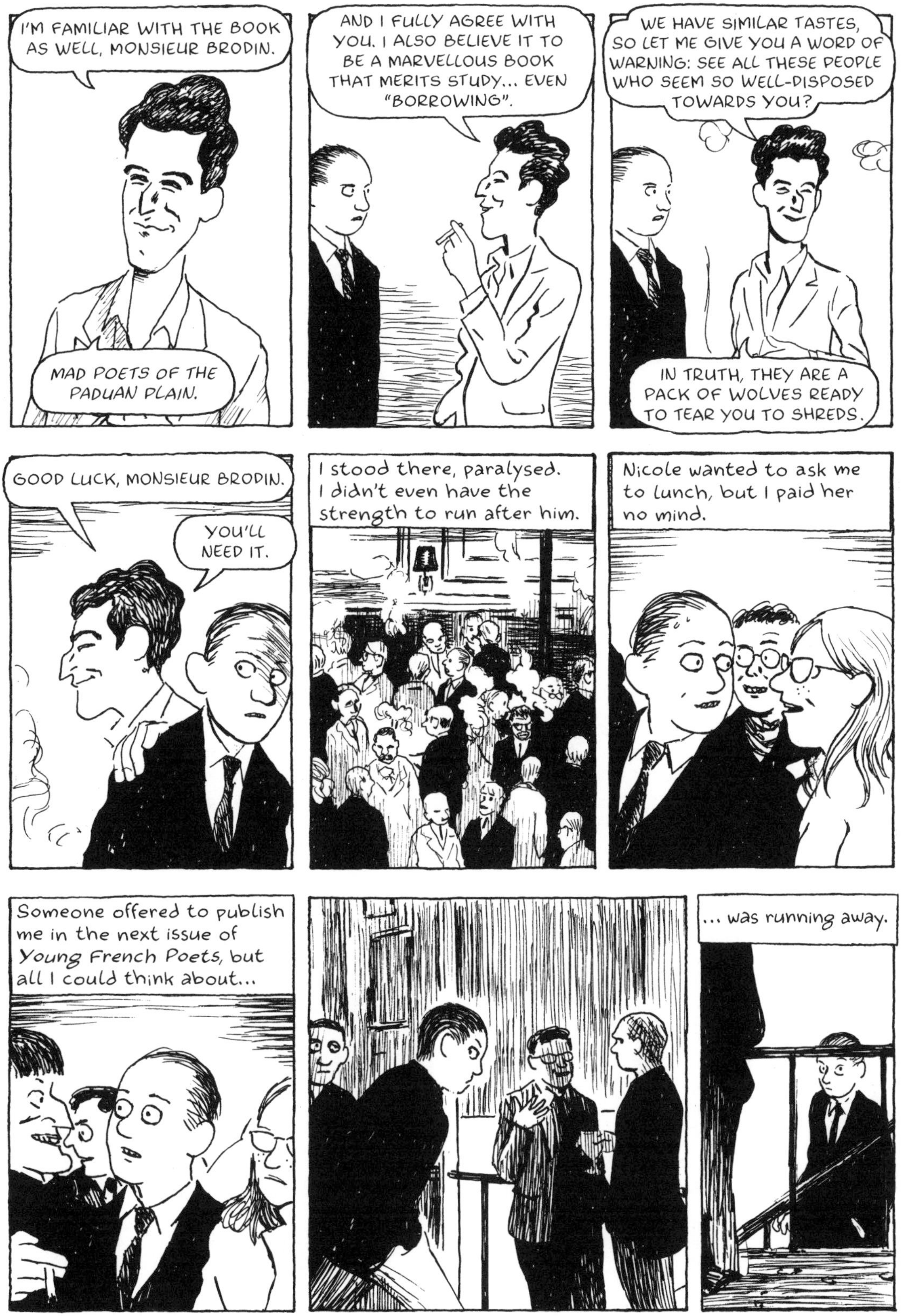
I'M FAMILIAR WITH THE BOOK AS WELL, MONSIEUR BRODIN.
MAD POETS OF THE PADUAN PLAIN.
AND I FULLY AGREE WITH YOU. I ALSO BELIEVE IT TO BE A MARVELLOUS BOOK THAT MERITS STUDY... EVEN "BORROWING".
WE HAVE SIMILAR TASTES, SO LET ME GIVE YOU A WORD OF WARNING: SEE ALL THESE PEOPLE WHO SEEM SO WELL-DISPOSED TOWARDS YOU?
IN TRUTH, THEY ARE A PACK OF WOLVES READY TO TEAR YOU TO SHREDS.
GOOD LUCK, MONSIEUR BRODIN.
YOU'LL NEED IT.
I stood there, paralysed. I didn't even have the strength to run after him.
Nicole wanted to ask me to lunch, but I paid her no mind.
Someone offered to publish me in the next issue of *Young French Poets*, but all I could think about...
... was running away.

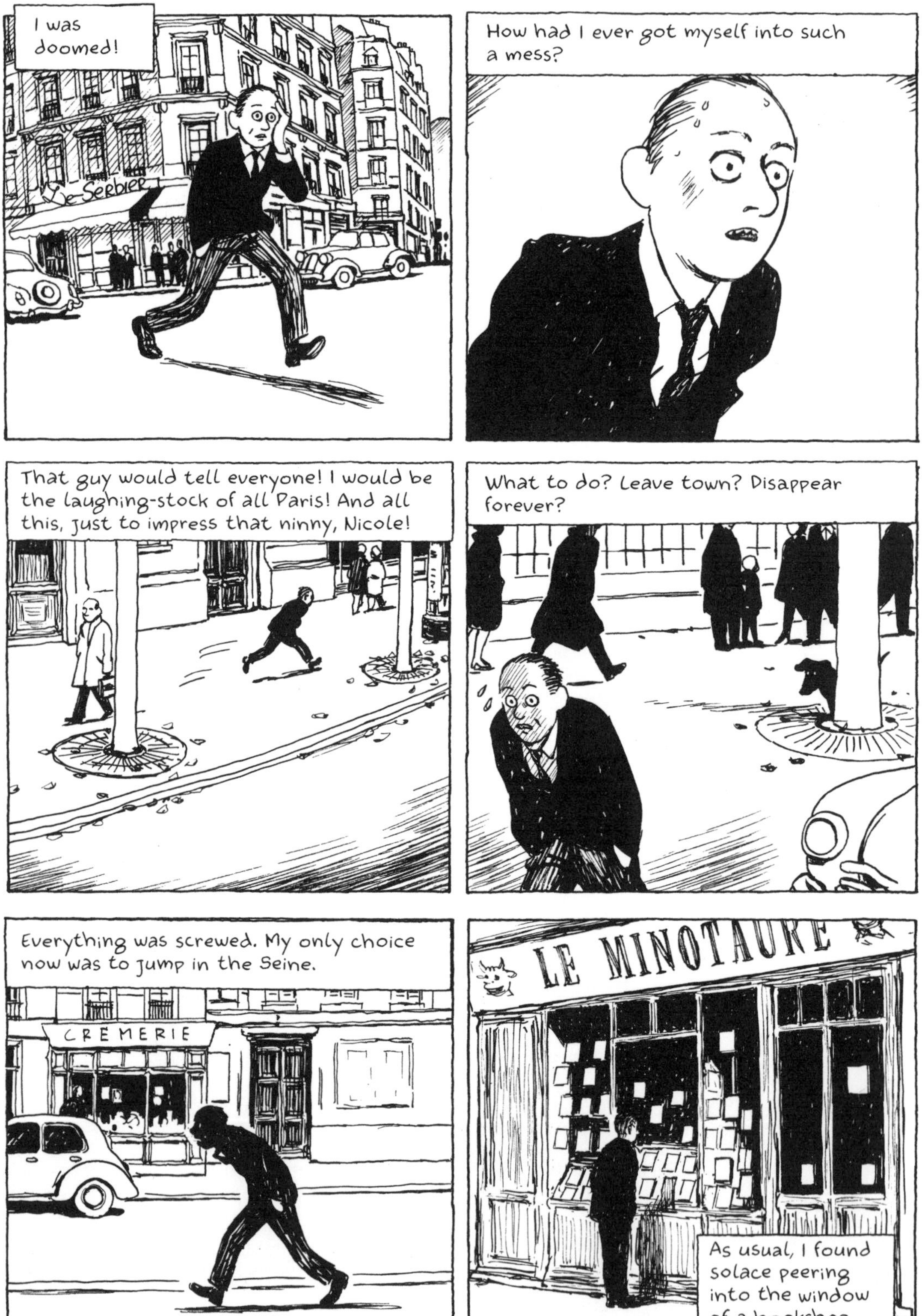
I was doomed!
How had I ever got myself into such a mess?
That guy would tell everyone! I would be the laughing-stock of all Paris! And all this, just to impress that ninny, Nicole!
What to do? Leave town? Disappear forever?
Everything was screwed. My only choice now was to jump in the Seine.
CREMERIE
LE MINOTAURE
As usual, I found solace peering into the window of a bookshop.

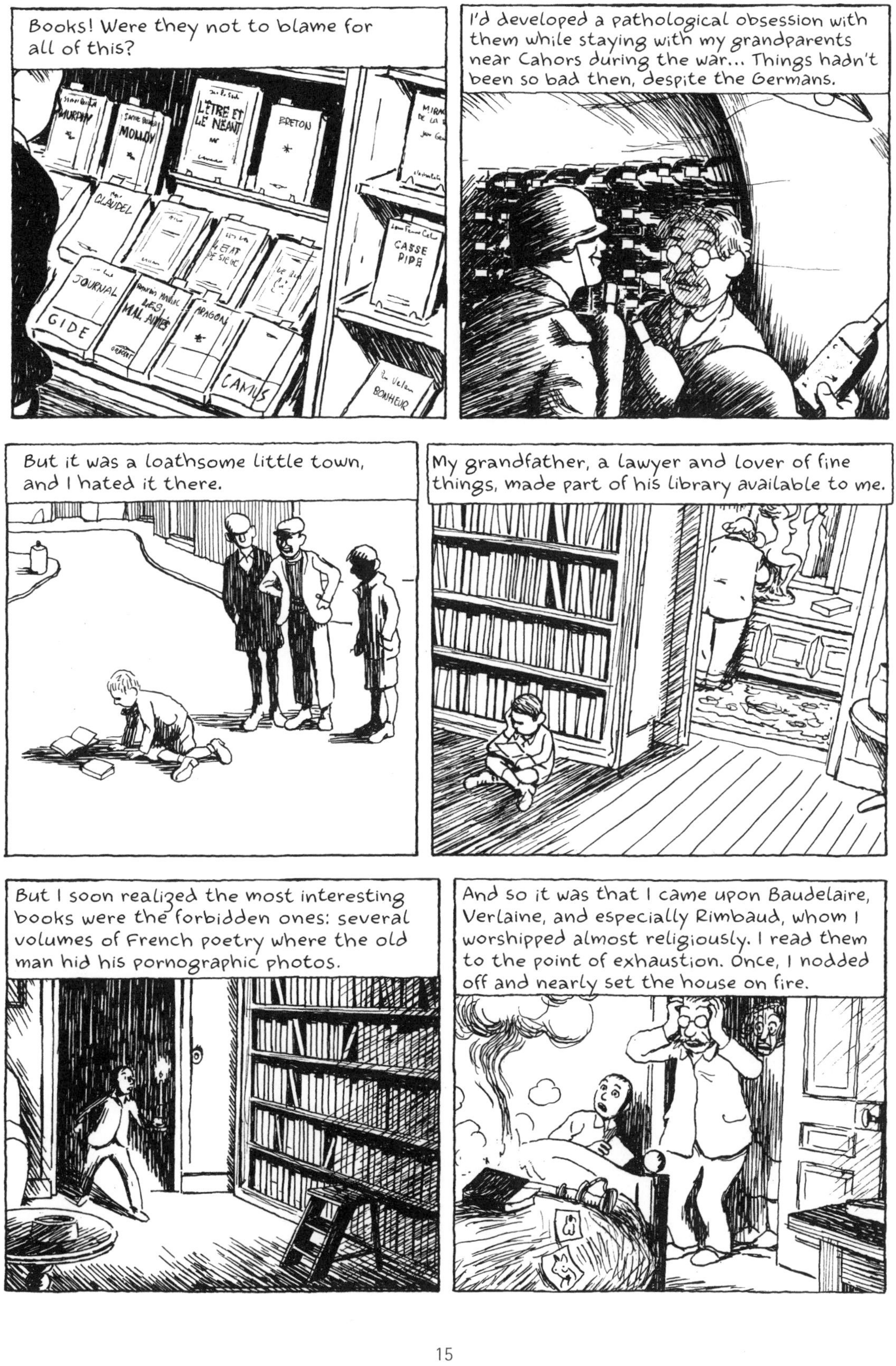
Books! Were they not to blame for all of this?
MURPHY
MOLLOY
L'ETRE ET LE NEANT
BRETON
CLAUDEL
JOURNAL
GIDE
ARAGON
CAMUS
CASSE PIPE
BONHEUR
I'd developed a pathological obsession with them while staying with my grandparents near Cahors during the war... Things hadn't been so bad then, despite the Germans.
But it was a loathsome little town, and I hated it there.
My grandfather, a lawyer and lover of fine things, made part of his library available to me.
But I soon realized the most interesting books were the forbidden ones: several volumes of French poetry where the old man hid his pornographic photos.
And so it was that I came upon Baudelaire, Verlaine, and especially Rimbaud, whom I worshipped almost religiously. I read them to the point of exhaustion. Once, I nodded off and nearly set the house on fire.

That should have been a warning sign. I should've stopped and cultivated other pastimes.

Instead, I hurled myself headlong into writing, an activity that gave me enormous erections.

But in such a provincial environment, writing was but a waste of time.

When I was sent to study law in Paris, it felt like a liberation.

"PARIS, HERE I COME!"

I moved in with my aunt and uncle, ex-Resistance fighters and Communist Party diehards. Good people, if a bit fanatical.

From then on, my passion for books only grew. To sate it, I began to steal. It was an irresistible urge: I was even forced to find a secret hiding place to stash all my loot.

AU TERMINUS RESTAURANT

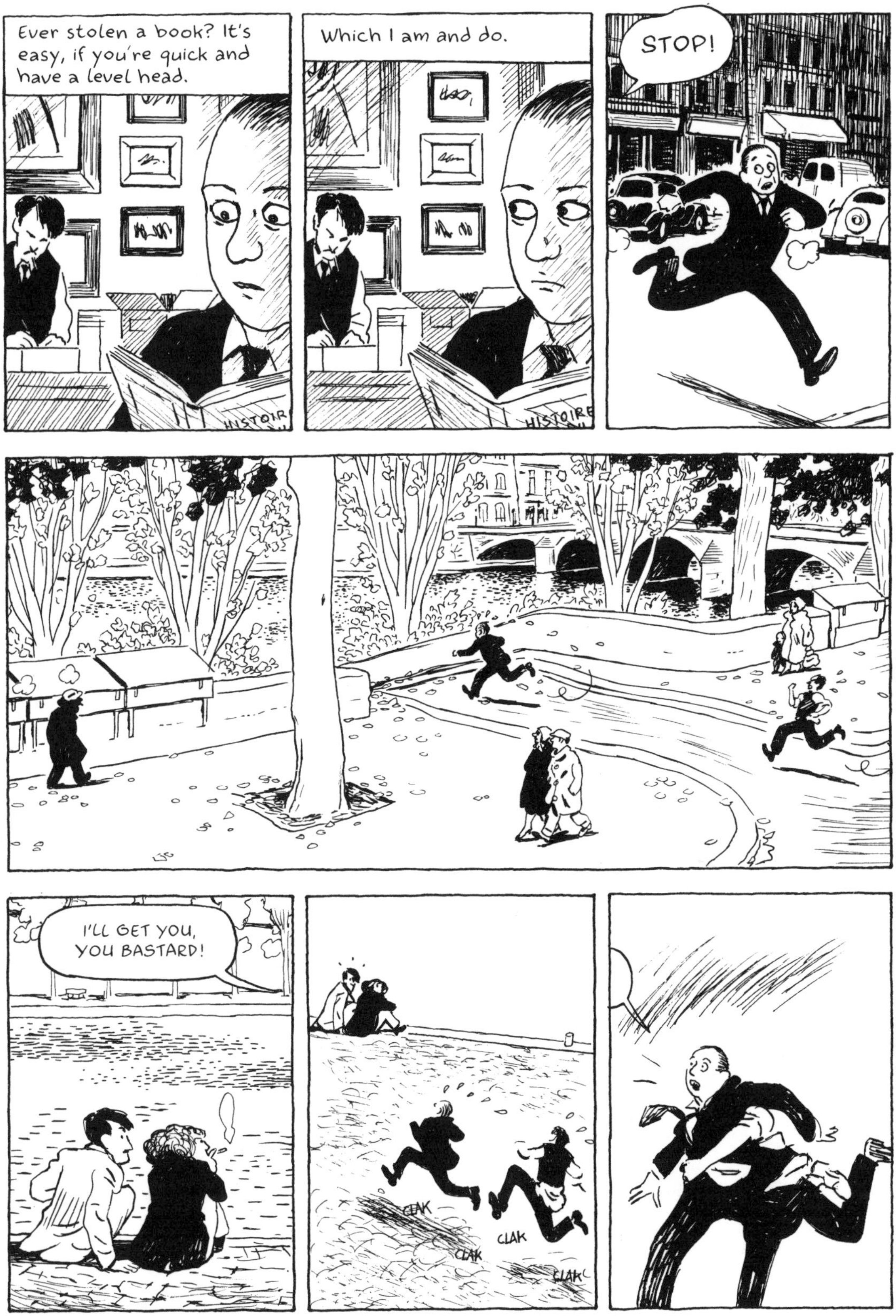
Ever stolen a book? It's easy, if you're quick and have a level head.
HISTOIR
Which I am and do.
HISTOIRE
STOP!
I'LL GET YOU, YOU BASTARD!
CLAK
CLAK
CLAK
CLAK

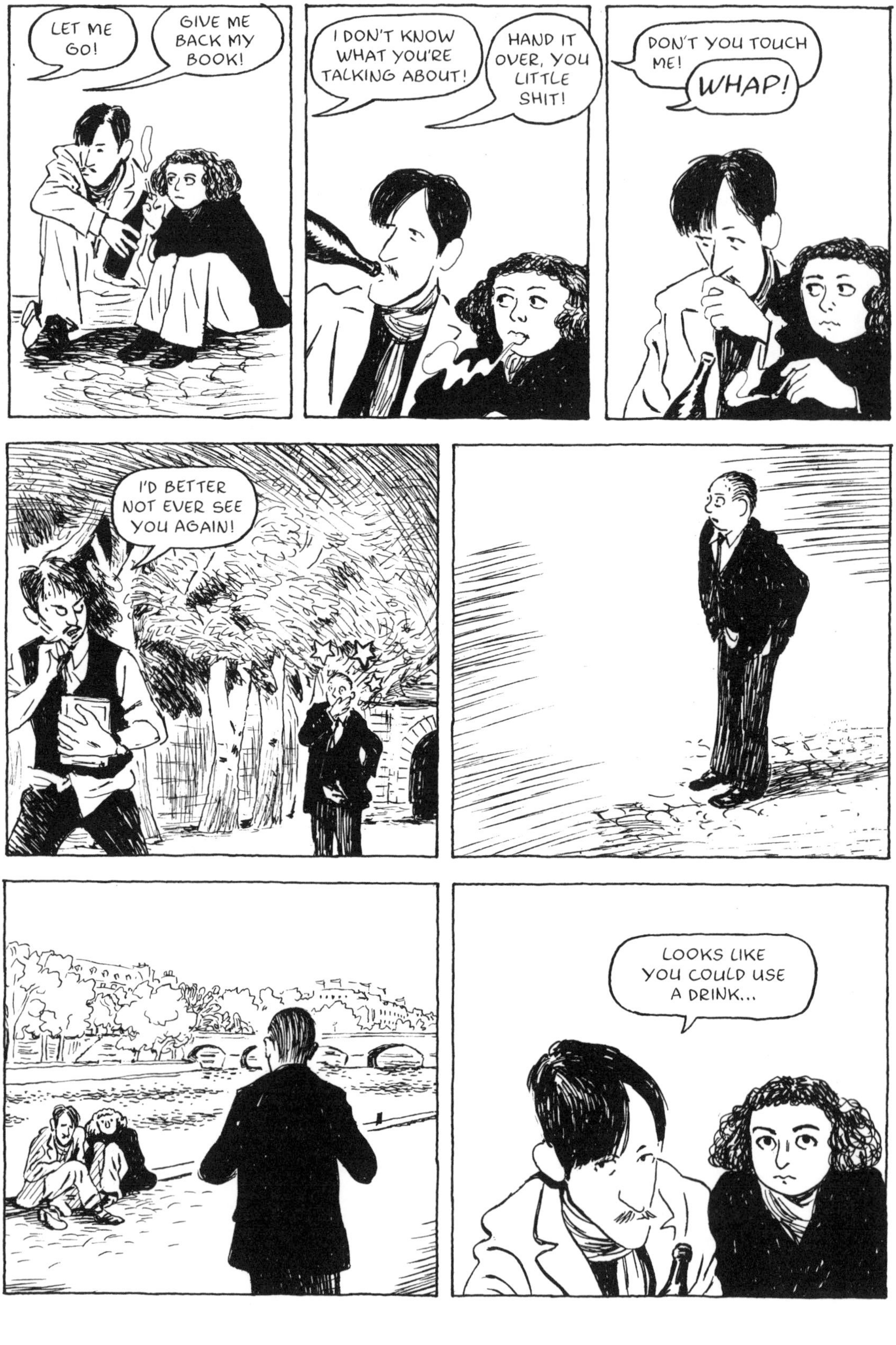
LET ME GO!
GIVE ME BACK MY BOOK!
I DON'T KNOW WHAT YOU'RE TALKING ABOUT!
HAND IT OVER, YOU LITTLE SHIT!
DON'T YOU TOUCH ME!
WHAP!
I'D BETTER NOT EVER SEE YOU AGAIN!
LOOKS LIKE YOU COULD USE A DRINK...

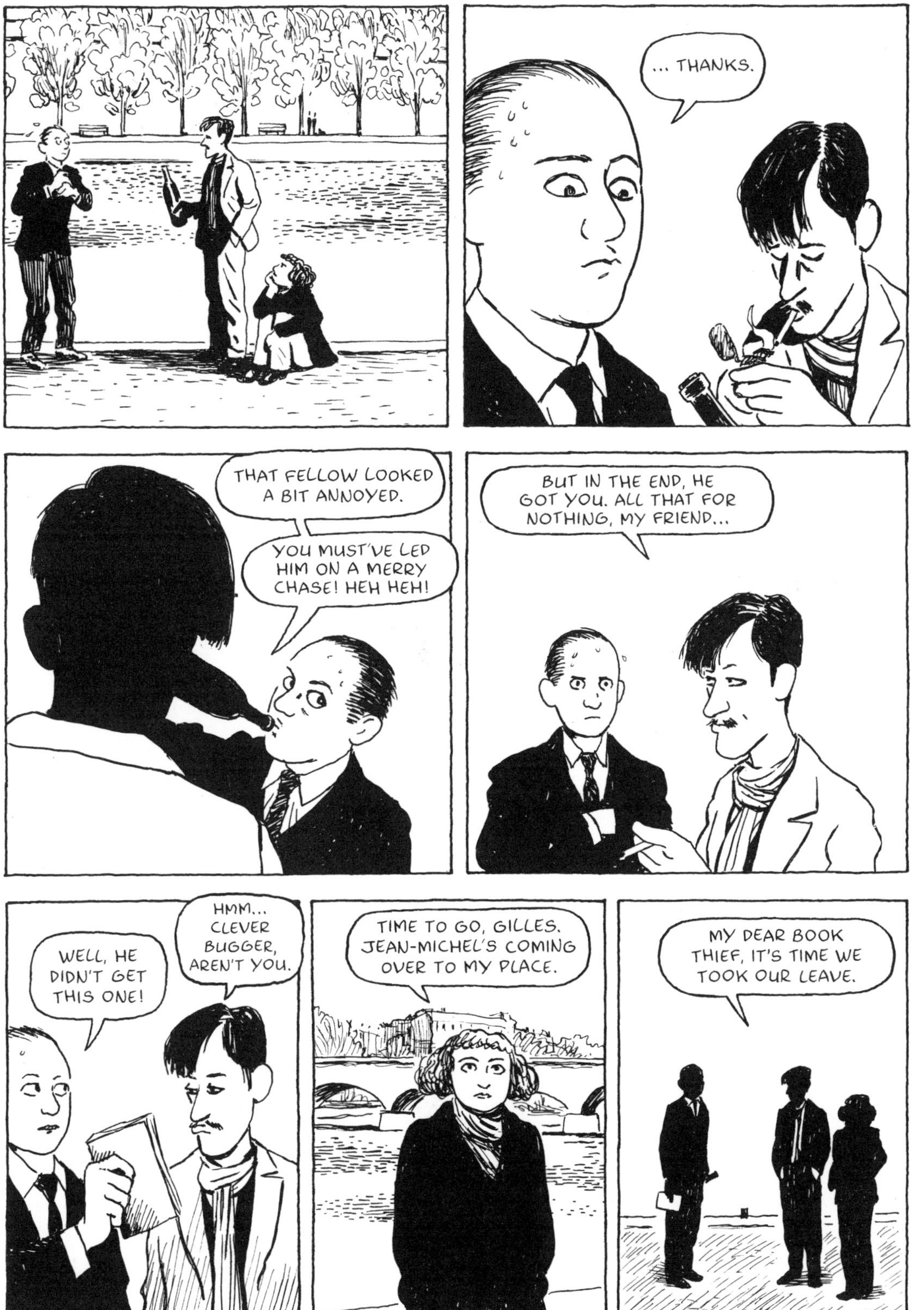
... THANKS.
THAT FELLOW LOOKED A BIT ANNOYED.
YOU MUST'VE LED HIM ON A MERRY CHASE! HEH HEH!
BUT IN THE END, HE GOT YOU. ALL THAT FOR NOTHING, MY FRIEND...
WELL, HE DIDN'T GET THIS ONE!
HMM... CLEVER BUGGER, AREN'T YOU.
TIME TO GO, GILLES. JEAN-MICHEL'S COMING OVER TO MY PLACE.
MY DEAR BOOK THIEF, IT'S TIME WE TOOK OUR LEAVE.

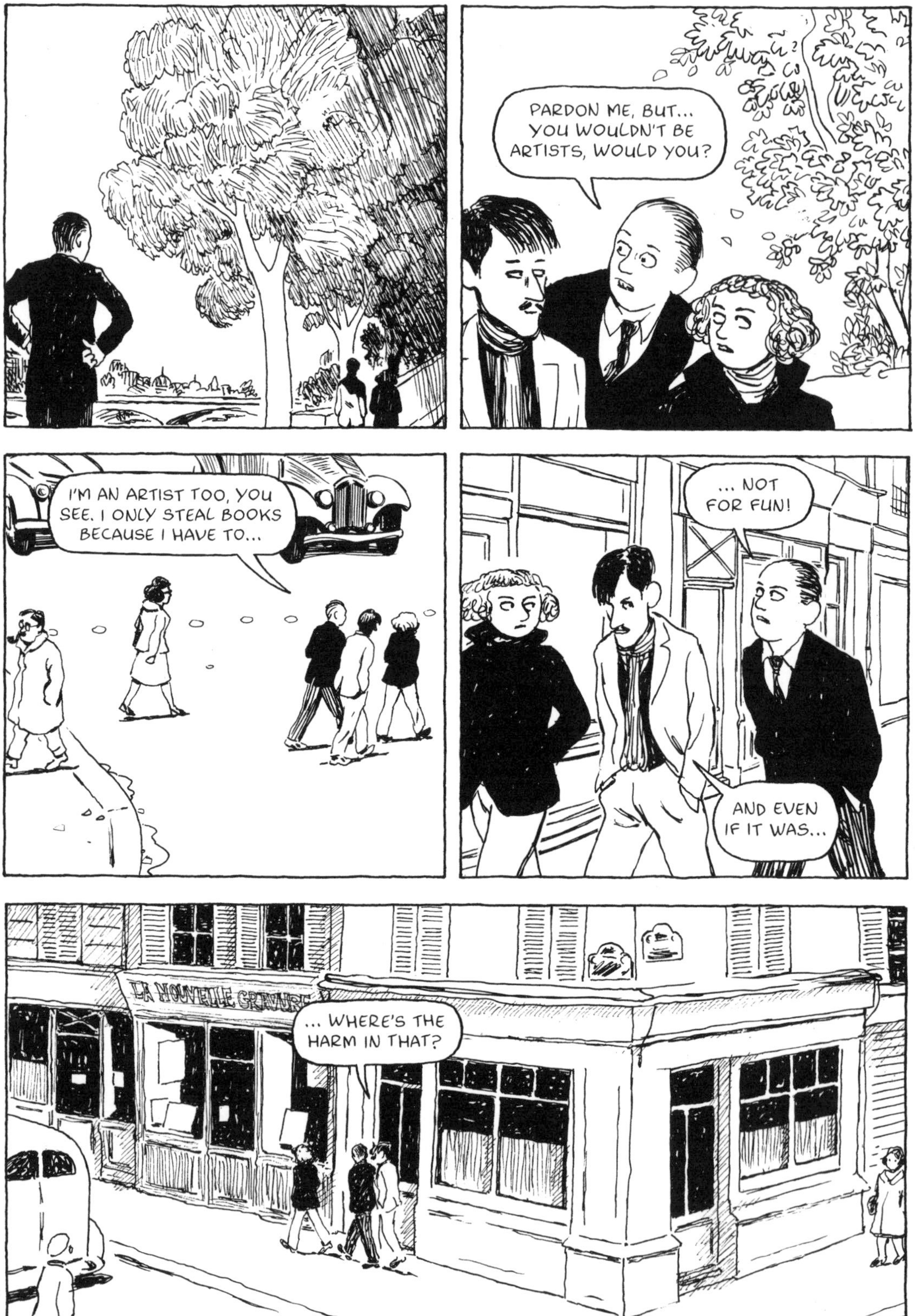
PARDON ME, BUT... YOU WOULDN'T BE ARTISTS, WOULD YOU?
I'M AN ARTIST TOO, YOU SEE. I ONLY STEAL BOOKS BECAUSE I HAVE TO...
... NOT FOR FUN!
AND EVEN IF IT WAS...
LA NOUVELLE GRAVURE
... WHERE'S THE HARM IN THAT?

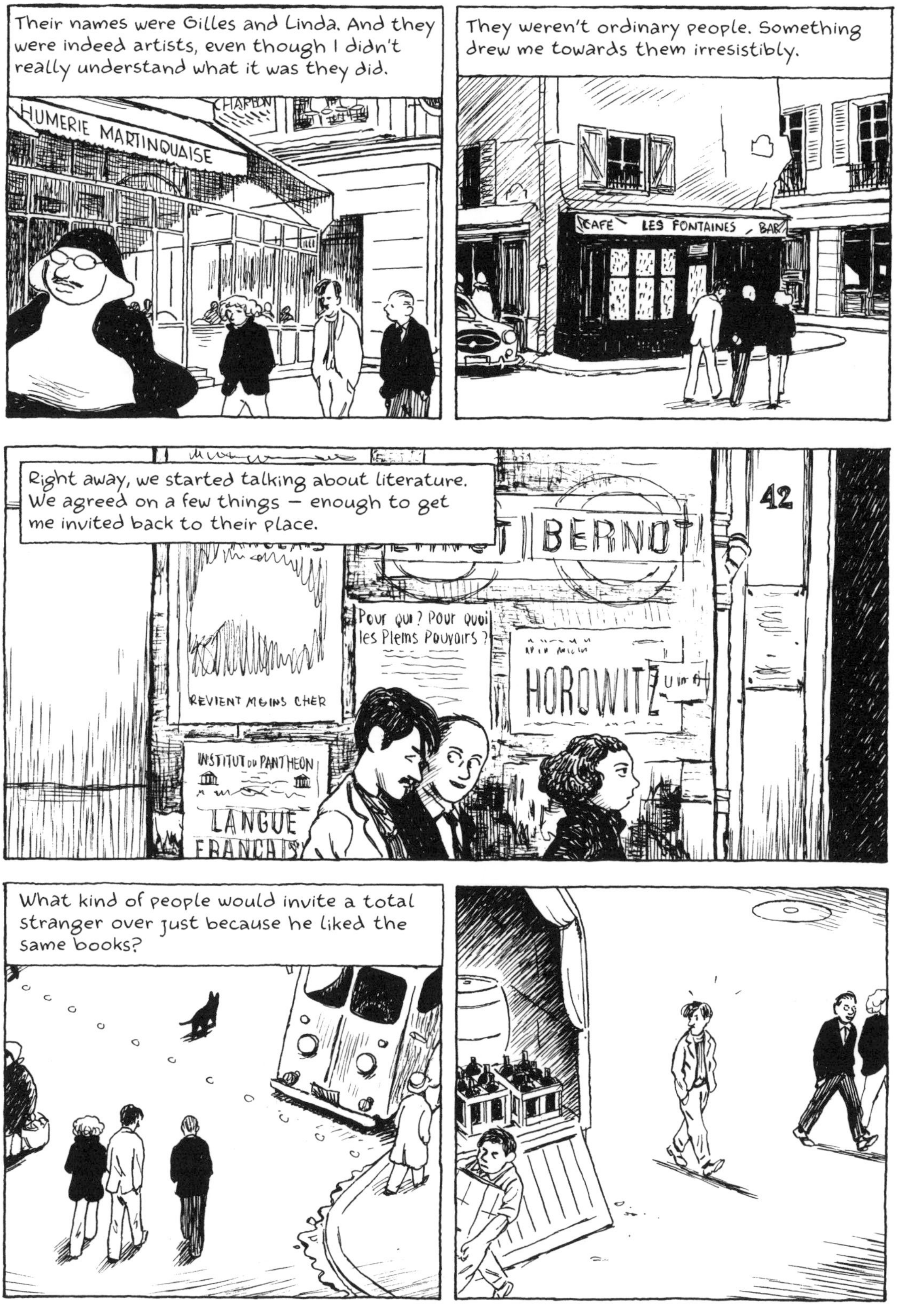
Their names were Gilles and Linda. And they were indeed artists, even though I didn't really understand what it was they did.
HUMERIE MARTINQUAISE
They weren't ordinary people. Something drew me towards them irresistibly.
CAFÉ LES FONTAINES BAR
Right away, we started talking about literature. We agreed on a few things – enough to get me invited back to their place.
42
BERNOT
Pour qui ? Pour quoi les Pleins Pouvoirs ?
REVIENT MOINS CHER
HOROWITZ
INSTITUT DU PANTHEON
LANGUE
What kind of people would invite a total stranger over just because he liked the same books?

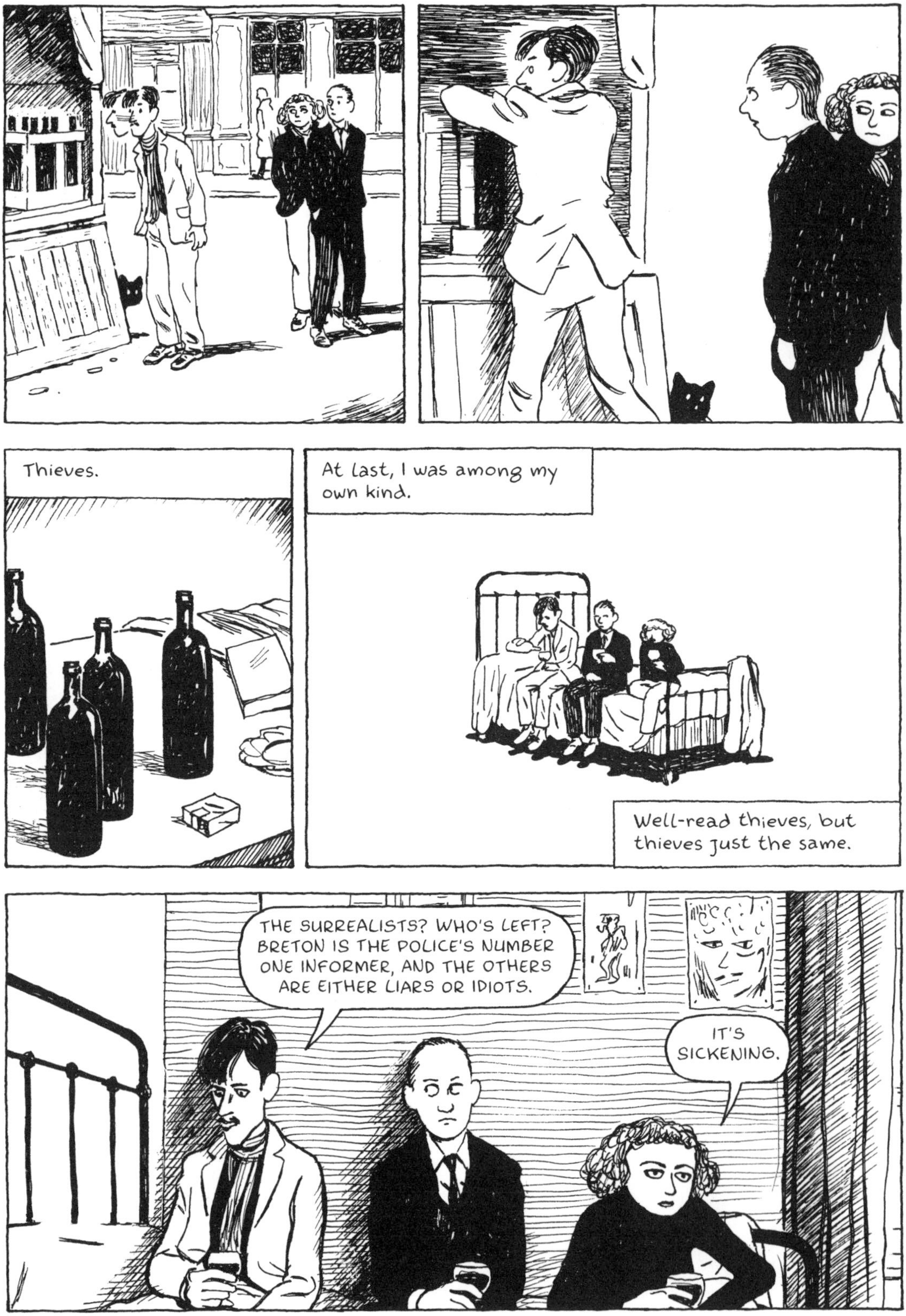
Thieves.
At last, I was among my own kind.
Well-read thieves, but thieves just the same.
THE SURREALISTS? WHO'S LEFT? BRETON IS THE POLICE'S NUMBER ONE INFORMER, AND THE OTHERS ARE EITHER LIARS OR IDIOTS.
IT'S SICKENING.

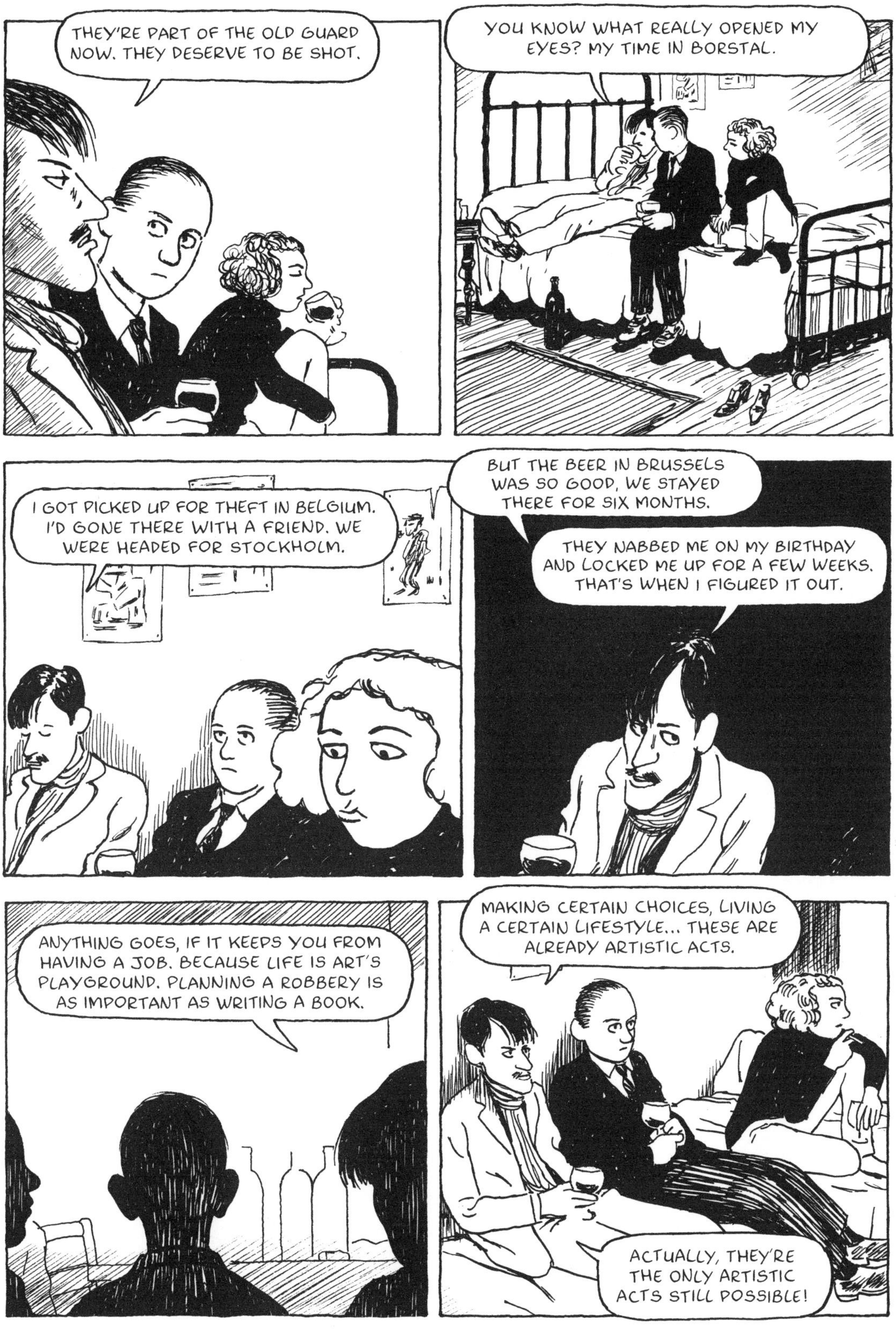
THEY'RE PART OF THE OLD GUARD NOW. THEY DESERVE TO BE SHOT.
YOU KNOW WHAT REALLY OPENED MY EYES? MY TIME IN BORSTAL.
I GOT PICKED UP FOR THEFT IN BELGIUM. I'D GONE THERE WITH A FRIEND. WE WERE HEADED FOR STOCKHOLM.
BUT THE BEER IN BRUSSELS WAS SO GOOD, WE STAYED THERE FOR SIX MONTHS.
THEY NABBED ME ON MY BIRTHDAY AND LOCKED ME UP FOR A FEW WEEKS. THAT'S WHEN I FIGURED IT OUT.
ANYTHING GOES, IF IT KEEPS YOU FROM HAVING A JOB. BECAUSE LIFE IS ART'S PLAYGROUND. PLANNING A ROBBERY IS AS IMPORTANT AS WRITING A BOOK.
MAKING CERTAIN CHOICES, LIVING A CERTAIN LIFESTYLE... THESE ARE ALREADY ARTISTIC ACTS.
ACTUALLY, THEY'RE THE ONLY ARTISTIC ACTS STILL POSSIBLE!

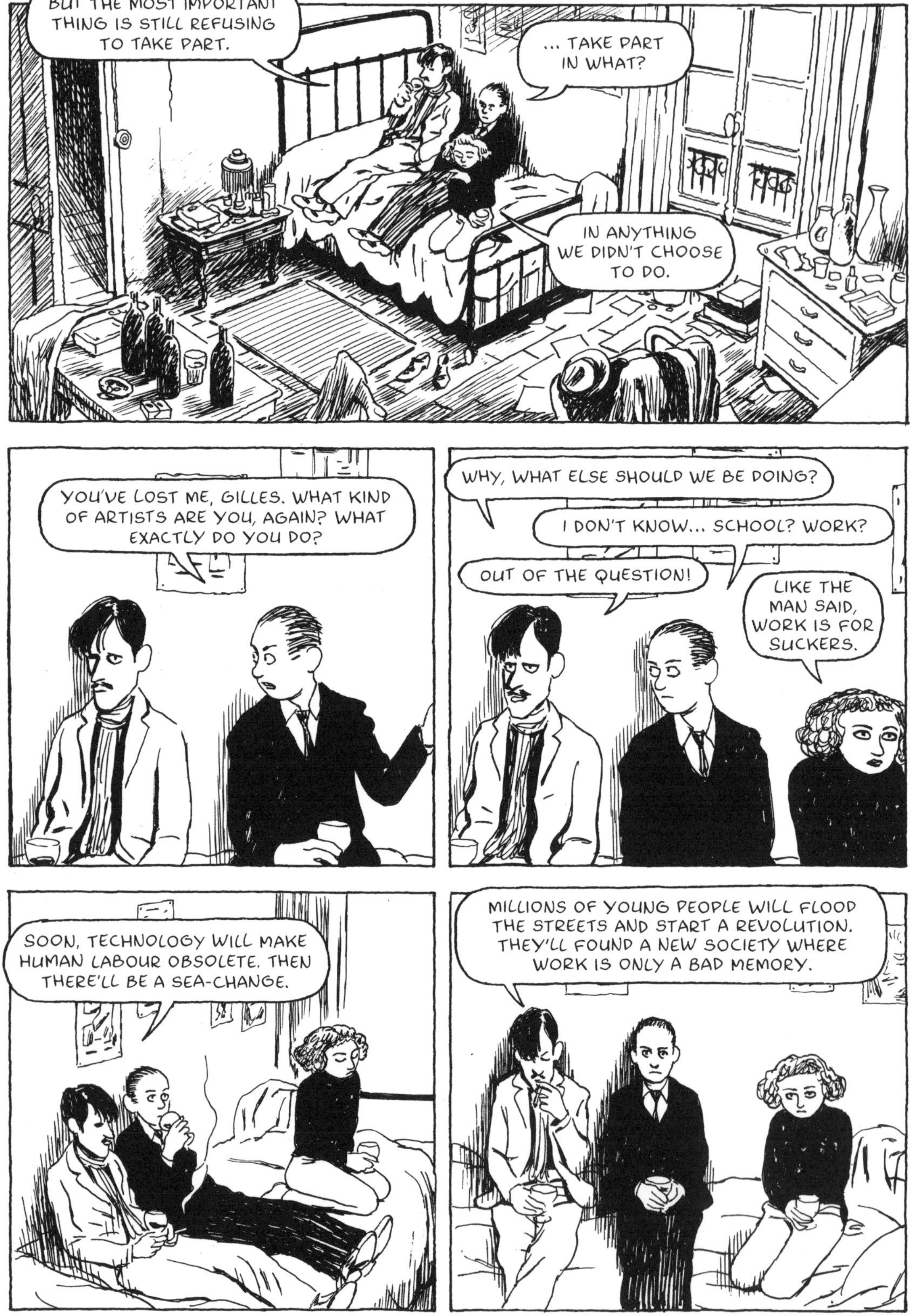

BUT THE MOST IMPORTANT THING IS STILL REFUSING TO TAKE PART.
... TAKE PART IN WHAT?
IN ANYTHING WE DIDN'T CHOOSE TO DO.
YOU'VE LOST ME, GILLES. WHAT KIND OF ARTISTS ARE YOU, AGAIN? WHAT EXACTLY DO YOU DO?
WHY, WHAT ELSE SHOULD WE BE DOING?
I DON'T KNOW... SCHOOL? WORK?
OUT OF THE QUESTION!
LIKE THE MAN SAID, WORK IS FOR SUCKERS.
SOON, TECHNOLOGY WILL MAKE HUMAN LABOUR OBSOLETE. THEN THERE'LL BE A SEA-CHANGE.
MILLIONS OF YOUNG PEOPLE WILL FLOOD THE STREETS AND START A REVOLUTION. THEY'LL FOUND A NEW SOCIETY WHERE WORK IS ONLY A BAD MEMORY.

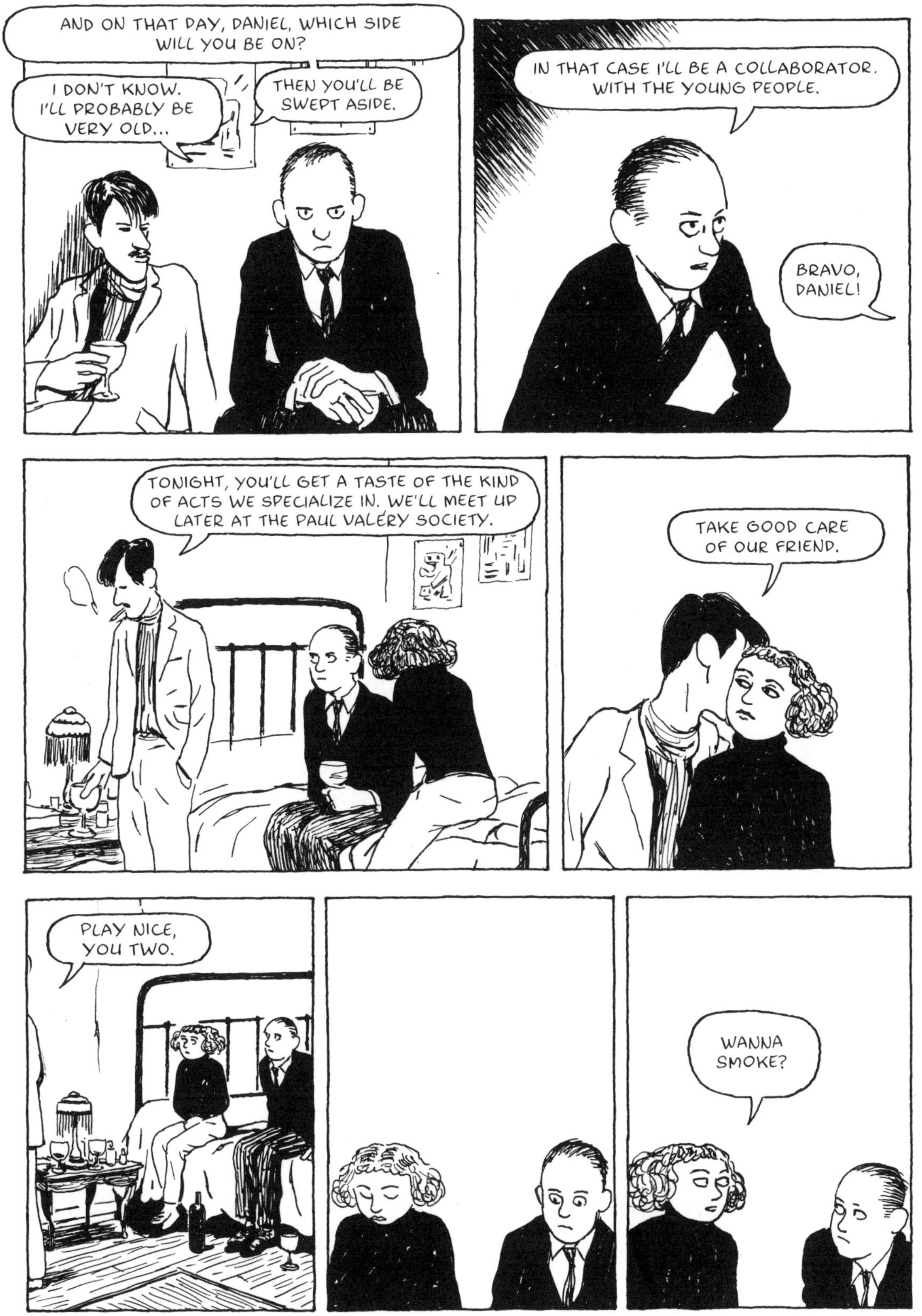
AND ON THAT DAY, DANIEL, WHICH SIDE WILL YOU BE ON?
I DON'T KNOW. I'LL PROBABLY BE VERY OLD...
THEN YOU'LL BE SWEPT ASIDE.
IN THAT CASE I'LL BE A COLLABORATOR. WITH THE YOUNG PEOPLE.
BRAVO, DANIEL!
TONIGHT, YOU'LL GET A TASTE OF THE KIND OF ACTS WE SPECIALIZE IN. WE'LL MEET UP LATER AT THE PAUL VALÉRY SOCIETY.
TAKE GOOD CARE OF OUR FRIEND.
PLAY NICE, YOU TWO.
WANNA SMOKE?

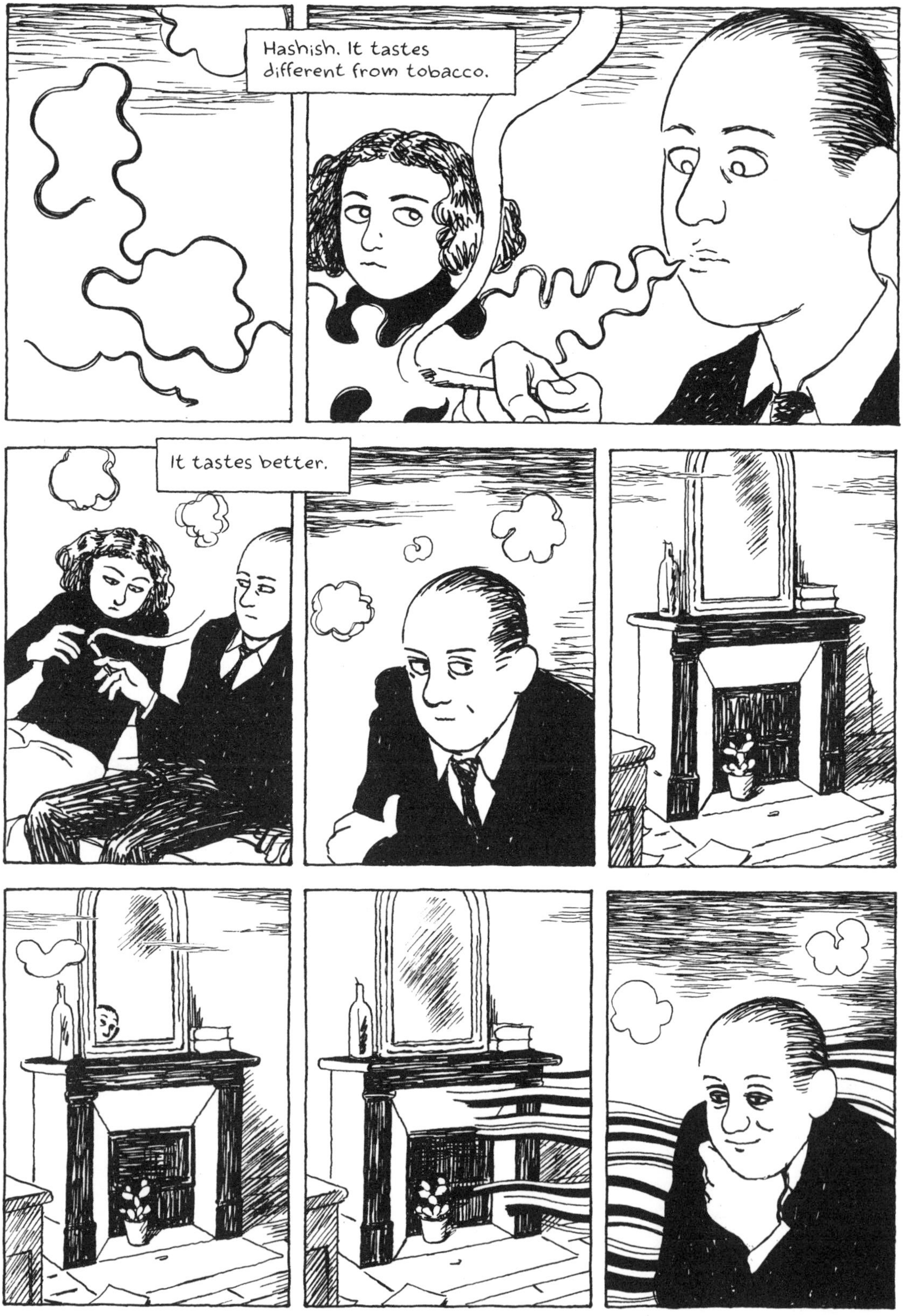
Hashish. It tastes different from tobacco.
It tastes better.

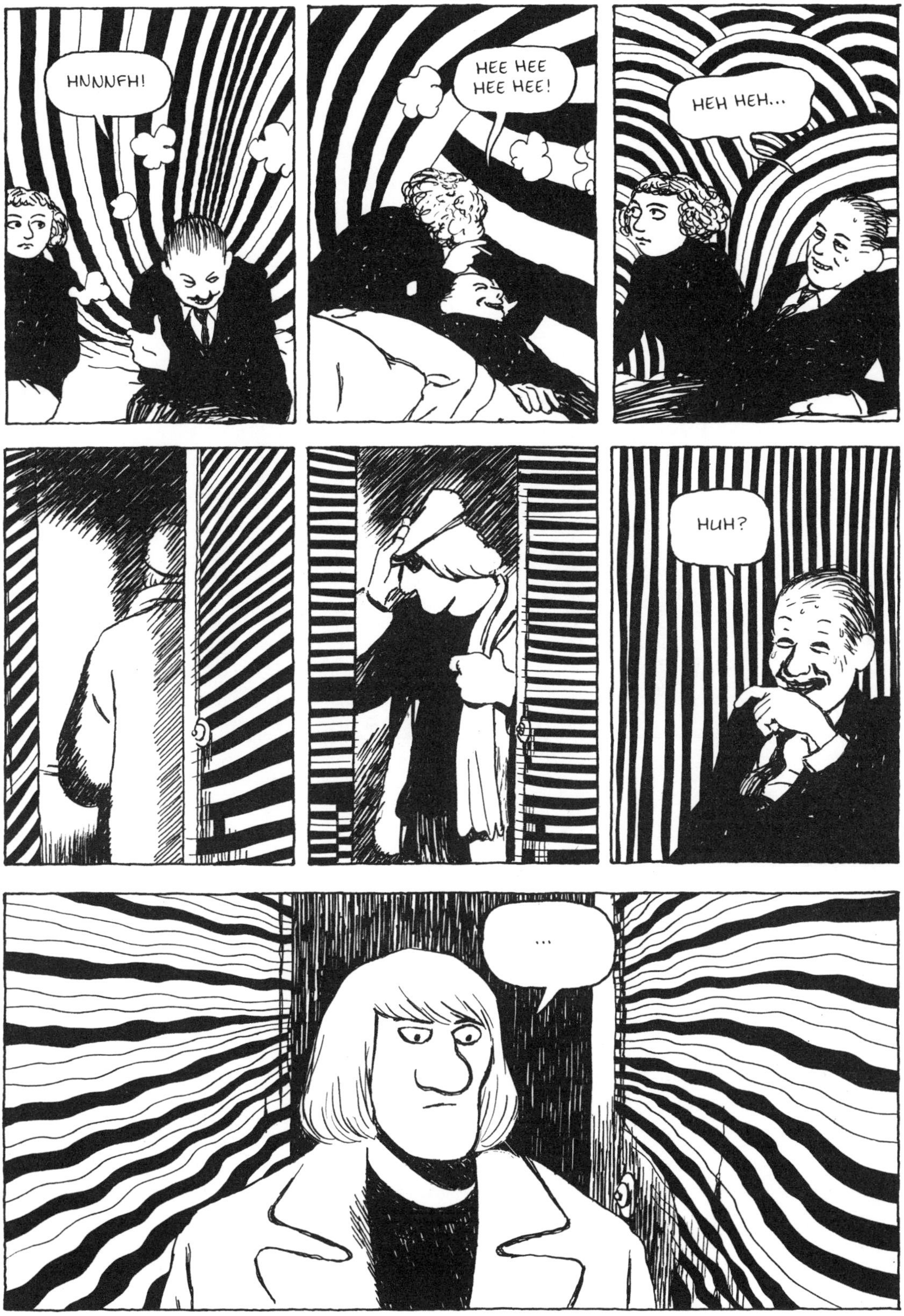
HNNNFH!
HEE HEE HEE HEE!
HEH HEH...
HUH?
...

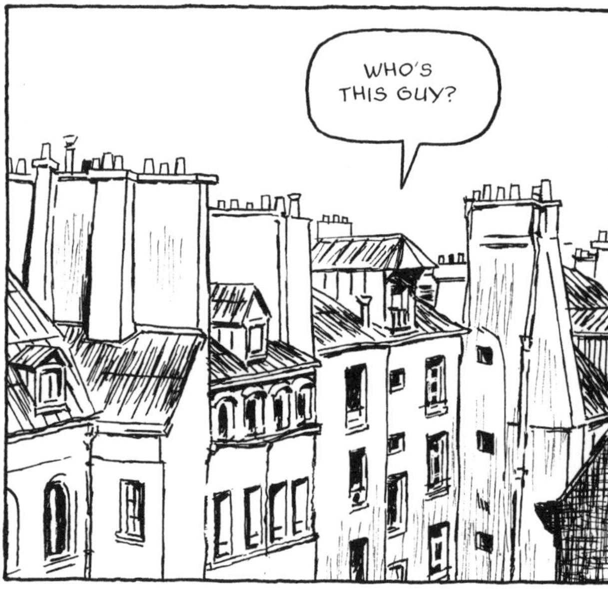
WHO'S
THIS GUY?

CHAPTER 2

"IF I WIN, EVERYONE DIES."
Gaspard D.

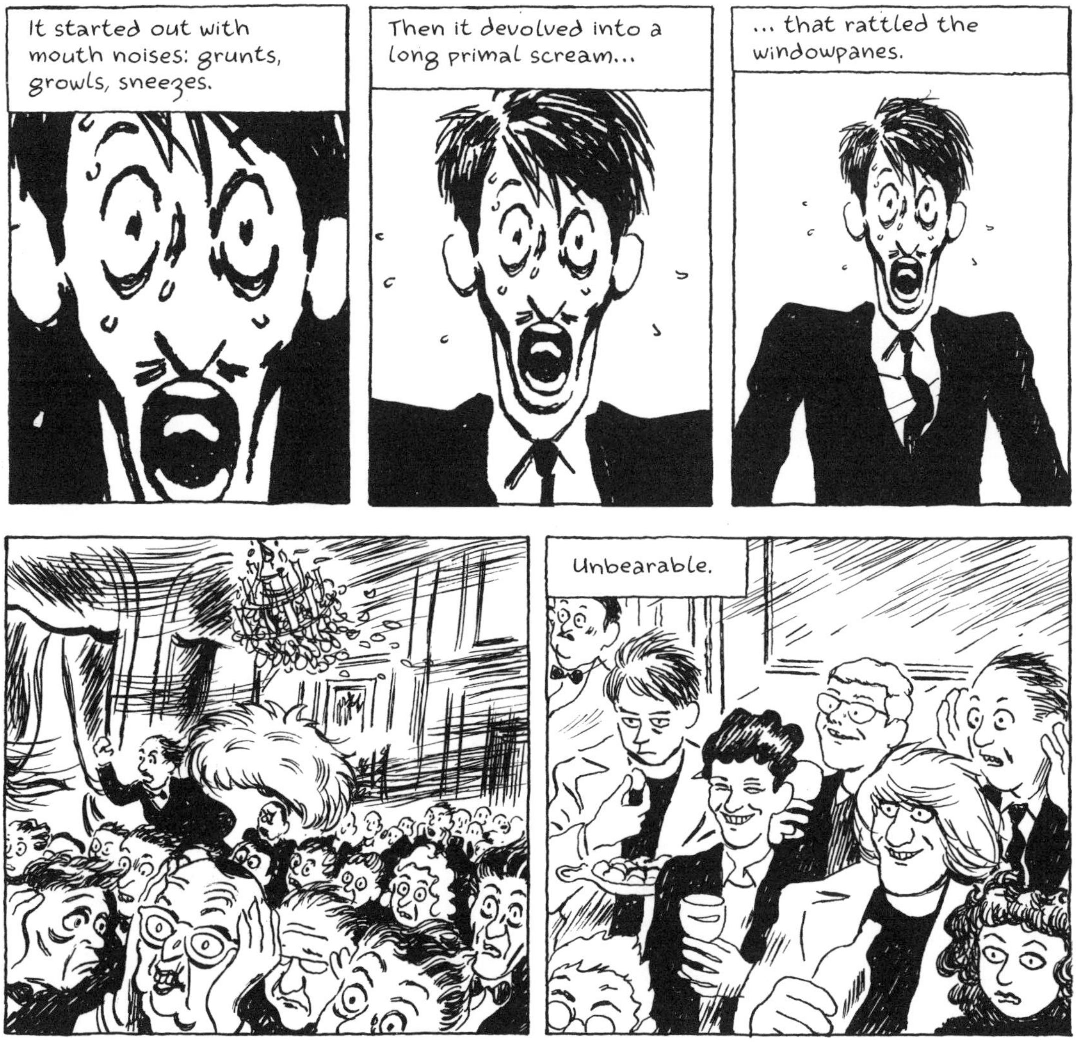
It started out with mouth noises: grunts, growls, sneezes.
Then it devolved into a long primal scream...
... that rattled the windowpanes.
Unbearable.

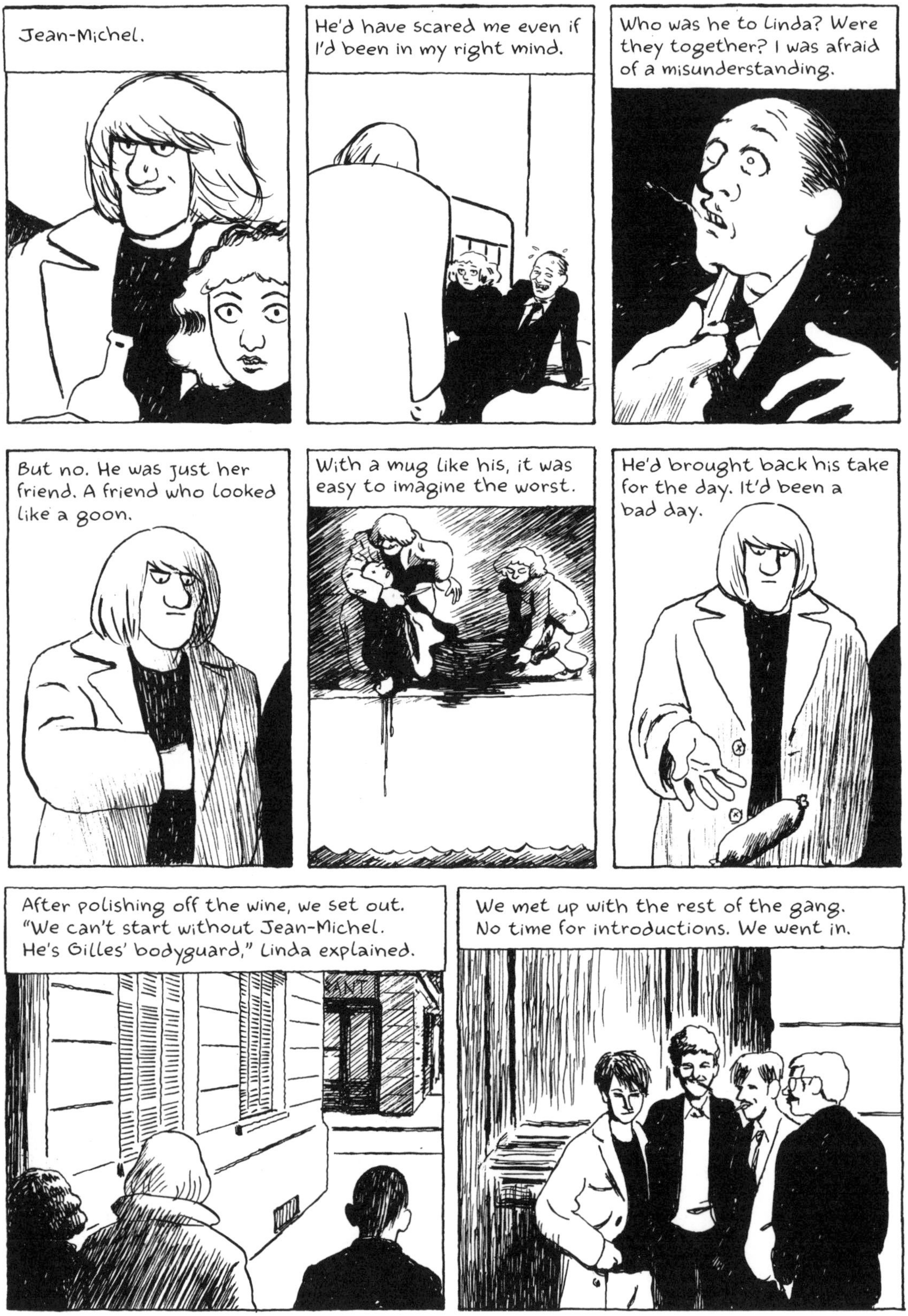
Jean-Michel.
He'd have scared me even if I'd been in my right mind.
Who was he to Linda? Were they together? I was afraid of a misunderstanding.
But no. He was just her friend. A friend who looked like a goon.
With a mug like his, it was easy to imagine the worst.
He'd brought back his take for the day. It'd been a bad day.
After polishing off the wine, we set out. "We can't start without Jean-Michel. He's Gilles' bodyguard," Linda explained.
We met up with the rest of the gang. No time for introductions. We went in.

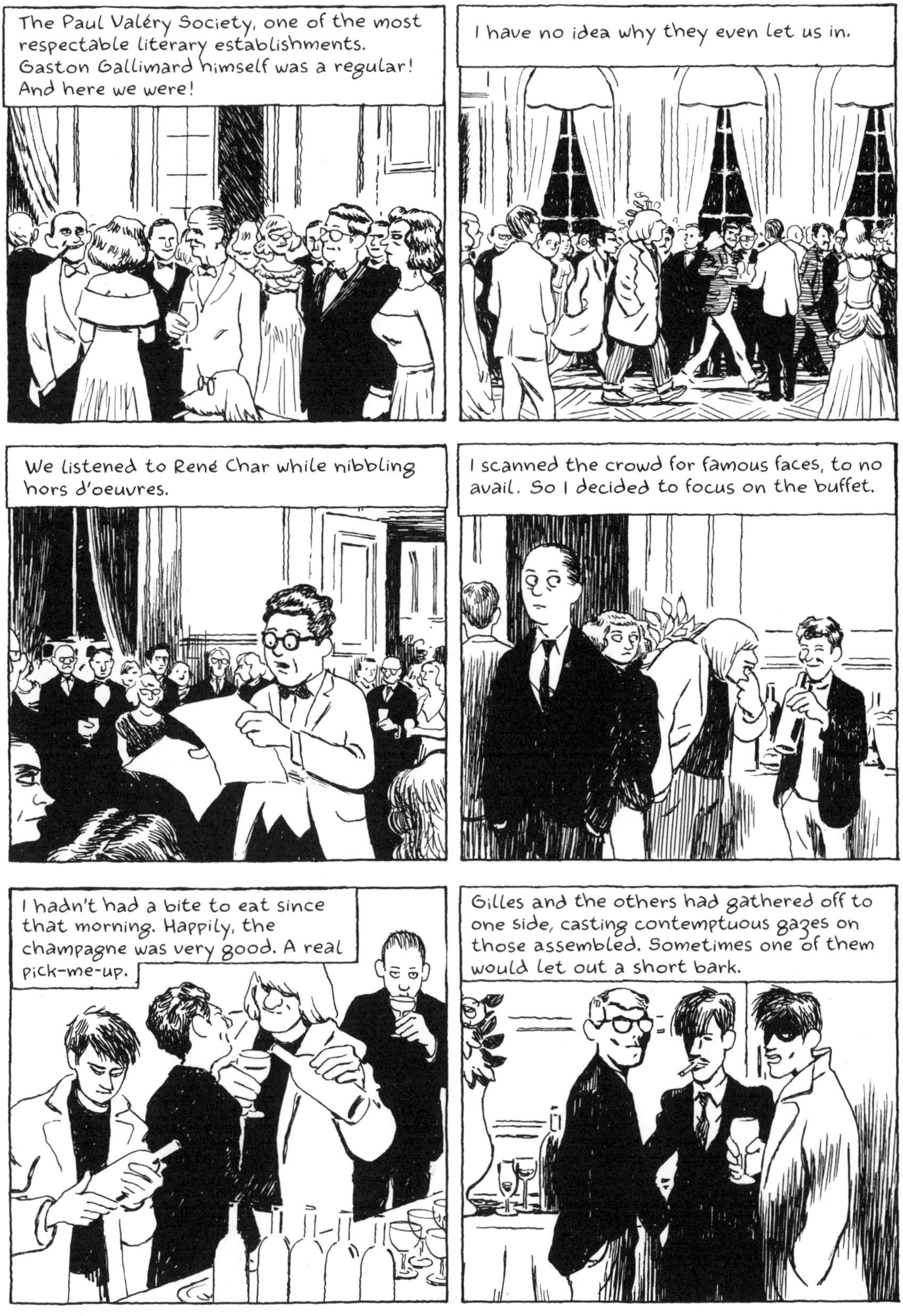
The Paul Valéry Society, one of the most respectable literary establishments. Gaston Gallimard himself was a regular! And here we were!
I have no idea why they even let us in.
We listened to René Char while nibbling hors d'oeuvres.
I scanned the crowd for famous faces, to no avail. So I decided to focus on the buffet.
I hadn't had a bite to eat since that morning. Happily, the champagne was very good. A real pick-me-up.
Gilles and the others had gathered off to one side, casting contemptuous gazes on those assembled. Sometimes one of them would let out a short bark.

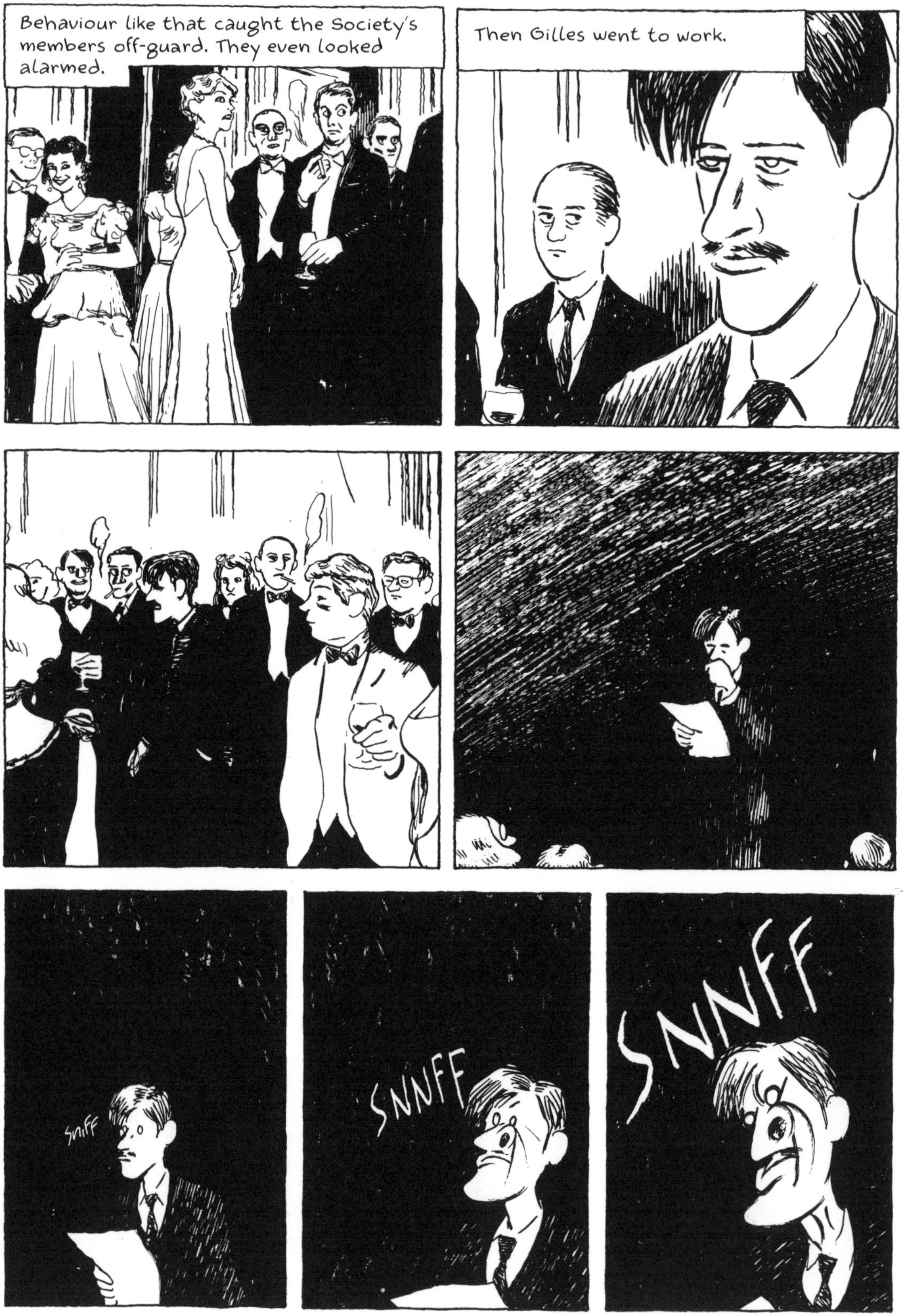
Behaviour like that caught the Society's members off-guard. They even looked alarmed.
Then Gilles went to work.
SNIFF
SNNFF
SNNFF

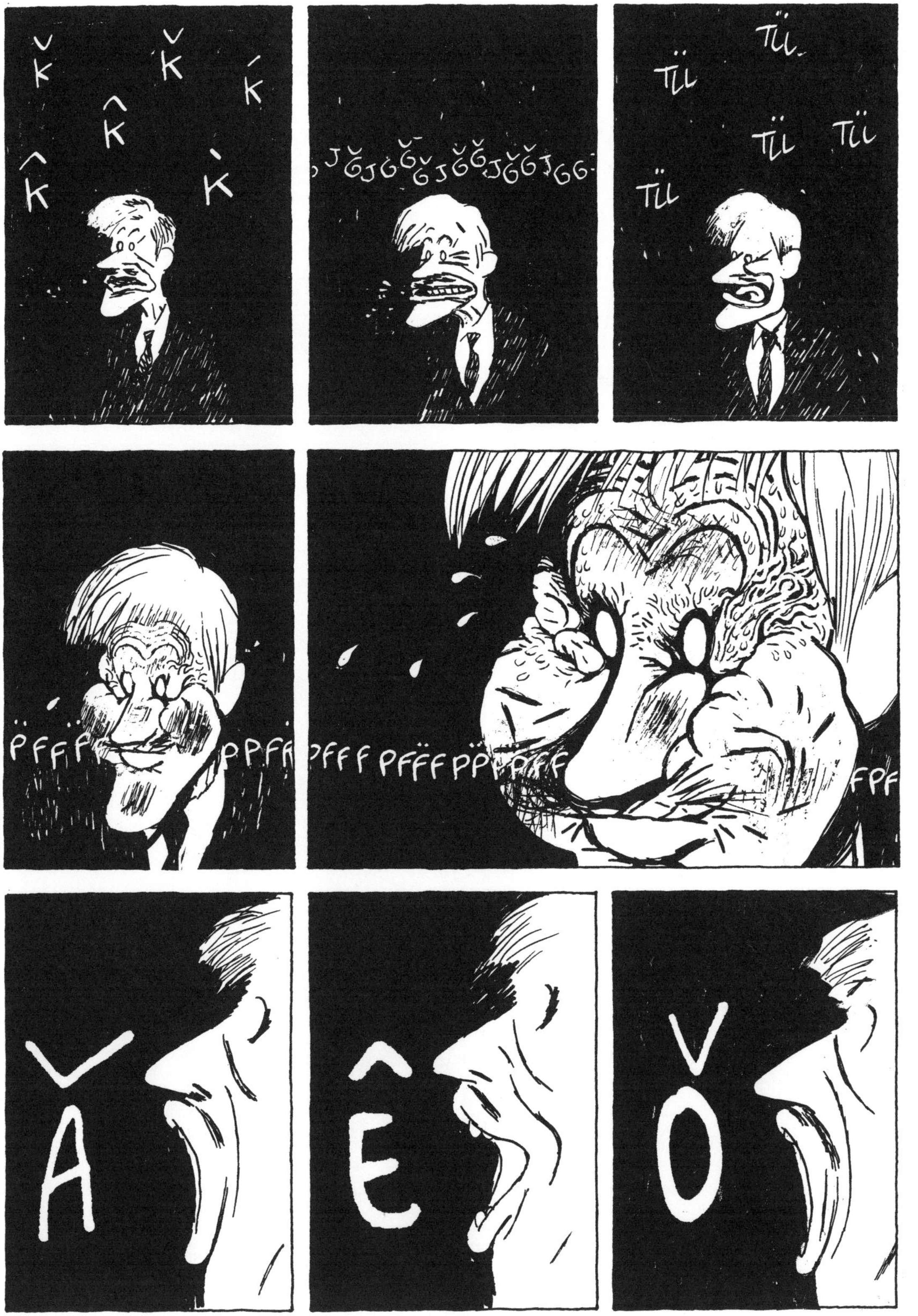
Ǩ Ǩ Ḱ K̂ K̂ K̀
JǦJǦǦJǦǦJǦǦJǦǦ
TÜL TÜL TÜL TÜL TÜL
PFFF PPFF
PFFF PFFF PPFFF FPF
Ă
Ê
Ǒ

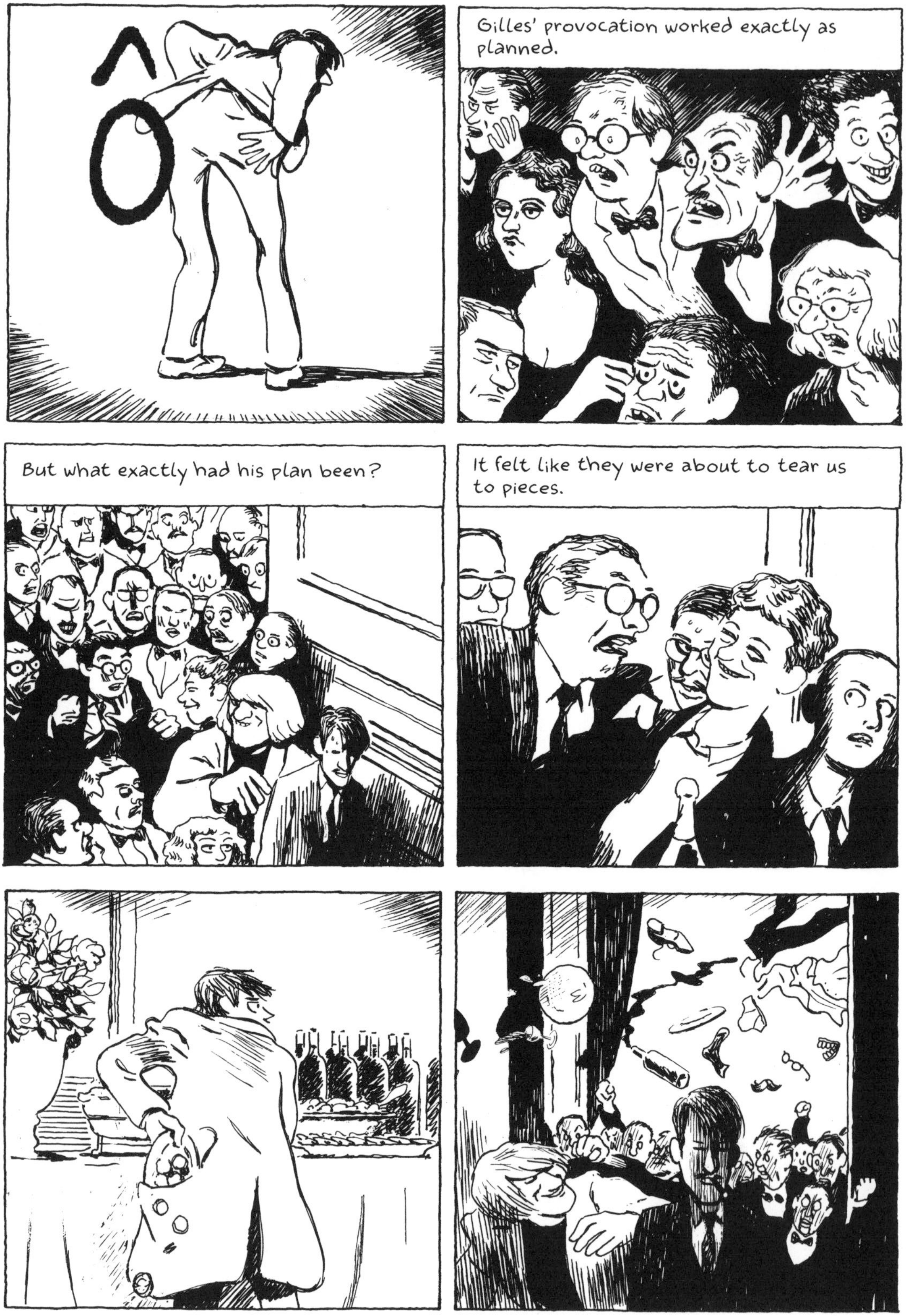
Ô
Gilles' provocation worked exactly as planned.
But what exactly had his plan been?
It felt like they were about to tear us to pieces.

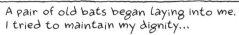
A pair of old bats began laying into me. I tried to maintain my dignity...

But it wasn't easy.

IS THAT...?

I HAVE NO IDEA WHOSE IT IS.

HEY, YOU REALLY ARE A KLEPTO.

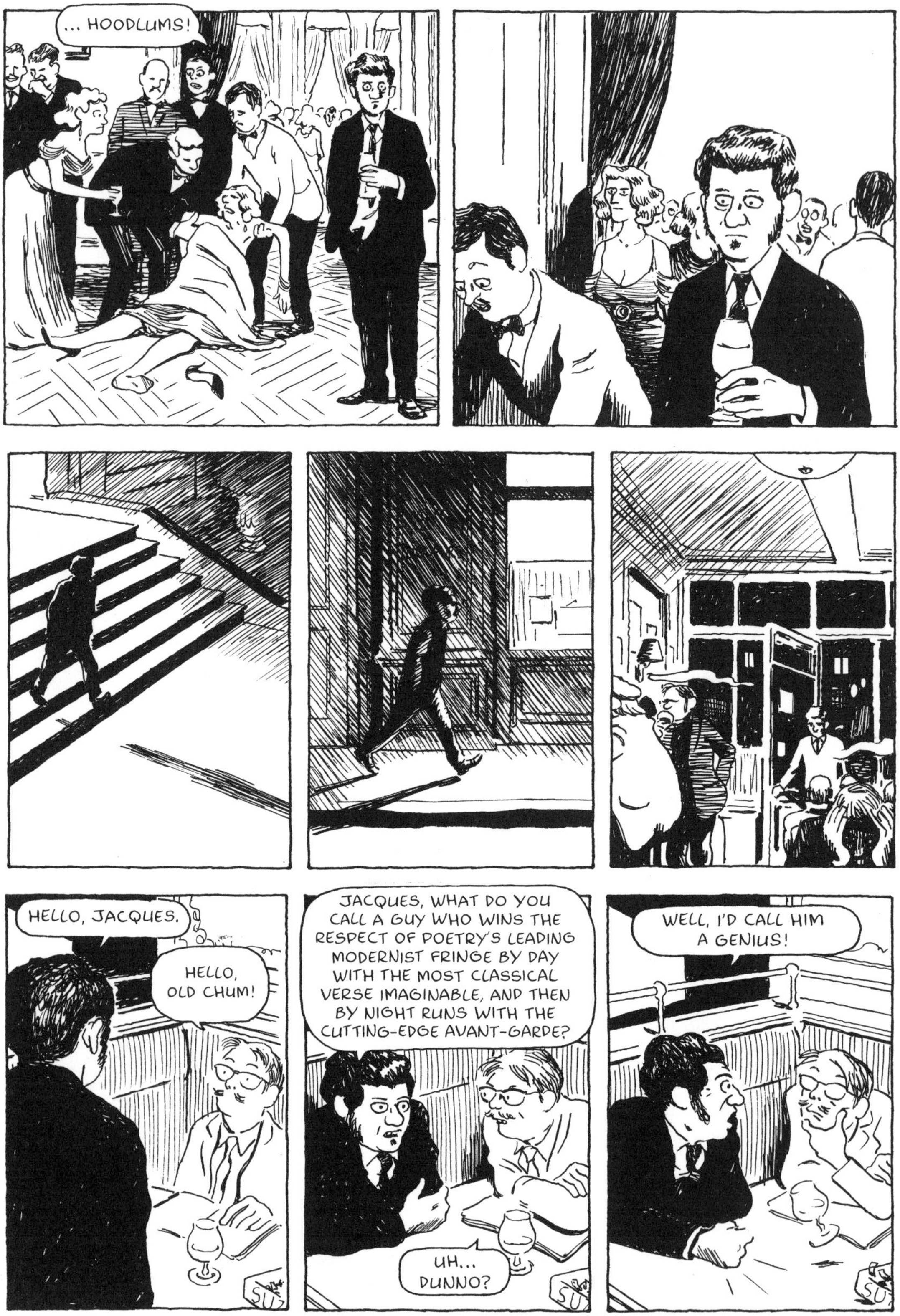
... HOODLUMS!
HELLO, JACQUES.
HELLO, OLD CHUM!
JACQUES, WHAT DO YOU CALL A GUY WHO WINS THE RESPECT OF POETRY'S LEADING MODERNIST FRINGE BY DAY WITH THE MOST CLASSICAL VERSE IMAGINABLE, AND THEN BY NIGHT RUNS WITH THE CUTTING-EDGE AVANT-GARDE?
UH... DUNNO?
WELL, I'D CALL HIM A GENIUS!

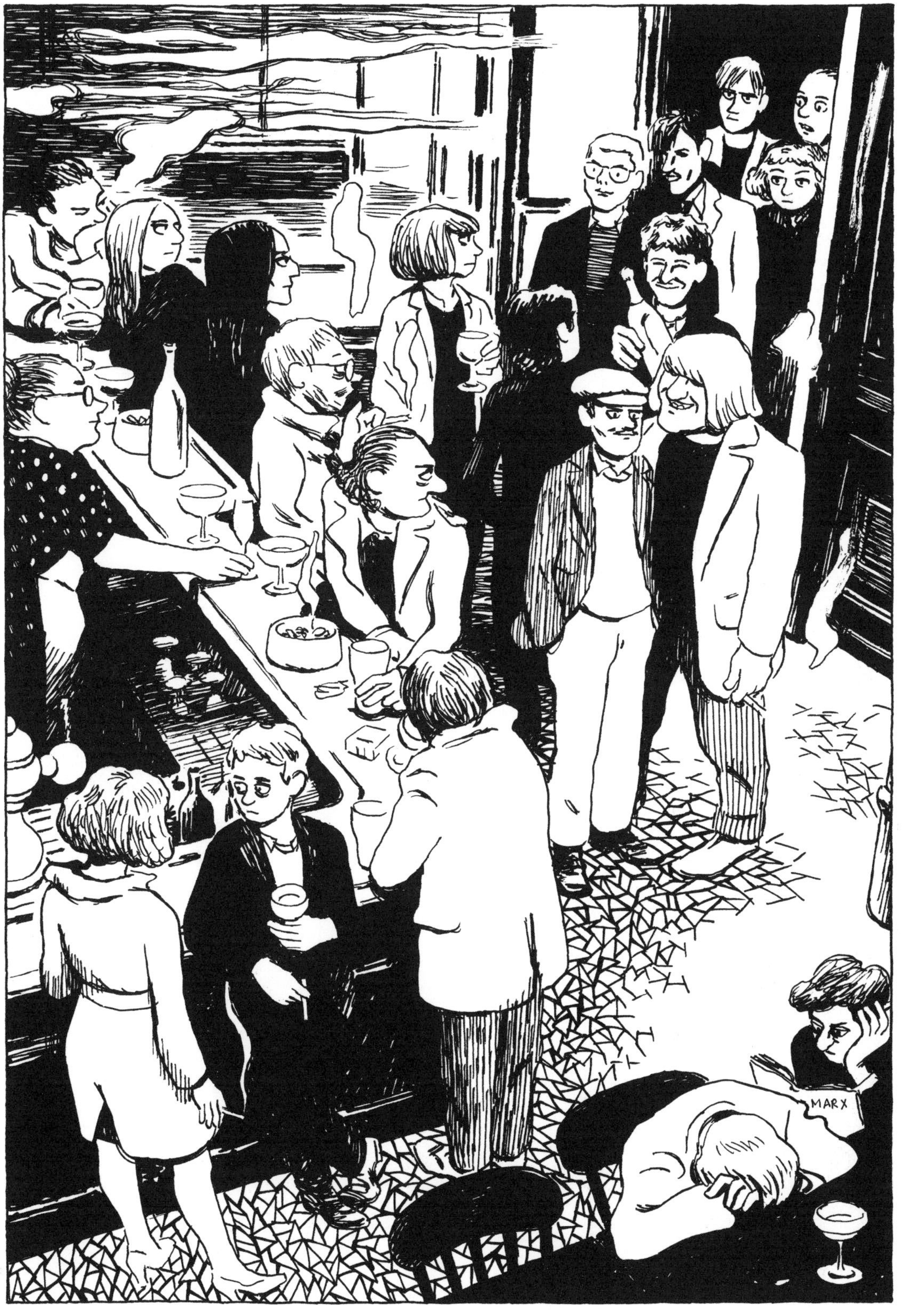
MARX

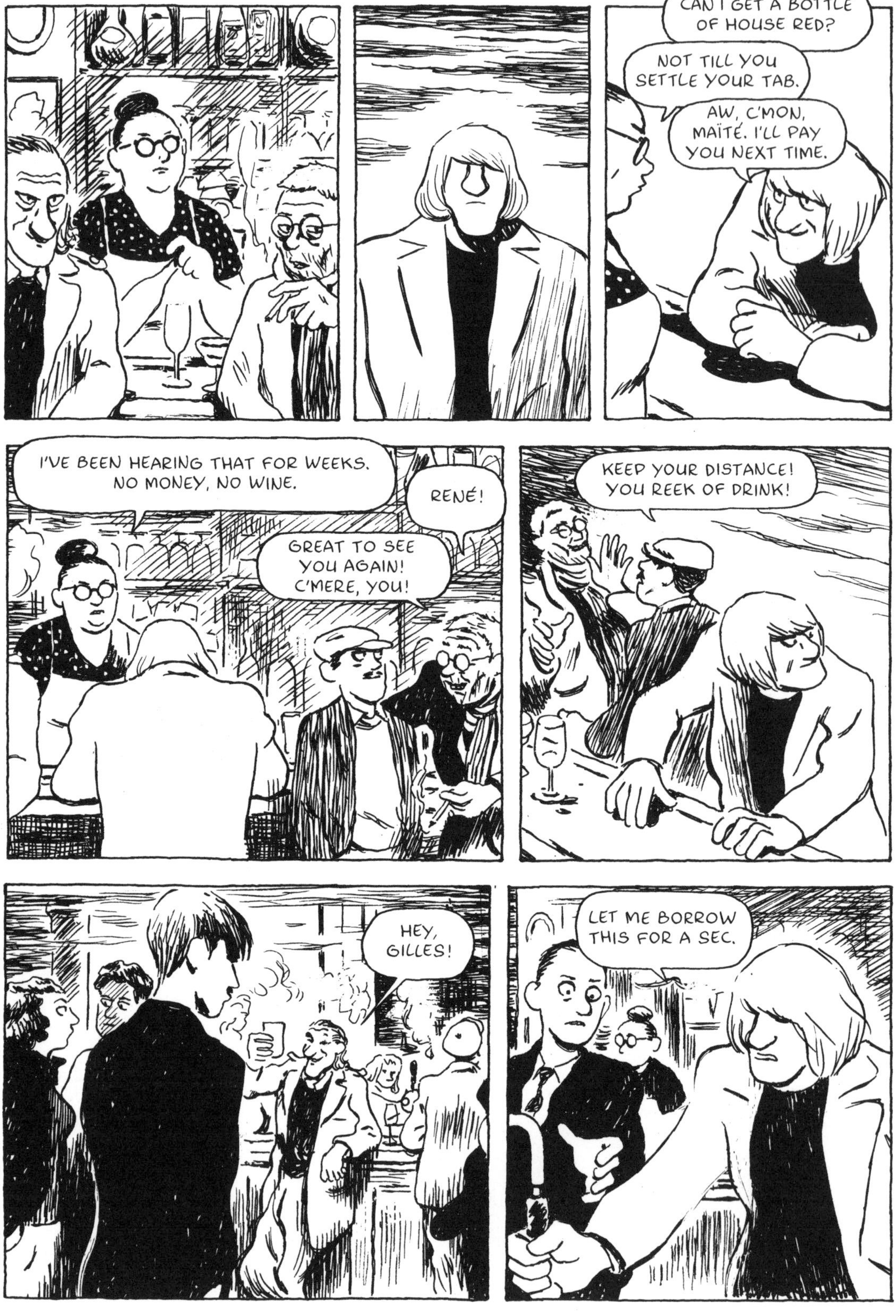

CAN I GET A BOTTLE OF HOUSE RED?
NOT TILL YOU SETTLE YOUR TAB.
AW, C'MON, MAÏTÉ. I'LL PAY YOU NEXT TIME.
I'VE BEEN HEARING THAT FOR WEEKS. NO MONEY, NO WINE.
RENÉ!
GREAT TO SEE YOU AGAIN! C'MERE, YOU!
KEEP YOUR DISTANCE! YOU REEK OF DRINK!
HEY, GILLES!
LET ME BORROW THIS FOR A SEC.

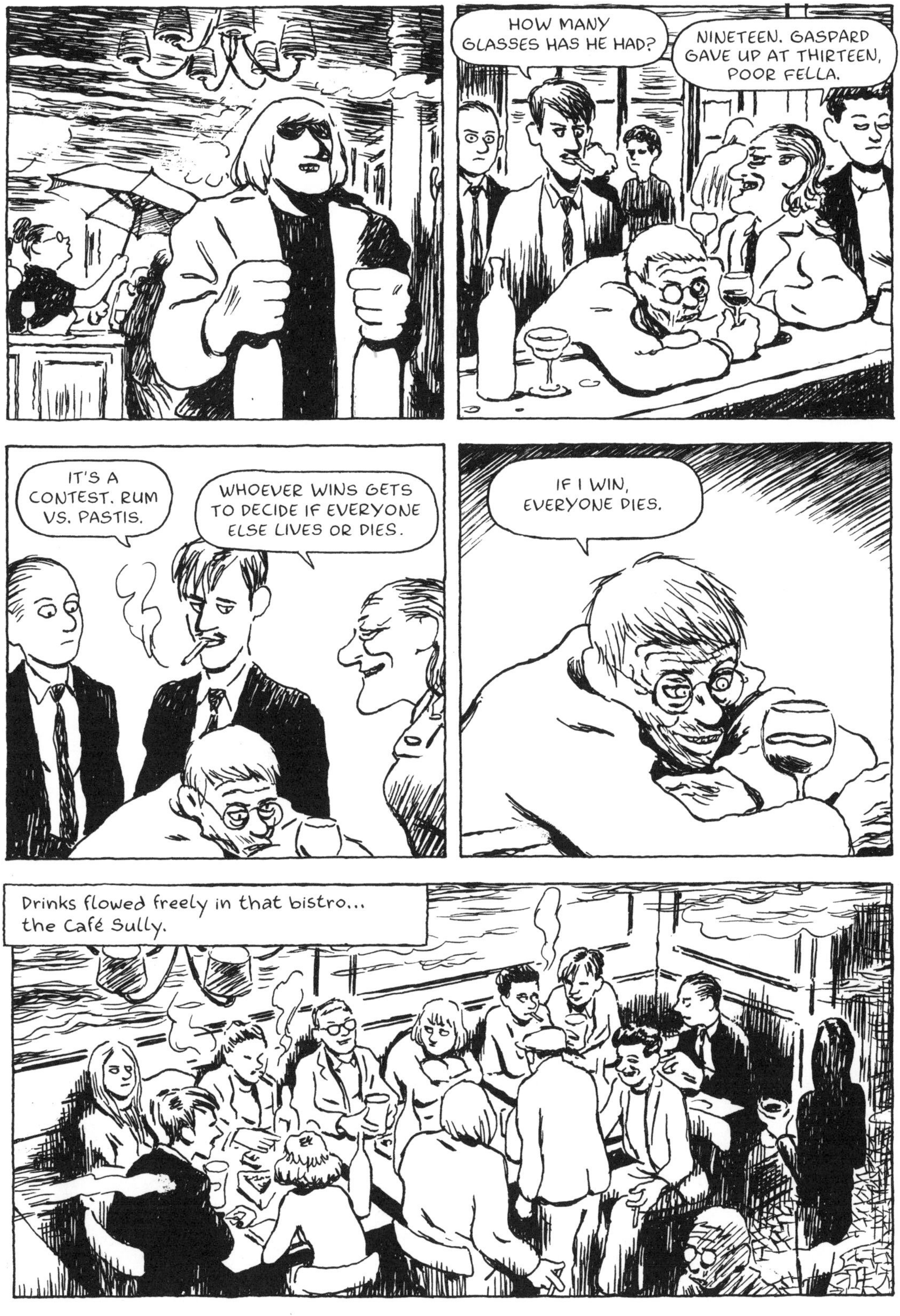
HOW MANY GLASSES HAS HE HAD?
NINETEEN. GASPARD GAVE UP AT THIRTEEN, POOR FELLA.
IT'S A CONTEST. RUM VS. PASTIS.
WHOEVER WINS GETS TO DECIDE IF EVERYONE ELSE LIVES OR DIES.
IF I WIN, EVERYONE DIES.
Drinks flowed freely in that bistro... the Café Sully.

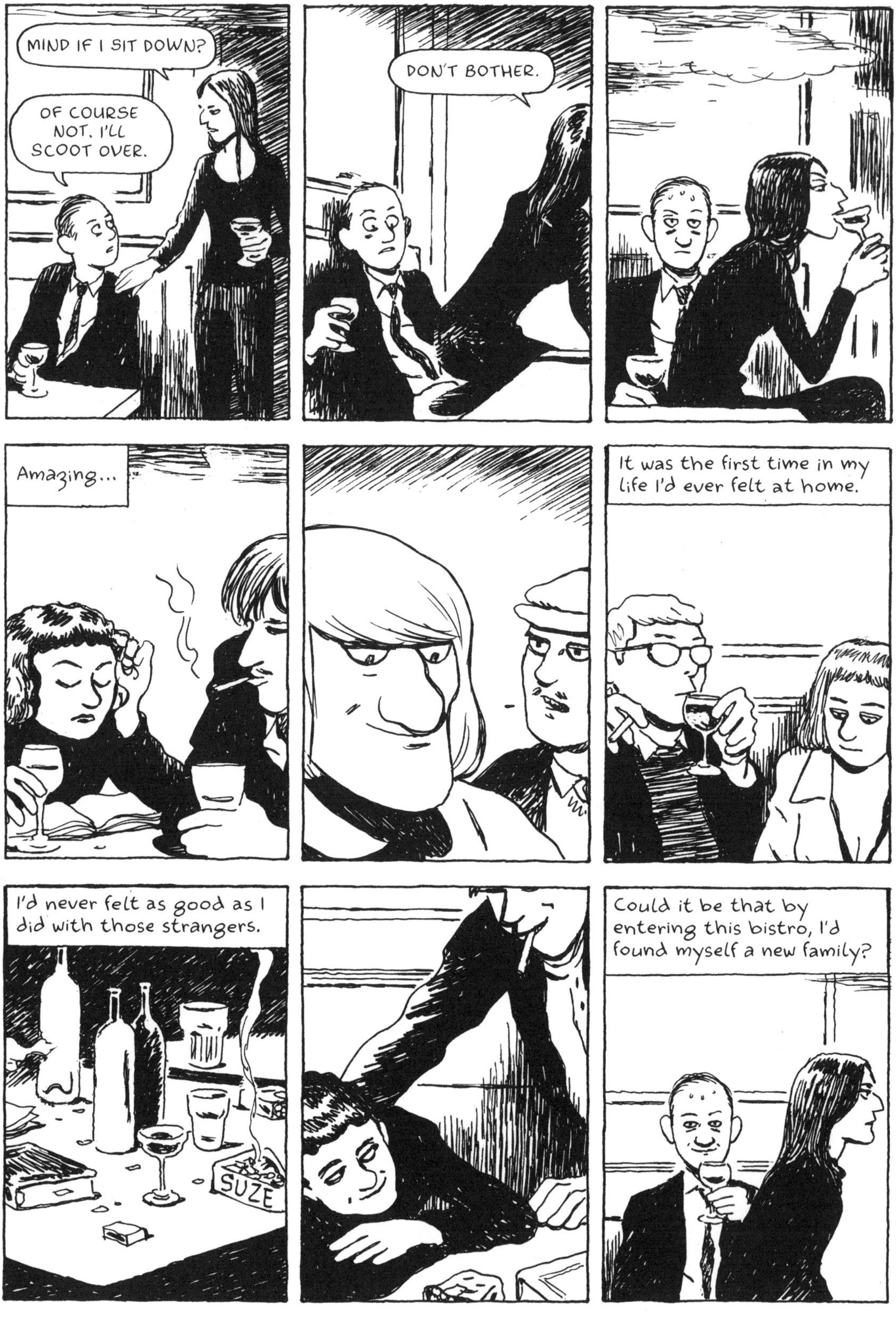
MIND IF I SIT DOWN?
OF COURSE NOT. I'LL SCOOT OVER.
DON'T BOTHER.
Amazing...
It was the first time in my life I'd ever felt at home.
I'd never felt as good as I did with those strangers.
SUZE
Could it be that by entering this bistro, I'd found myself a new family?

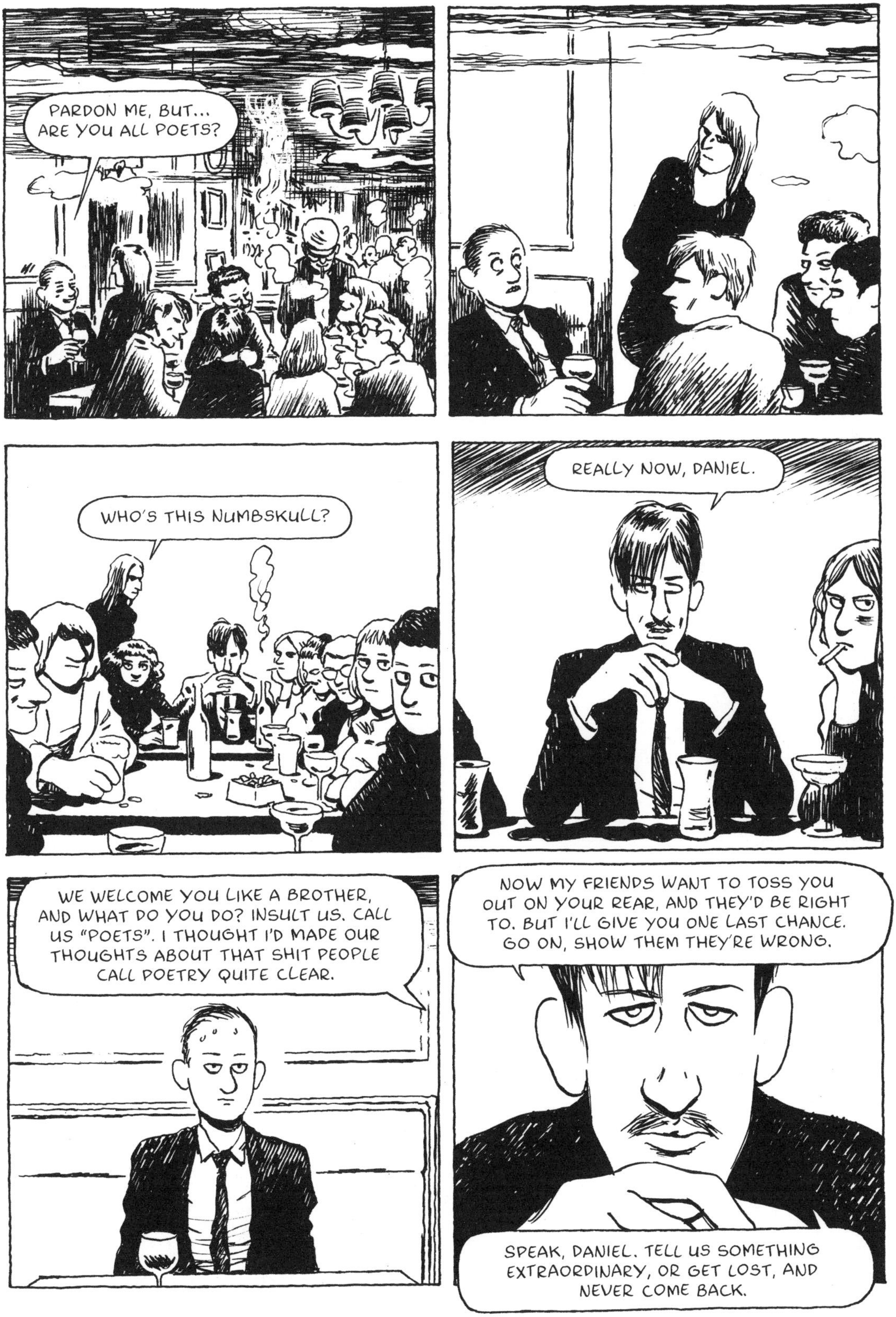
PARDON ME, BUT... ARE YOU ALL POETS?
WHO'S THIS NUMBSKULL?
REALLY NOW, DANIEL.
WE WELCOME YOU LIKE A BROTHER, AND WHAT DO YOU DO? INSULT US. CALL US "POETS". I THOUGHT I'D MADE OUR THOUGHTS ABOUT THAT SHIT PEOPLE CALL POETRY QUITE CLEAR.
NOW MY FRIENDS WANT TO TOSS YOU OUT ON YOUR REAR, AND THEY'D BE RIGHT TO. BUT I'LL GIVE YOU ONE LAST CHANCE. GO ON, SHOW THEM THEY'RE WRONG.
SPEAK, DANIEL. TELL US SOMETHING EXTRAORDINARY, OR GET LOST, AND NEVER COME BACK.

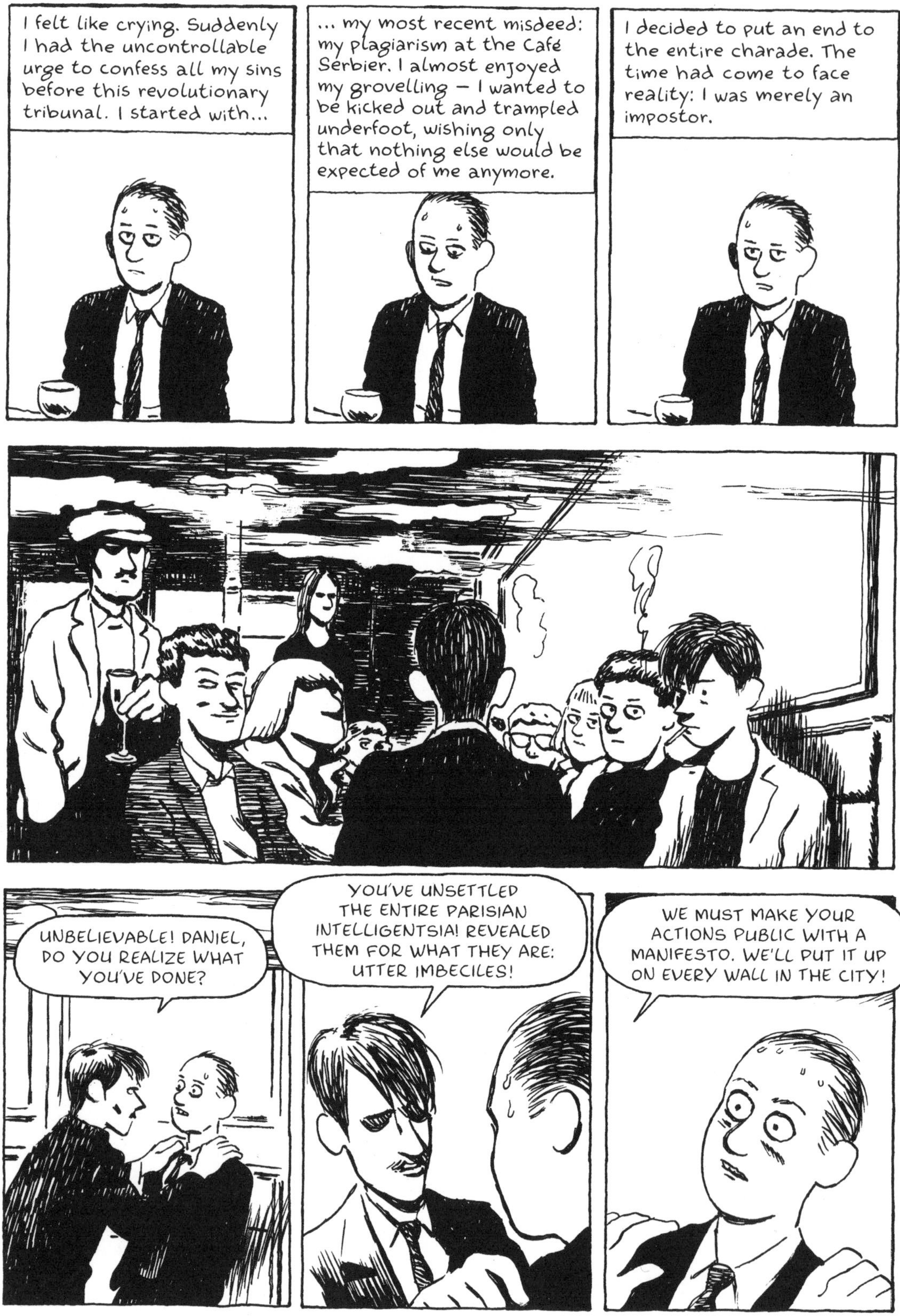
I felt like crying. Suddenly I had the uncontrollable urge to confess all my sins before this revolutionary tribunal. I started with...
... my most recent misdeed: my plagiarism at the Café Serbier. I almost enjoyed my grovelling – I wanted to be kicked out and trampled underfoot, wishing only that nothing else would be expected of me anymore.
I decided to put an end to the entire charade. The time had come to face reality: I was merely an impostor.
UNBELIEVABLE! DANIEL, DO YOU REALIZE WHAT YOU'VE DONE?
YOU'VE UNSETTLED THE ENTIRE PARISIAN INTELLIGENTSIA! REVEALED THEM FOR WHAT THEY ARE: UTTER IMBECILES!
WE MUST MAKE YOUR ACTIONS PUBLIC WITH A MANIFESTO. WE'LL PUT IT UP ON EVERY WALL IN THE CITY!

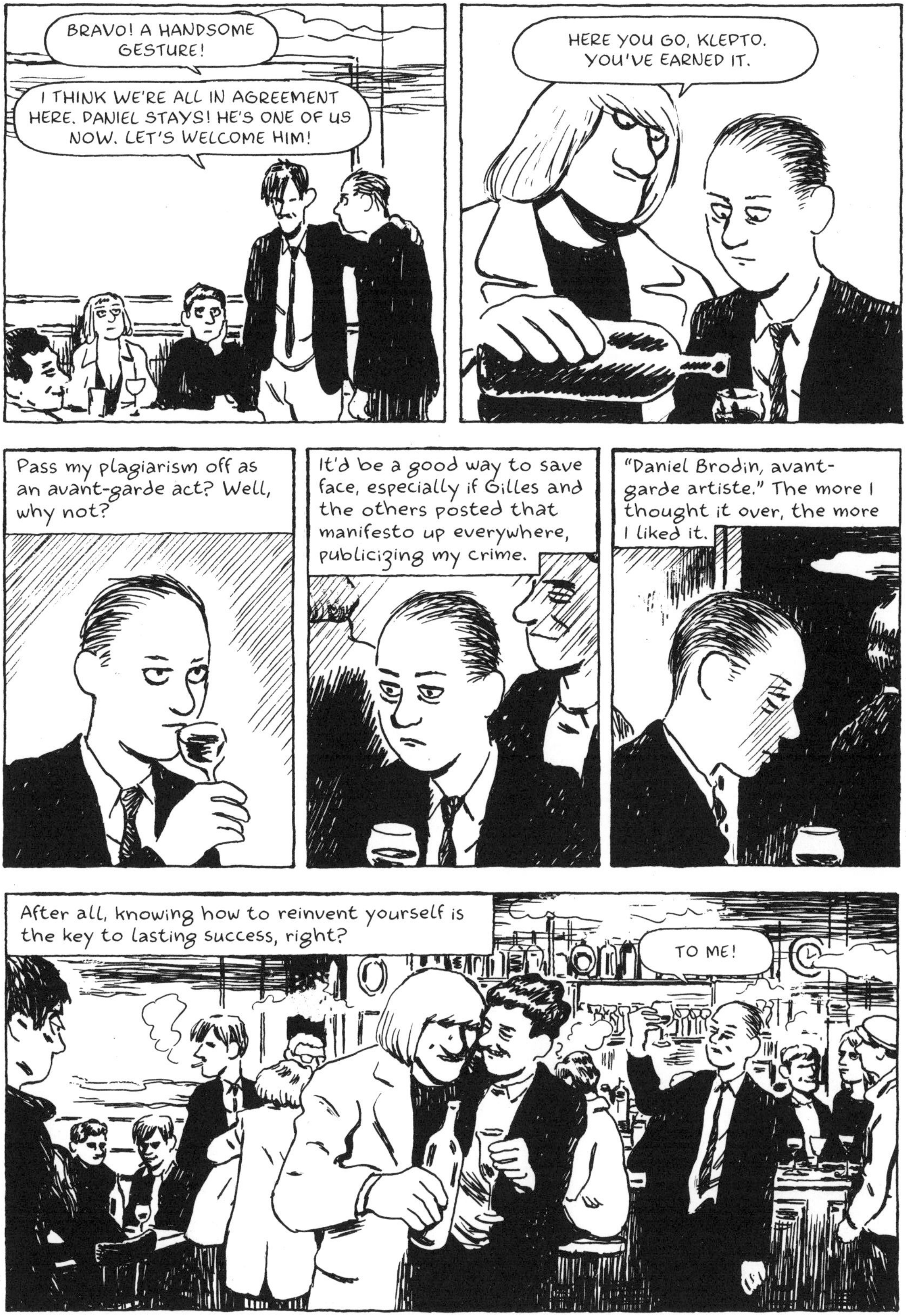
BRAVO! A HANDSOME GESTURE!
I THINK WE'RE ALL IN AGREEMENT HERE. DANIEL STAYS! HE'S ONE OF US NOW. LET'S WELCOME HIM!
HERE YOU GO, KLEPTO. YOU'VE EARNED IT.
Pass my plagiarism off as an avant-garde act? Well, why not?
It'd be a good way to save face, especially if Gilles and the others posted that manifesto up everywhere, publicizing my crime.
"Daniel Brodin, avant-garde artiste." The more I thought it over, the more I liked it.
After all, knowing how to reinvent yourself is the key to lasting success, right?
TO ME!

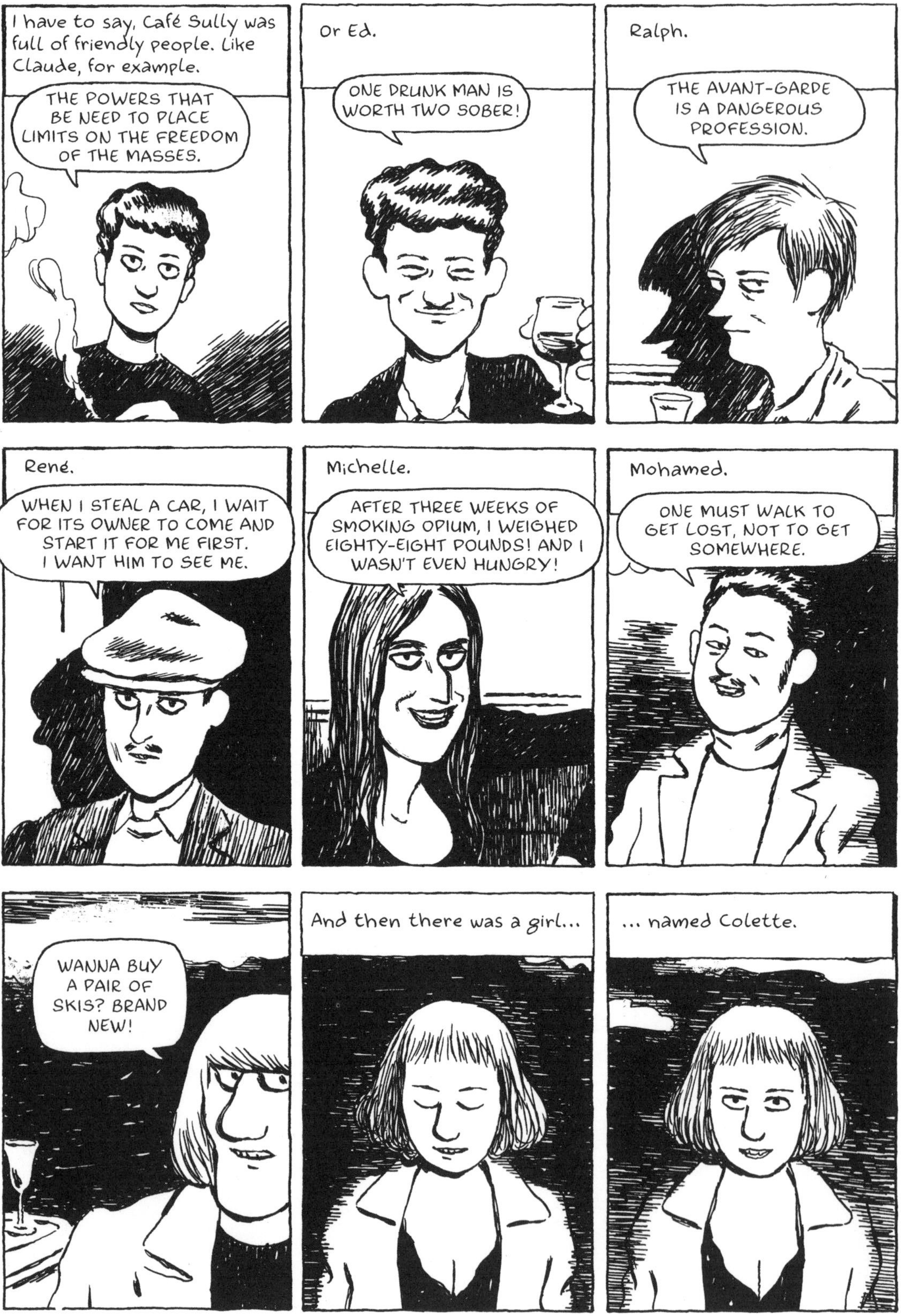
I have to say, Café Sully was full of friendly people. Like Claude, for example.
THE POWERS THAT BE NEED TO PLACE LIMITS ON THE FREEDOM OF THE MASSES.
Or Ed.
ONE DRUNK MAN IS WORTH TWO SOBER!
Ralph.
THE AVANT-GARDE IS A DANGEROUS PROFESSION.
René.
WHEN I STEAL A CAR, I WAIT FOR ITS OWNER TO COME AND START IT FOR ME FIRST. I WANT HIM TO SEE ME.
Michelle.
AFTER THREE WEEKS OF SMOKING OPIUM, I WEIGHED EIGHTY-EIGHT POUNDS! AND I WASN'T EVEN HUNGRY!
Mohamed.
ONE MUST WALK TO GET LOST, NOT TO GET SOMEWHERE.
WANNA BUY A PAIR OF SKIS? BRAND NEW!
And then there was a girl...
... named Colette.

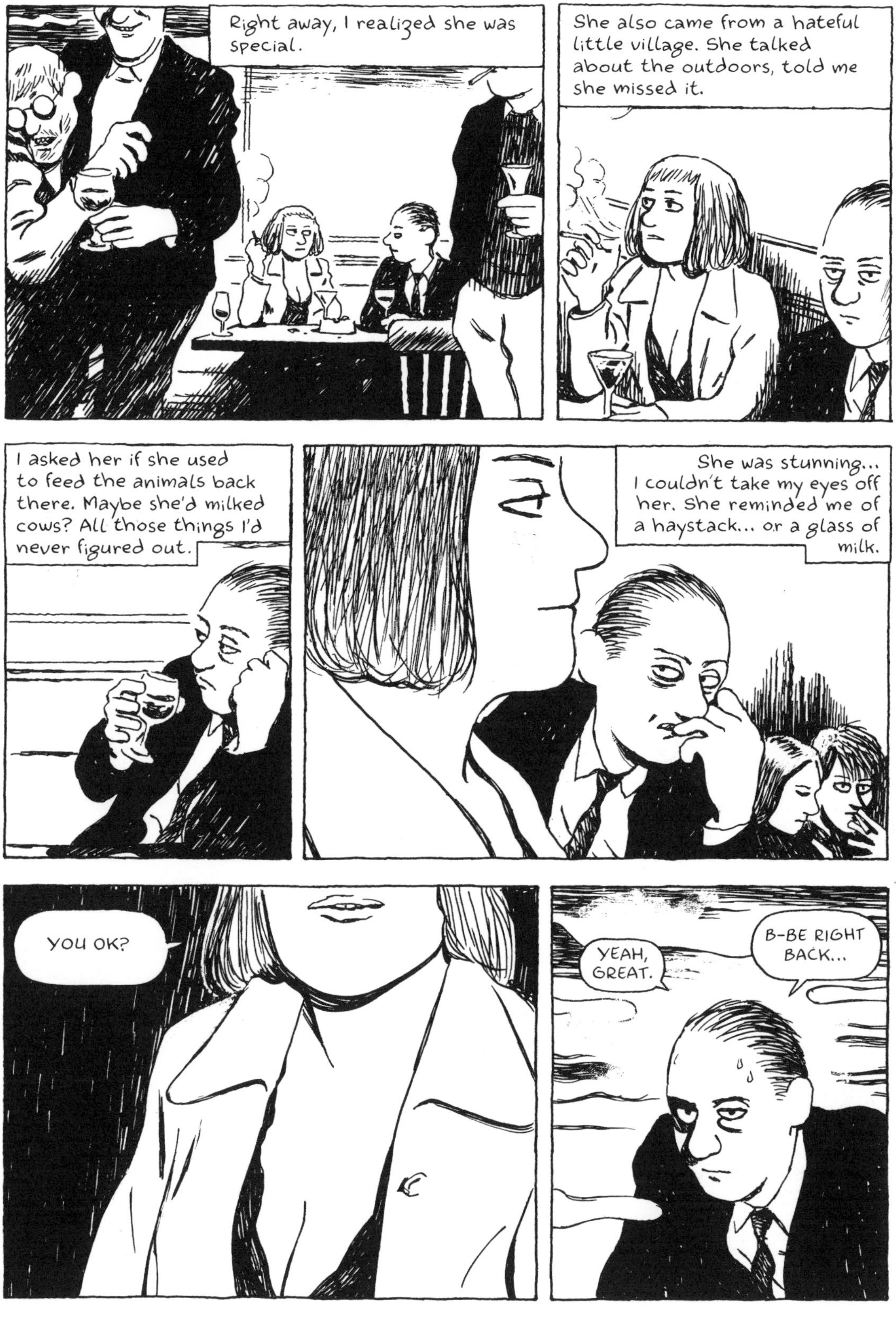
Right away, I realized she was special.
She also came from a hateful little village. She talked about the outdoors, told me she missed it.
I asked her if she used to feed the animals back there. Maybe she'd milked cows? All those things I'd never figured out.
She was stunning... I couldn't take my eyes off her. She reminded me of a haystack... or a glass of milk.
YOU OK?
YEAH, GREAT.
B-BE RIGHT BACK...

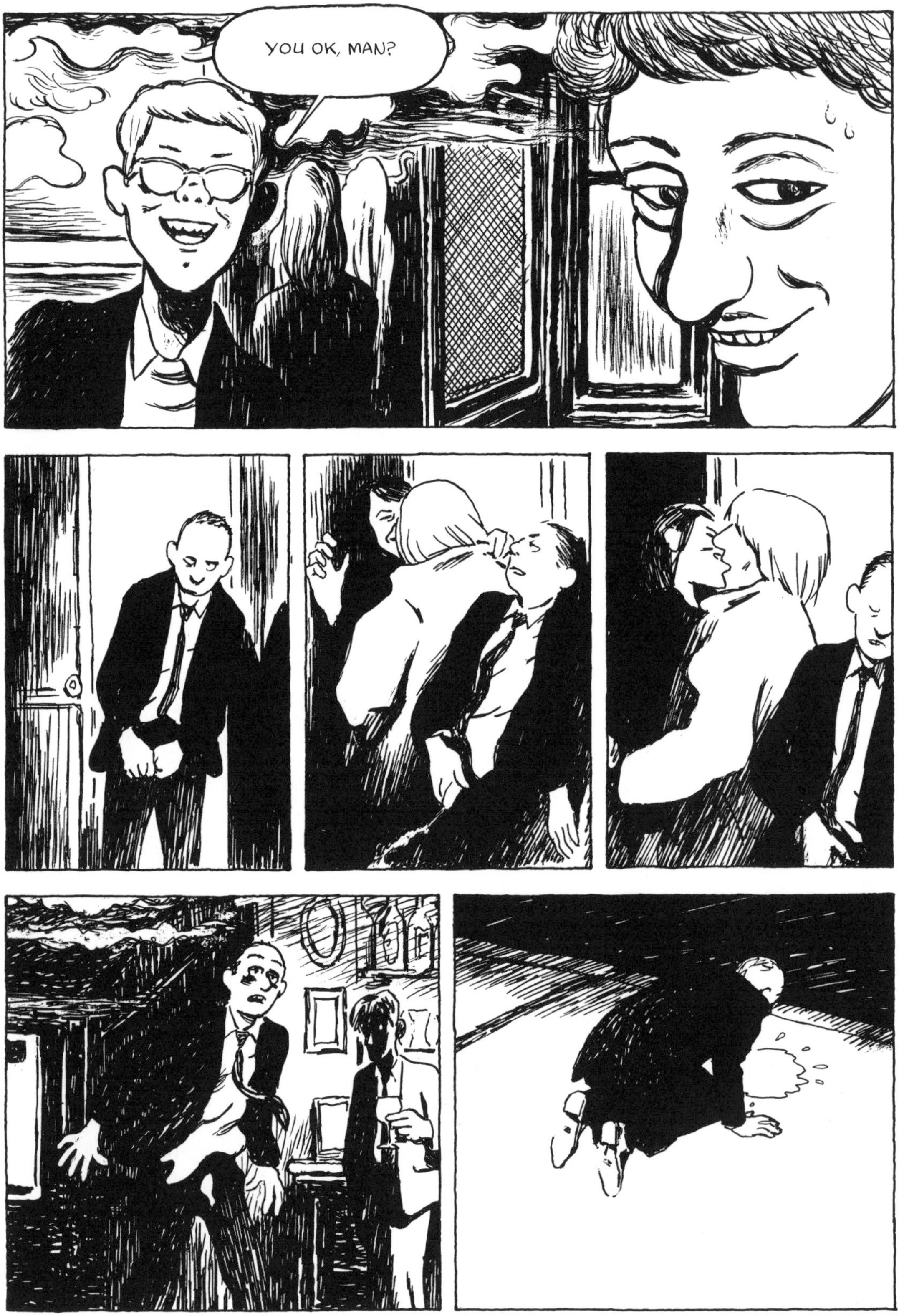
YOU OK, MAN?

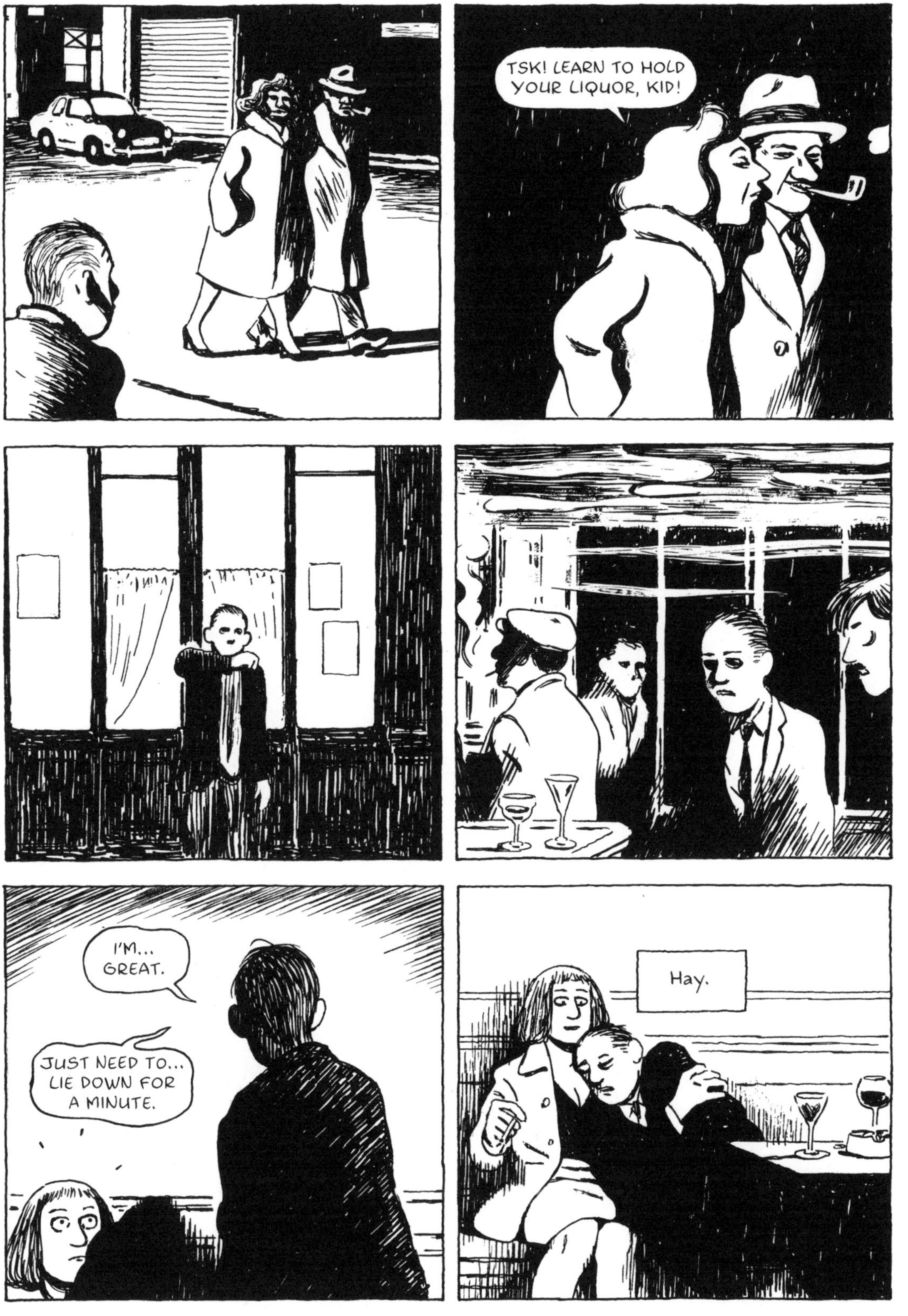
TSK! LEARN TO HOLD YOUR LIQUOR, KID!
I'M... GREAT.
JUST NEED TO... LIE DOWN FOR A MINUTE.
Hay.

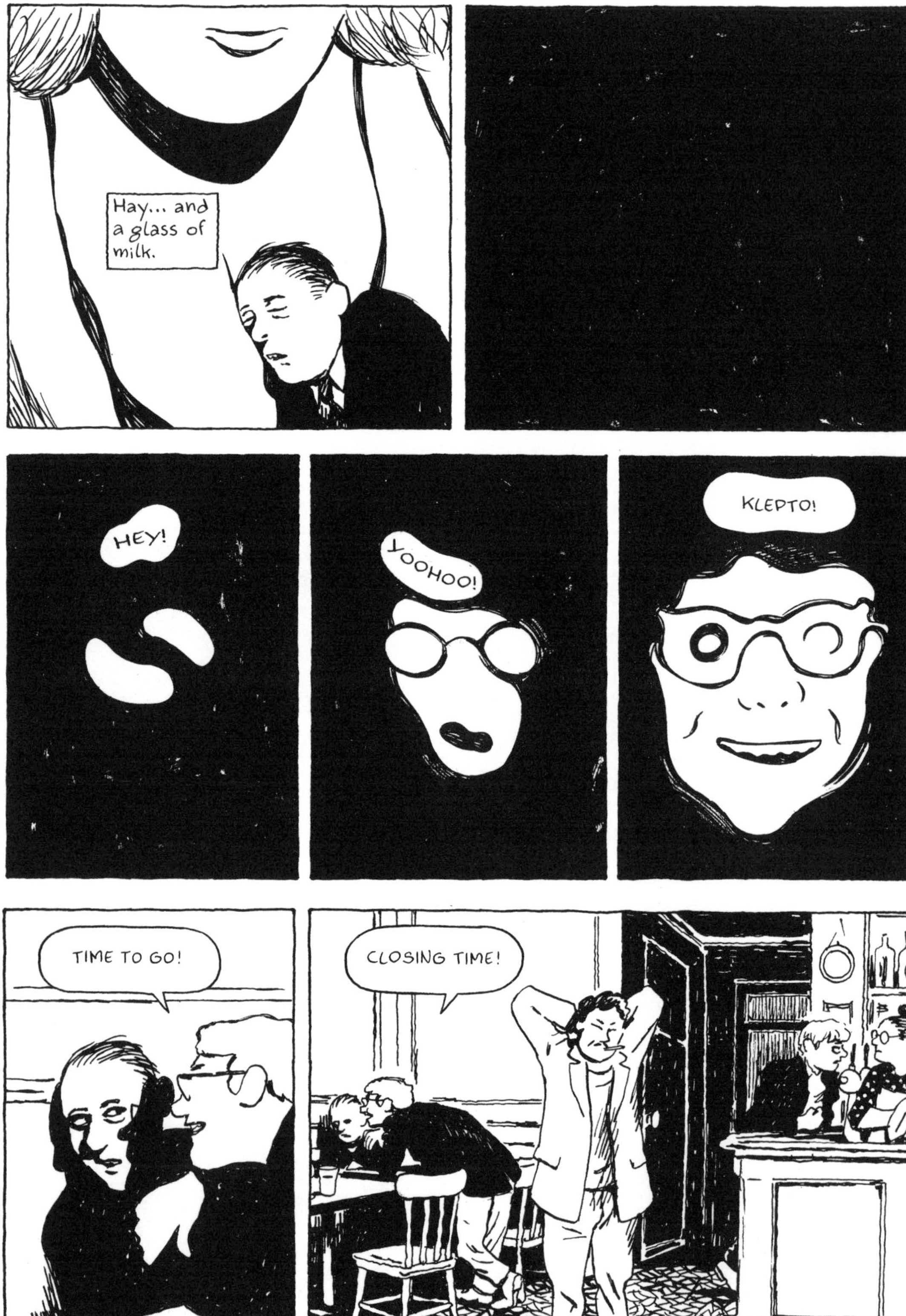
Hay... and a glass of milk.
HEY!
YOOHOO!
KLEPTO!
TIME TO GO!
CLOSING TIME!

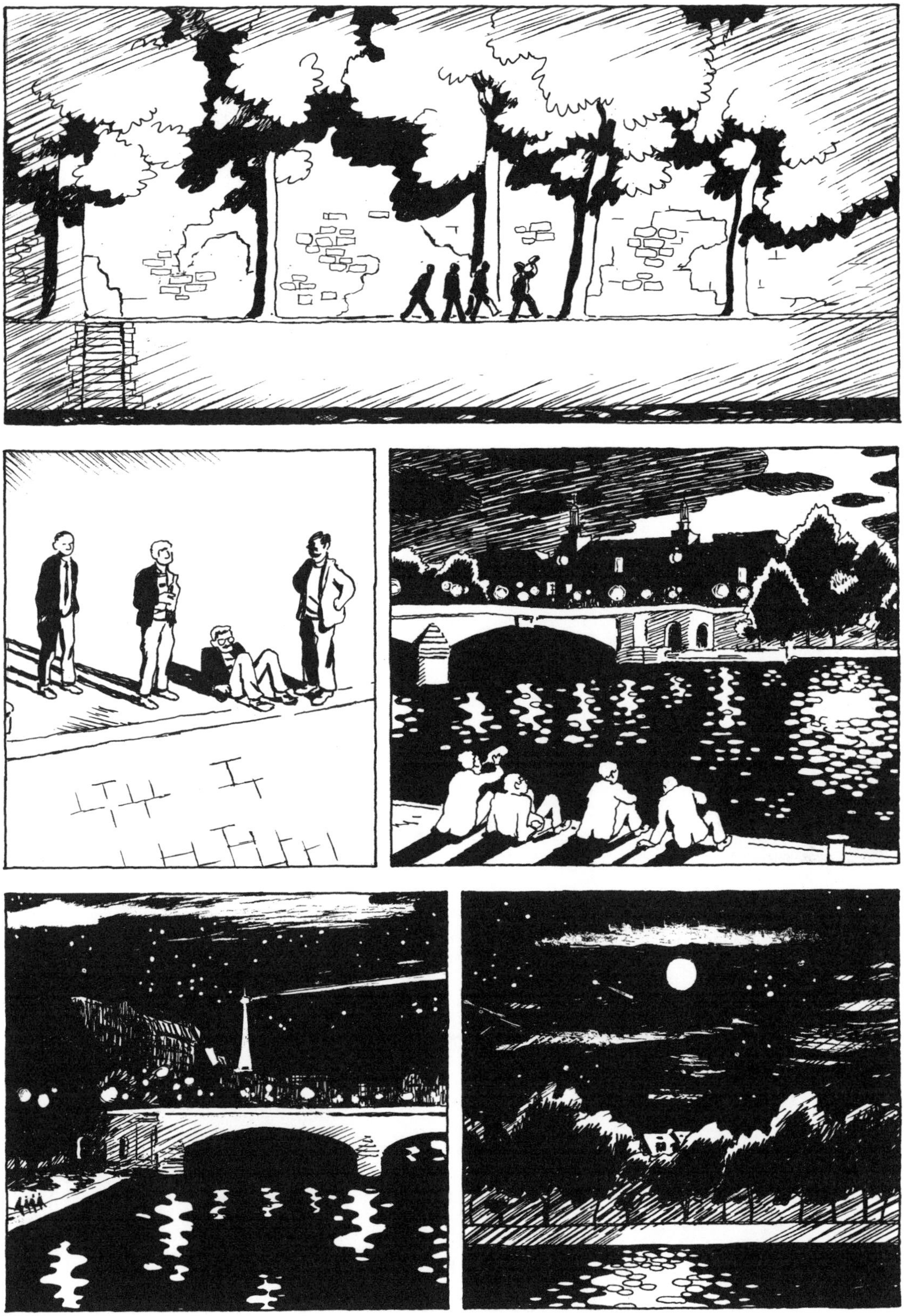

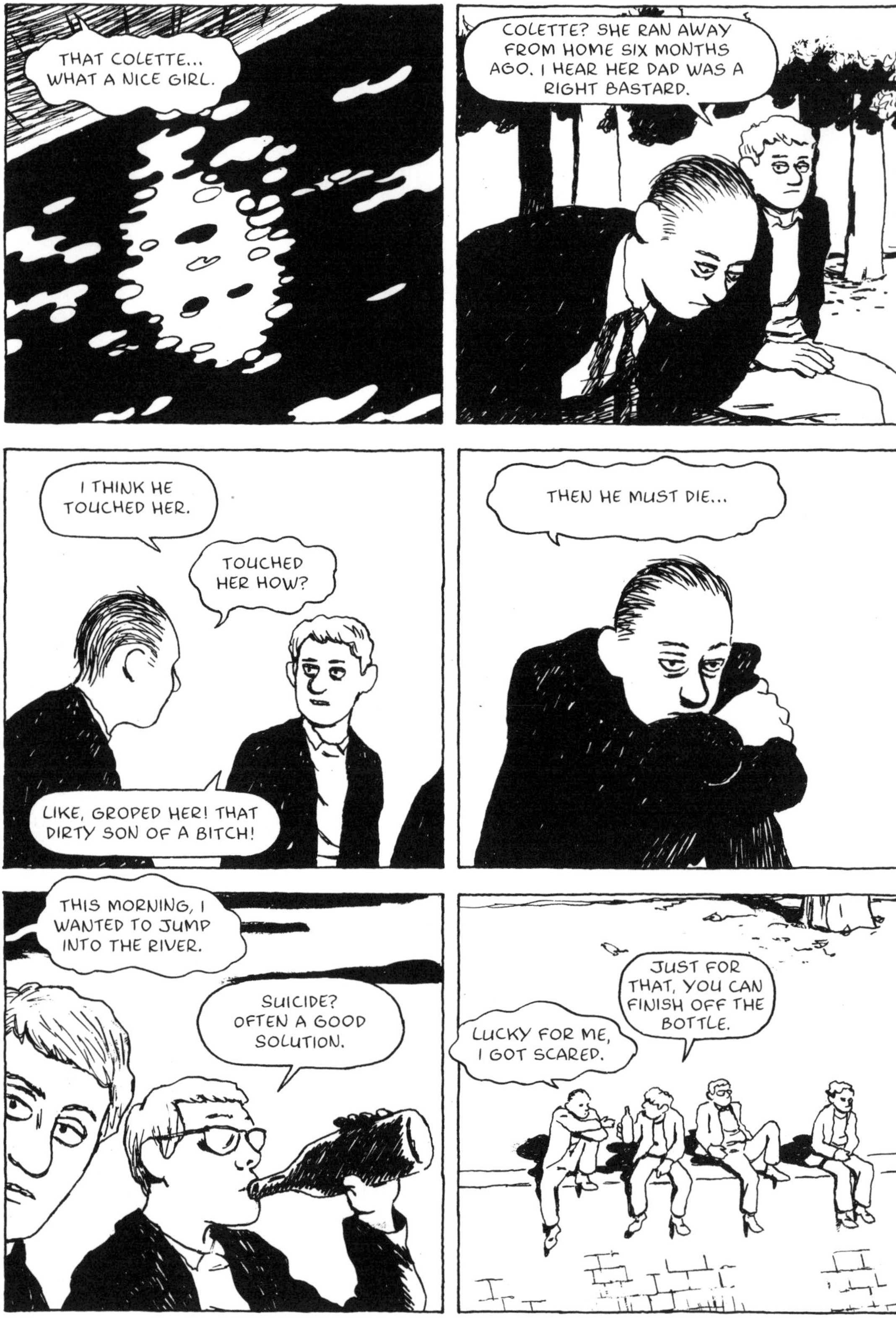
THAT COLETTE... WHAT A NICE GIRL.
COLETTE? SHE RAN AWAY FROM HOME SIX MONTHS AGO. I HEAR HER DAD WAS A RIGHT BASTARD.
I THINK HE TOUCHED HER.
TOUCHED HER HOW?
LIKE, GROPED HER! THAT DIRTY SON OF A BITCH!
THEN HE MUST DIE...
THIS MORNING, I WANTED TO JUMP INTO THE RIVER.
SUICIDE? OFTEN A GOOD SOLUTION.
LUCKY FOR ME, I GOT SCARED.
JUST FOR THAT, YOU CAN FINISH OFF THE BOTTLE.

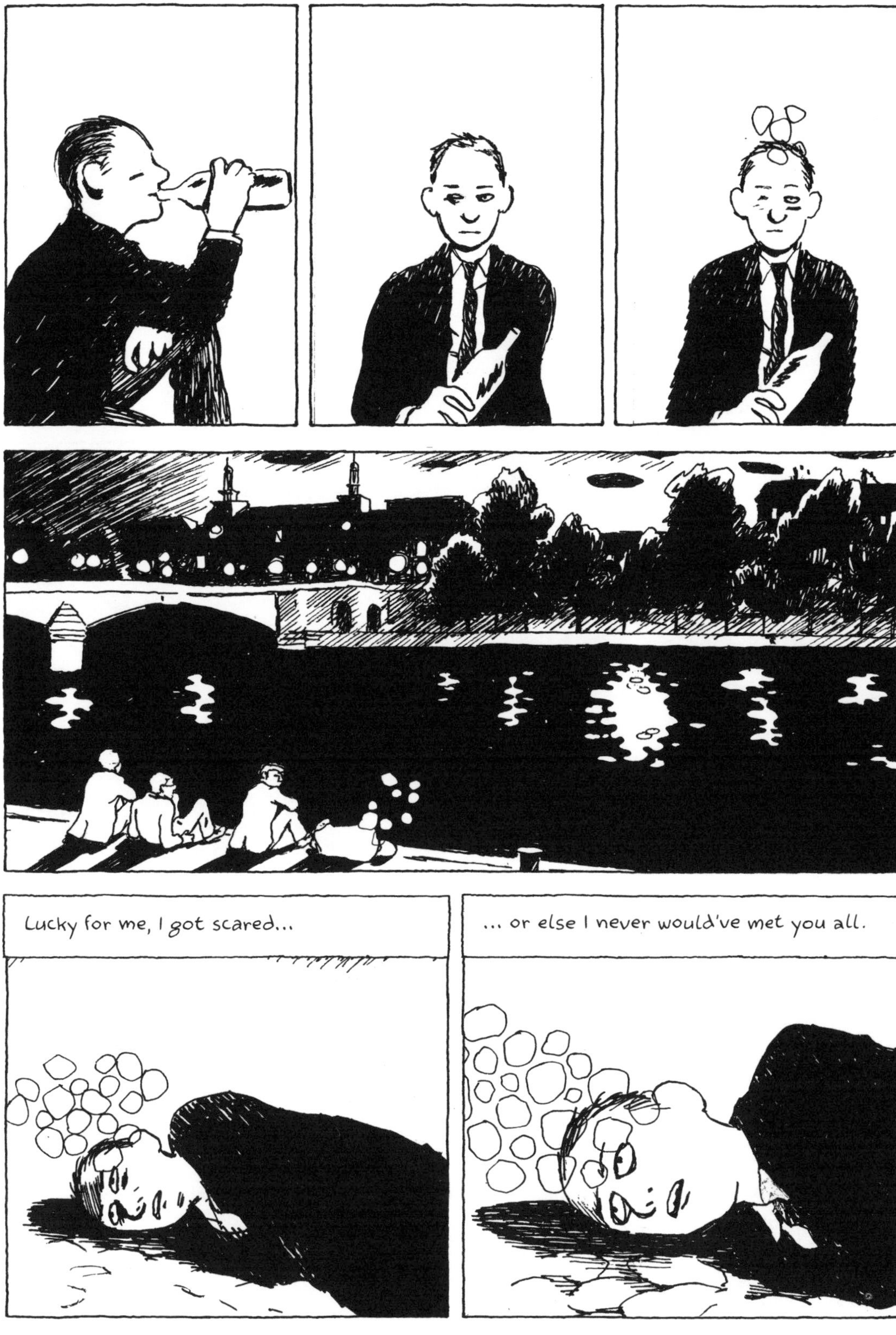
Lucky for me, I got scared...
... or else I never would've met you all.

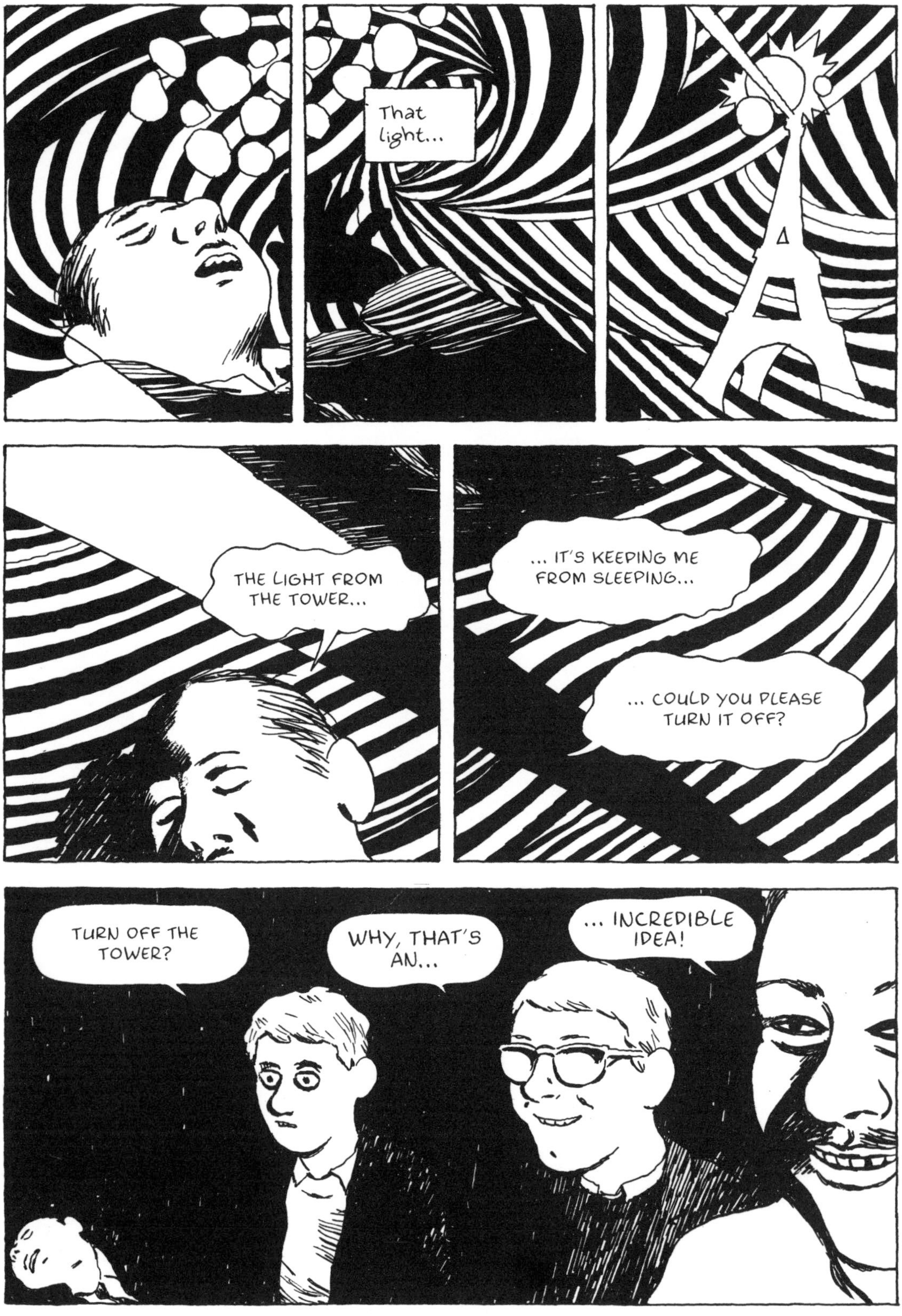
That light...
THE LIGHT FROM THE TOWER...
... IT'S KEEPING ME FROM SLEEPING...
... COULD YOU PLEASE TURN IT OFF?
TURN OFF THE TOWER?
WHY, THAT'S AN...
... INCREDIBLE IDEA!

CHAPTER 3

"YOU HAVE THE MAKINGS OF A TRUE POET! I CAN TELL!"
M. Bélanchon

Twenty-three poems and a letter.

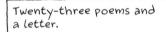

That's what I've written since getting back to my uncle's, in Aubervilliers.

I sing of the girls of Café Serbier.

The perfume of their hair, and the furious blaze in their eyes.

I sing of Gilles, his friends, and drink...

And the Seine. And Paris by night.

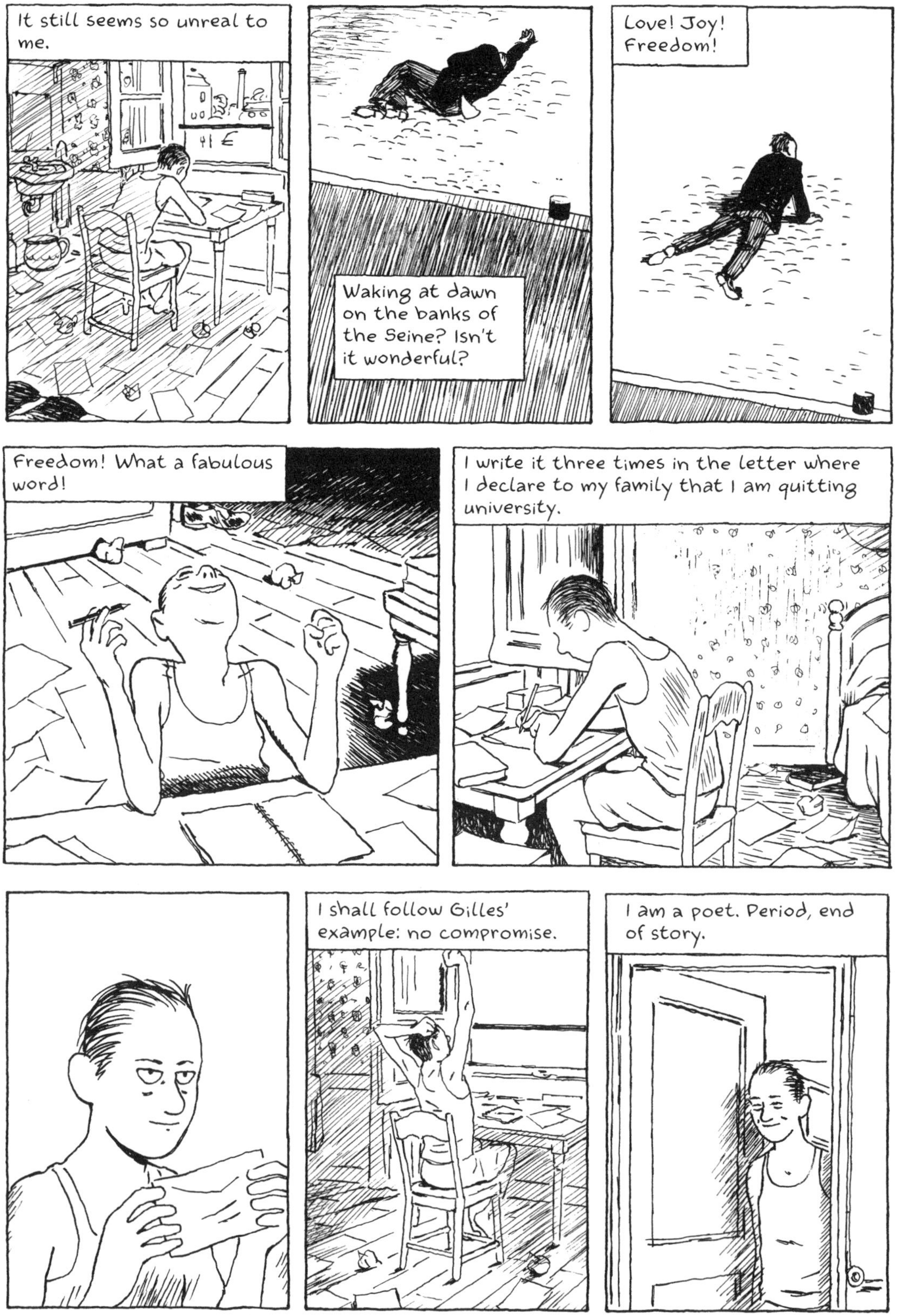
It still seems so unreal to me.
Waking at dawn on the banks of the Seine? Isn't it wonderful?
Love! Joy! Freedom!
Freedom! What a fabulous word!
I write it three times in the letter where I declare to my family that I am quitting university.
I shall follow Gilles' example: no compromise.
I am a poet. Period, end of story.

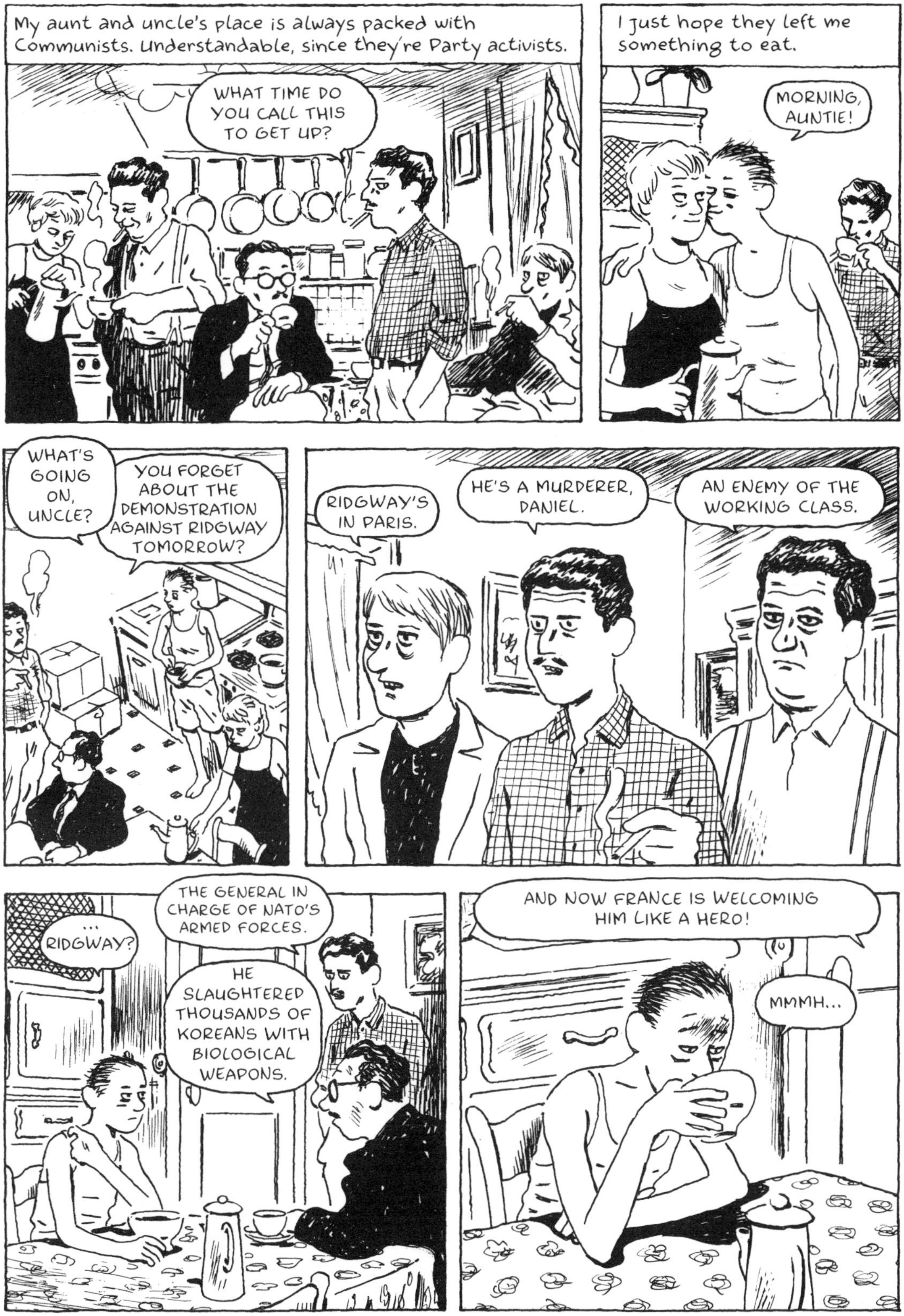
My aunt and uncle's place is always packed with Communists. Understandable, since they're Party activists.
WHAT TIME DO YOU CALL THIS TO GET UP?
I just hope they left me something to eat.
MORNING, AUNTIE!
WHAT'S GOING ON, UNCLE?
YOU FORGET ABOUT THE DEMONSTRATION AGAINST RIDGWAY TOMORROW?
RIDGWAY'S IN PARIS.
HE'S A MURDERER, DANIEL.
AN ENEMY OF THE WORKING CLASS.
... RIDGWAY?
THE GENERAL IN CHARGE OF NATO'S ARMED FORCES.
HE SLAUGHTERED THOUSANDS OF KOREANS WITH BIOLOGICAL WEAPONS.
AND NOW FRANCE IS WELCOMING HIM LIKE A HERO!
MMMH...

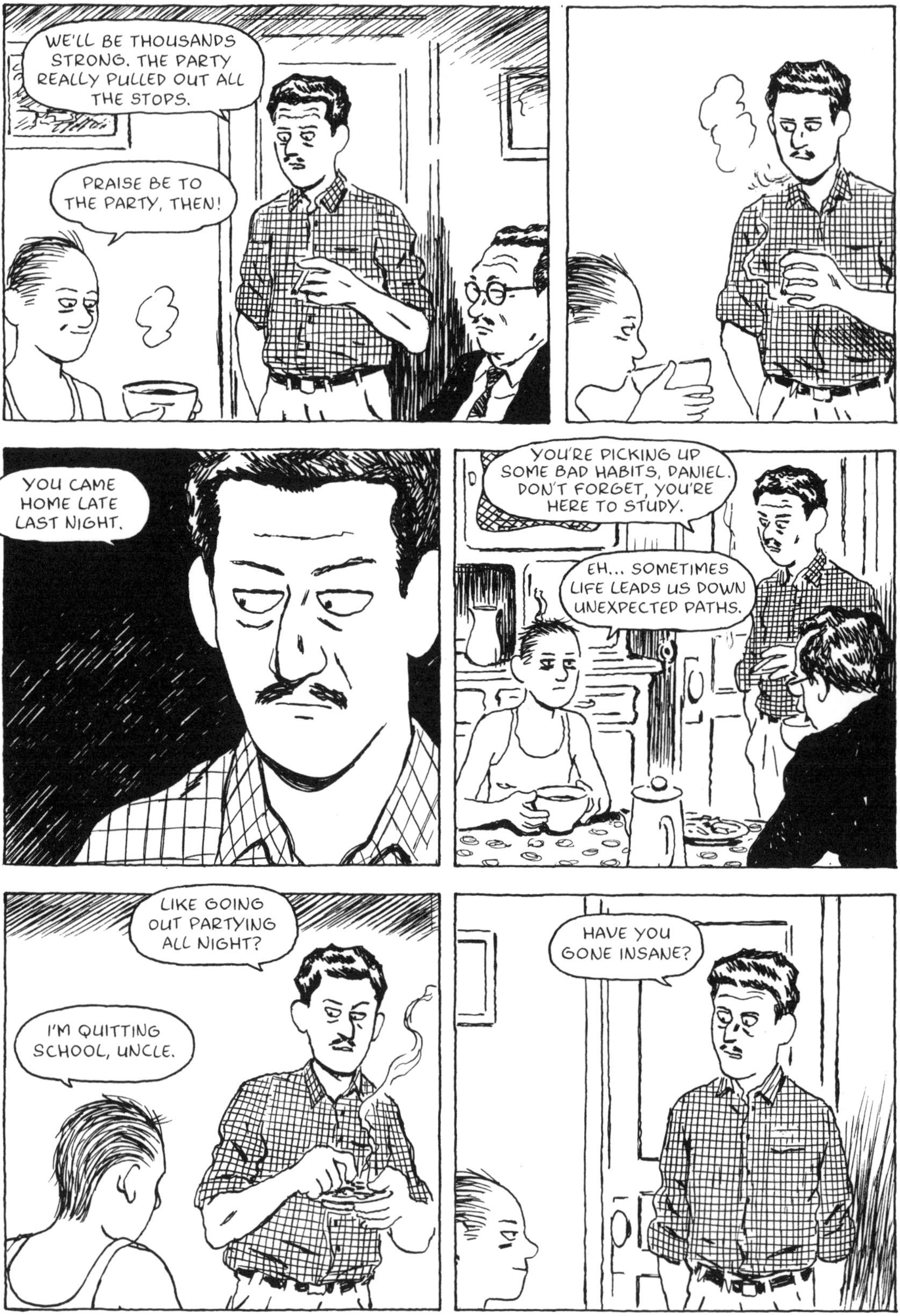
WE'LL BE THOUSANDS STRONG. THE PARTY REALLY PULLED OUT ALL THE STOPS.
PRAISE BE TO THE PARTY, THEN!
YOU CAME HOME LATE LAST NIGHT.
YOU'RE PICKING UP SOME BAD HABITS, DANIEL. DON'T FORGET, YOU'RE HERE TO STUDY.
EH... SOMETIMES LIFE LEADS US DOWN UNEXPECTED PATHS.
LIKE GOING OUT PARTYING ALL NIGHT?
I'M QUITTING SCHOOL, UNCLE.
HAVE YOU GONE INSANE?

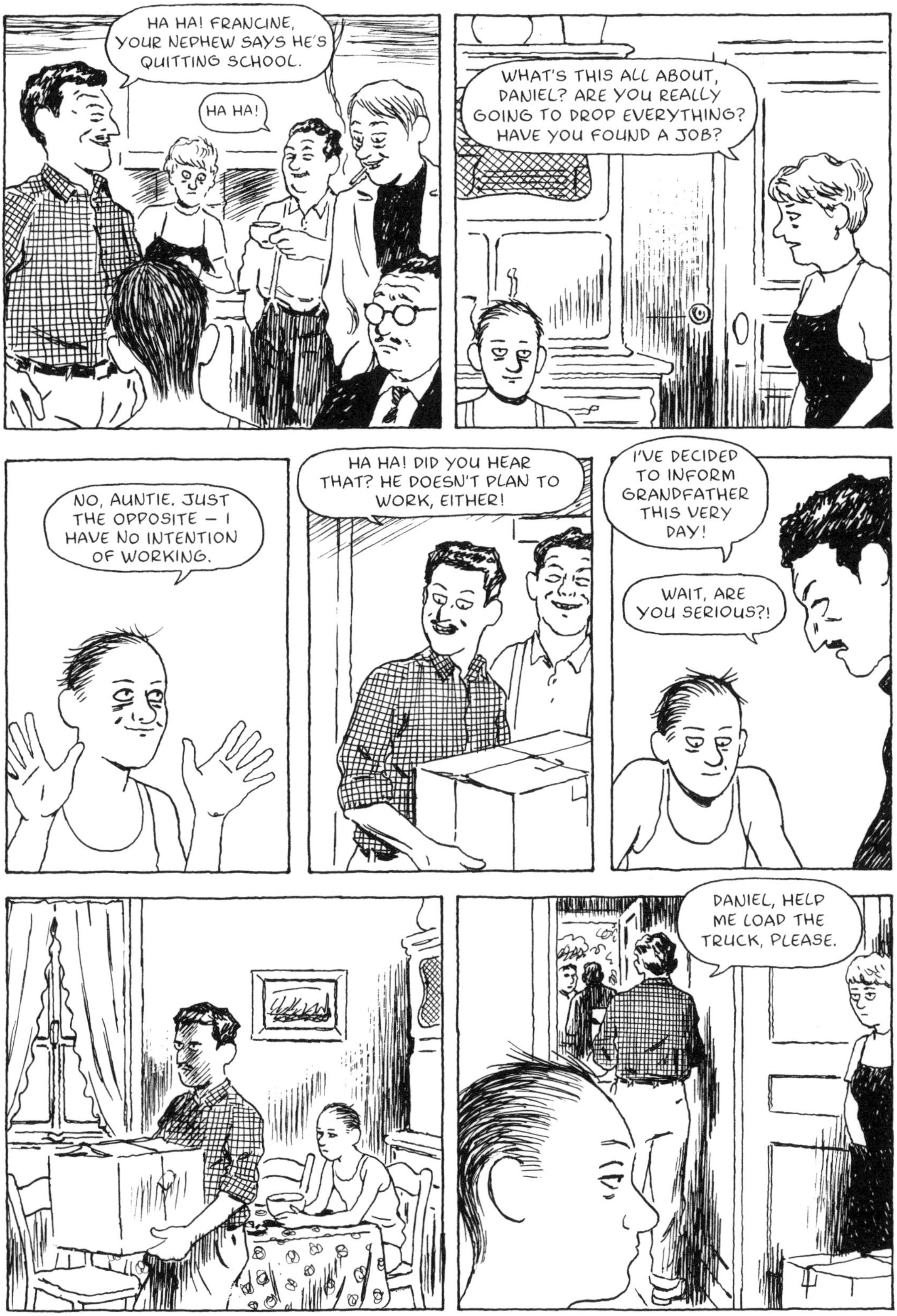
HA HA! FRANCINE, YOUR NEPHEW SAYS HE'S QUITTING SCHOOL.
HA HA!
WHAT'S THIS ALL ABOUT, DANIEL? ARE YOU REALLY GOING TO DROP EVERYTHING? HAVE YOU FOUND A JOB?
NO, AUNTIE. JUST THE OPPOSITE — I HAVE NO INTENTION OF WORKING.
HA HA! DID YOU HEAR THAT? HE DOESN'T PLAN TO WORK, EITHER!
I'VE DECIDED TO INFORM GRANDFATHER THIS VERY DAY!
WAIT, ARE YOU SERIOUS?!
DANIEL, HELP ME LOAD THE TRUCK, PLEASE.

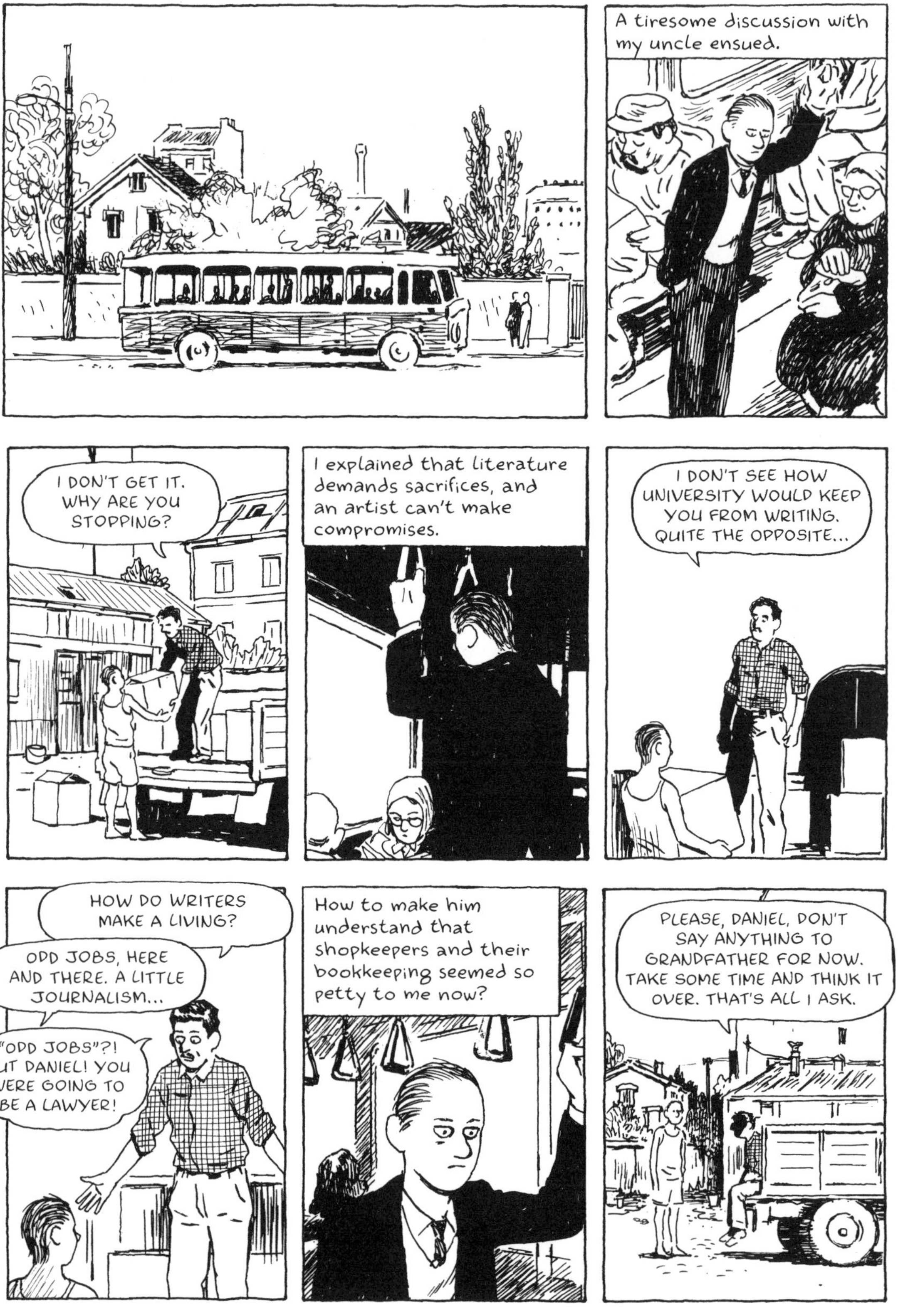
A tiresome discussion with my uncle ensued.
I DON'T GET IT. WHY ARE YOU STOPPING?
I explained that literature demands sacrifices, and an artist can't make compromises.
I DON'T SEE HOW UNIVERSITY WOULD KEEP YOU FROM WRITING. QUITE THE OPPOSITE...
HOW DO WRITERS MAKE A LIVING?
ODD JOBS, HERE AND THERE. A LITTLE JOURNALISM...
"ODD JOBS"?! BUT DANIEL! YOU WERE GOING TO BE A LAWYER!
How to make him understand that shopkeepers and their bookkeeping seemed so petty to me now?
PLEASE, DANIEL, DON'T SAY ANYTHING TO GRANDFATHER FOR NOW. TAKE SOME TIME AND THINK IT OVER. THAT'S ALL I ASK.

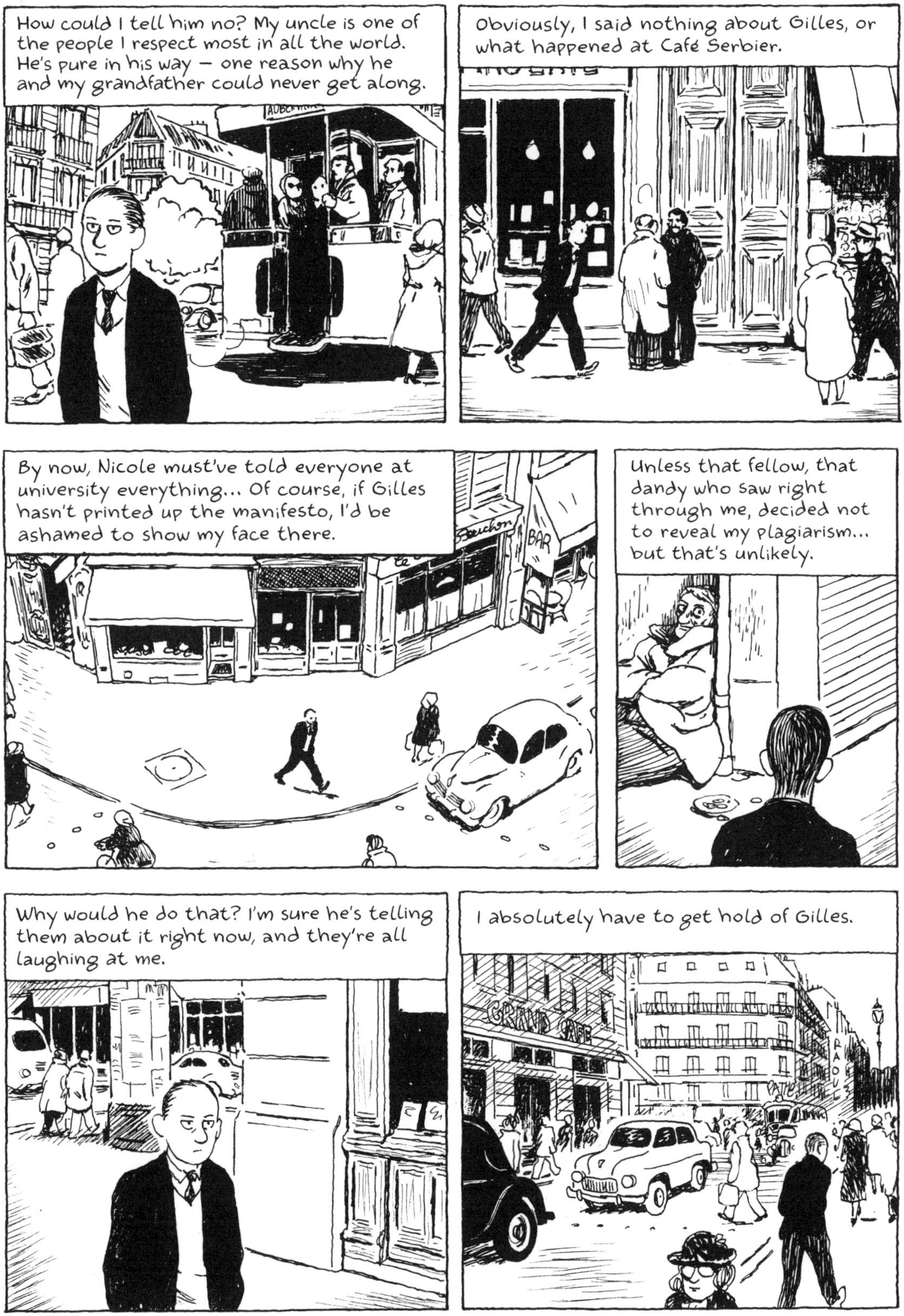
How could I tell him no? My uncle is one of the people I respect most in all the world. He's pure in his way — one reason why he and my grandfather could never get along.
Obviously, I said nothing about Gilles, or what happened at Café Serbier.
By now, Nicole must've told everyone at university everything... Of course, if Gilles hasn't printed up the manifesto, I'd be ashamed to show my face there.
BAR
Unless that fellow, that dandy who saw right through me, decided not to reveal my plagiarism... but that's unlikely.
Why would he do that? I'm sure he's telling them about it right now, and they're all laughing at me.
I absolutely have to get hold of Gilles.
GRAND CAFE
RAOUL

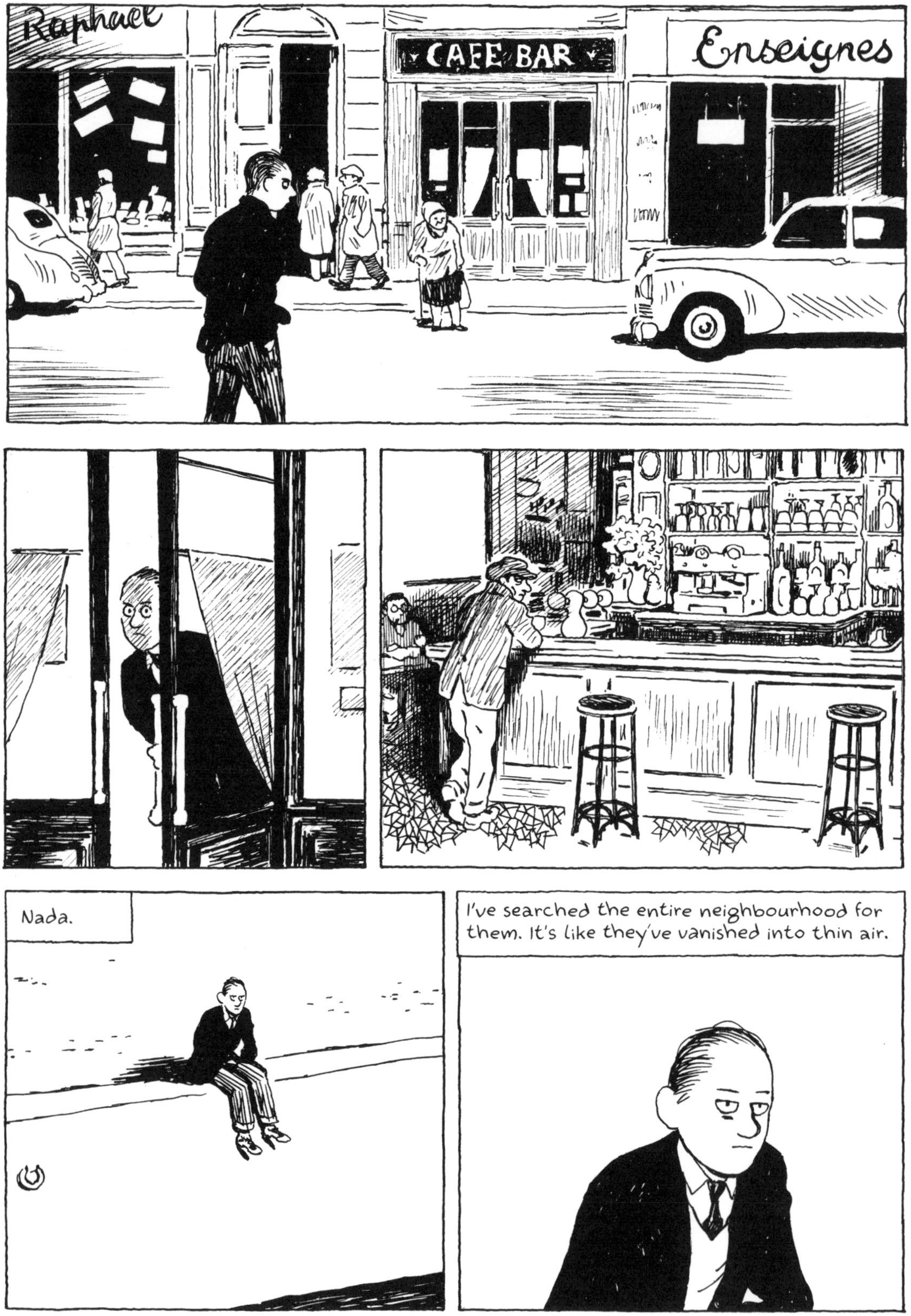
Raphael
CAFE BAR
Enseignes
Nada.
I've searched the entire neighbourhood for them. It's like they've vanished into thin air.

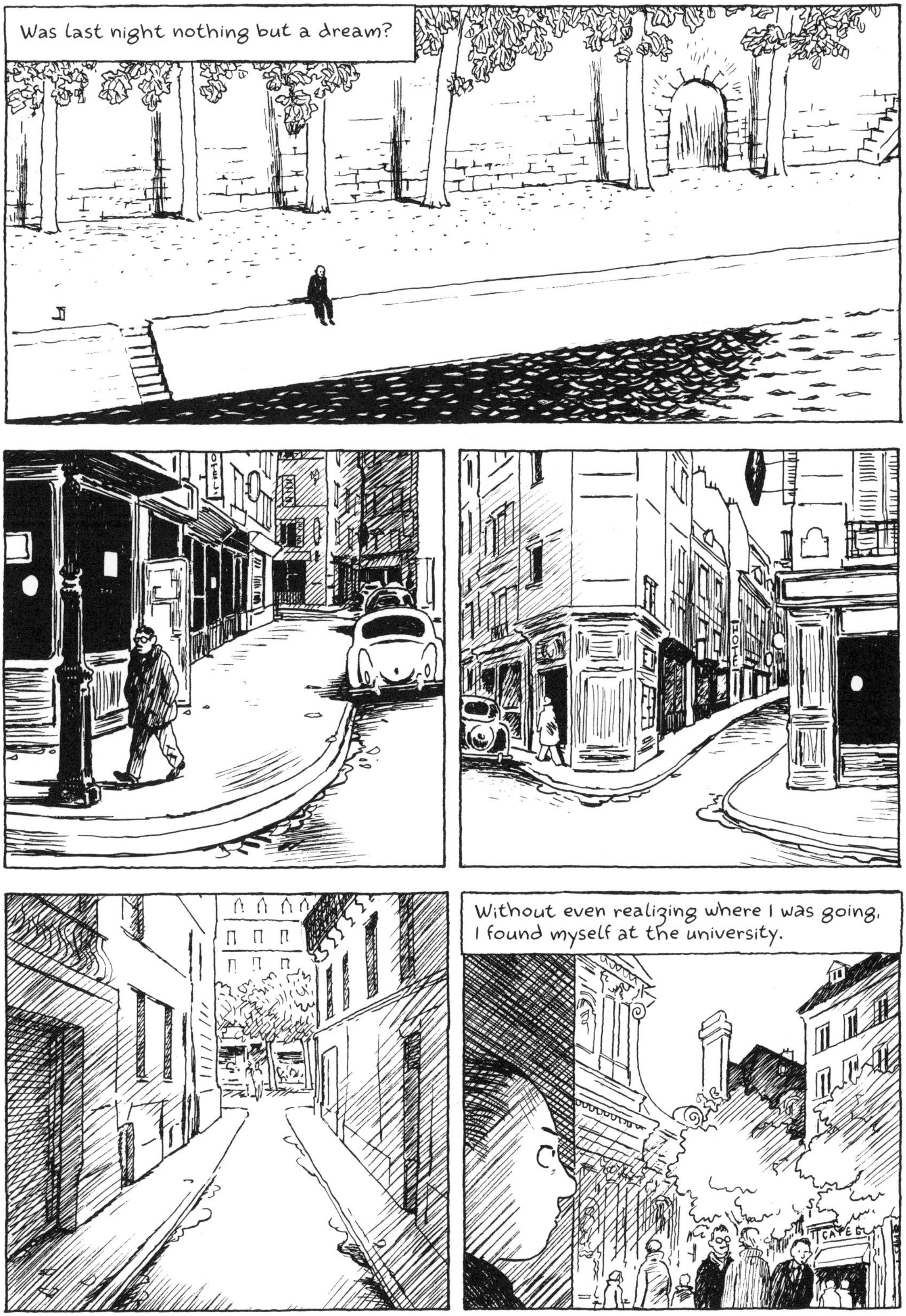
Was last night nothing but a dream?
Without even realizing where I was going, I found myself at the university.

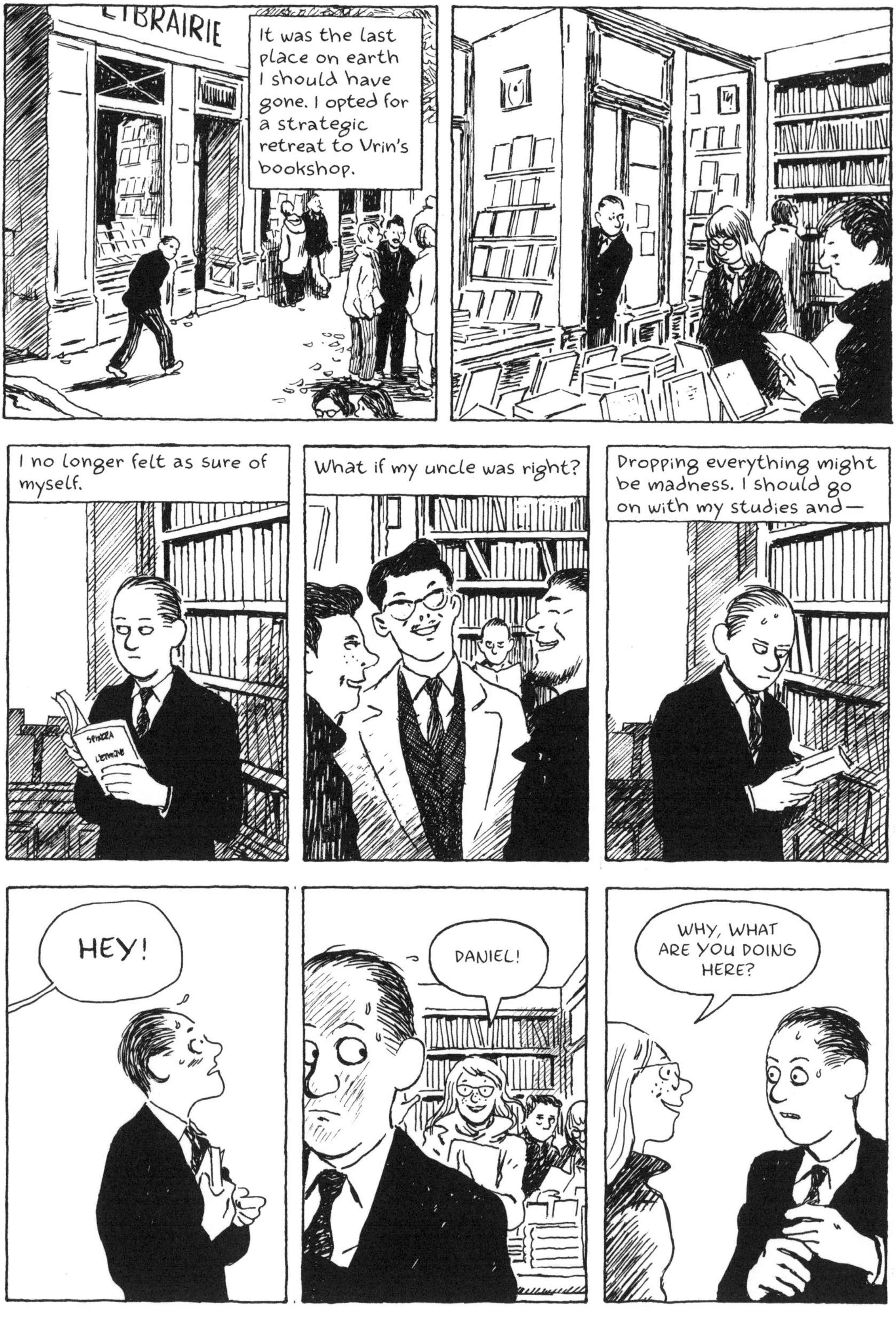

LIBRAIRIE
It was the last place on earth I should have gone. I opted for a strategic retreat to Vrin's bookshop.
I no longer felt as sure of myself.
SPINOZA L'ÉTHIQUE
What if my uncle was right?
Dropping everything might be madness. I should go on with my studies and—
HEY!
DANIEL!
WHY, WHAT ARE YOU DOING HERE?

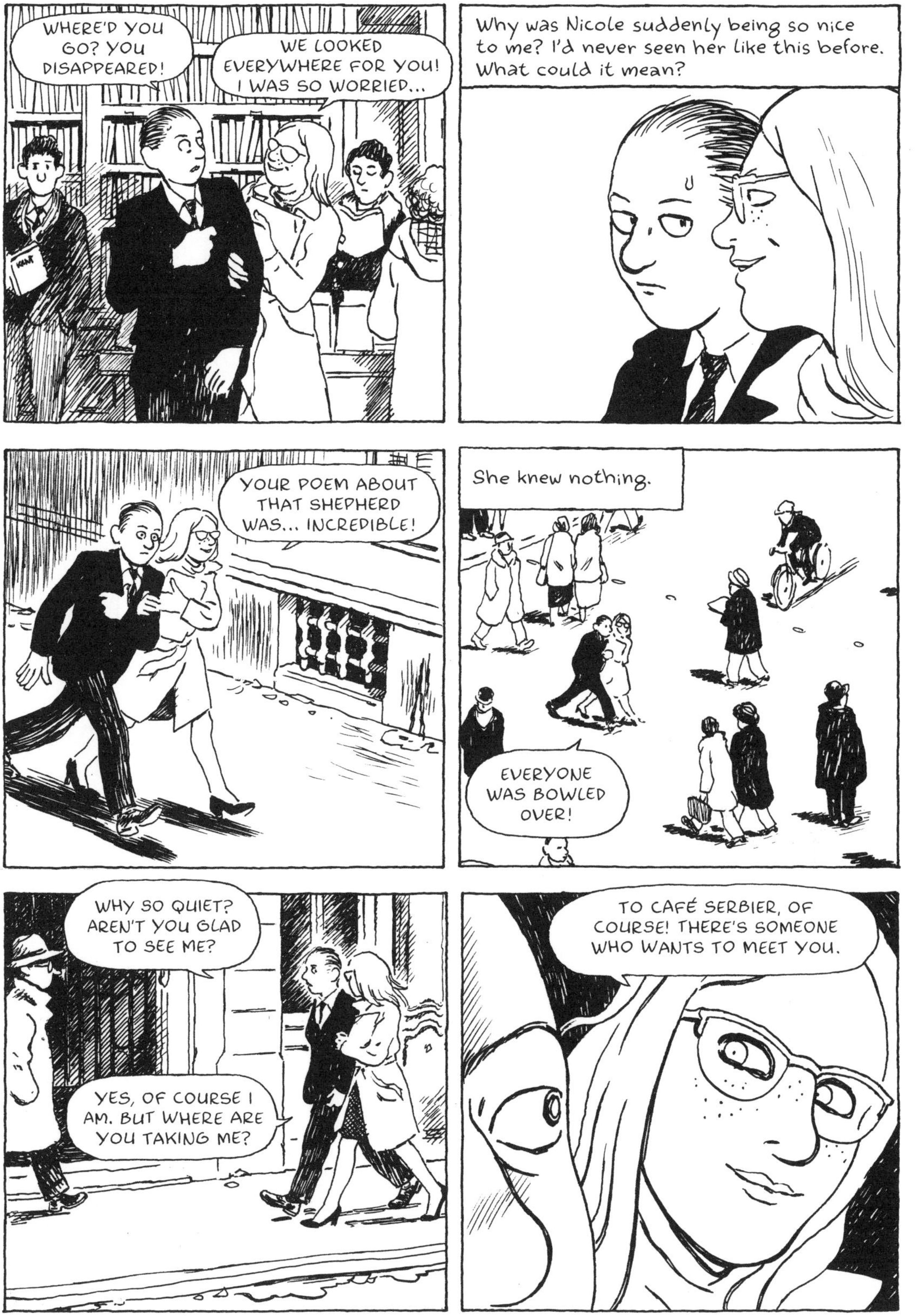
WHERE'D YOU GO? YOU DISAPPEARED!
WE LOOKED EVERYWHERE FOR YOU! I WAS SO WORRIED...
Why was Nicole suddenly being so nice to me? I'd never seen her like this before. What could it mean?
YOUR POEM ABOUT THAT SHEPHERD WAS... INCREDIBLE!
She knew nothing.
EVERYONE WAS BOWLED OVER!
WHY SO QUIET? AREN'T YOU GLAD TO SEE ME?
YES, OF COURSE I AM. BUT WHERE ARE YOU TAKING ME?
TO CAFÉ SERBIER, OF COURSE! THERE'S SOMEONE WHO WANTS TO MEET YOU.

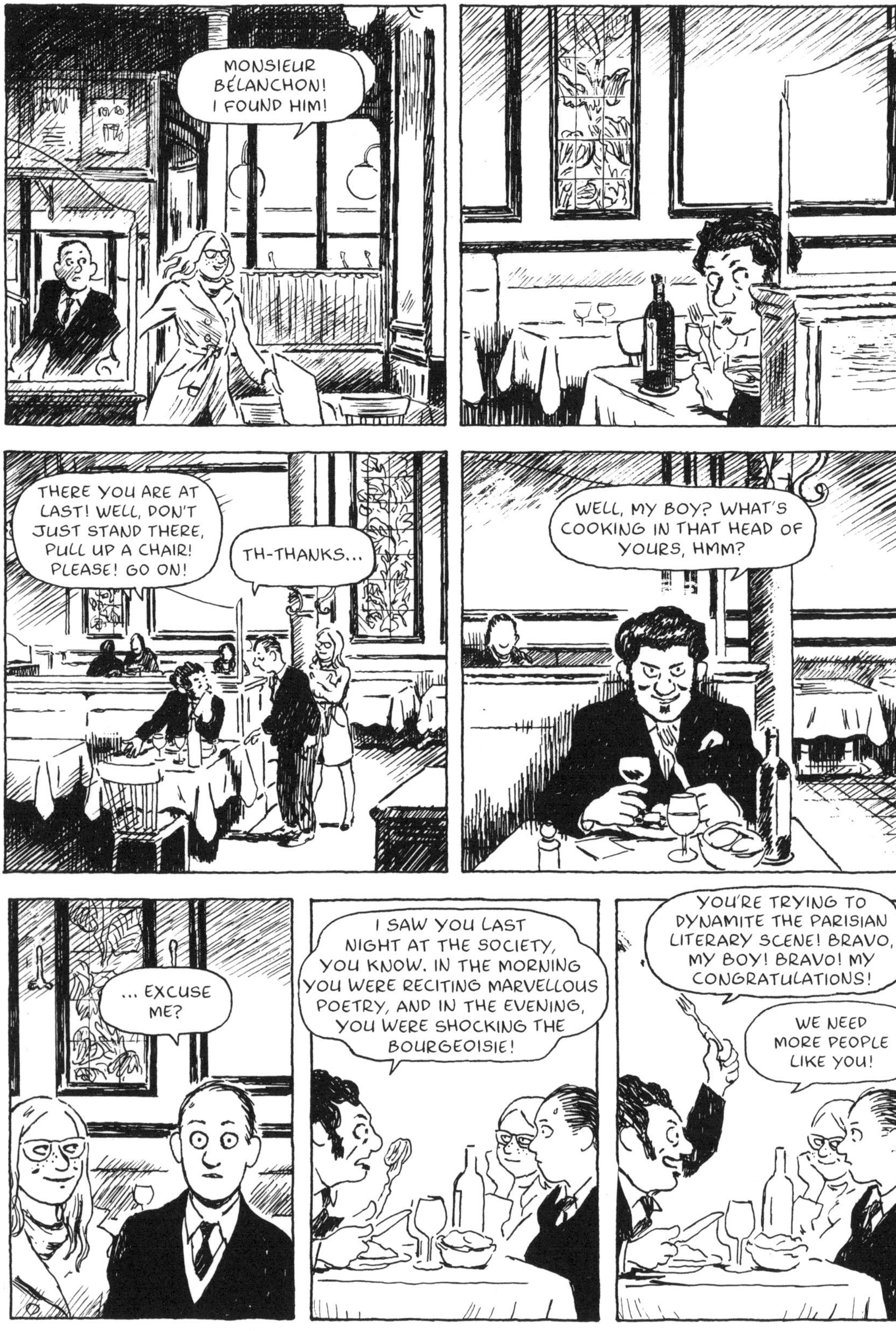
MONSIEUR BÉLANCHON! I FOUND HIM!
THERE YOU ARE AT LAST! WELL, DON'T JUST STAND THERE, PULL UP A CHAIR! PLEASE! GO ON!
TH-THANKS...
WELL, MY BOY? WHAT'S COOKING IN THAT HEAD OF YOURS, HMM?
... EXCUSE ME?
I SAW YOU LAST NIGHT AT THE SOCIETY, YOU KNOW. IN THE MORNING YOU WERE RECITING MARVELLOUS POETRY, AND IN THE EVENING, YOU WERE SHOCKING THE BOURGEOISIE!
YOU'RE TRYING TO DYNAMITE THE PARISIAN LITERARY SCENE! BRAVO, MY BOY! BRAVO! MY CONGRATULATIONS!
WE NEED MORE PEOPLE LIKE YOU!

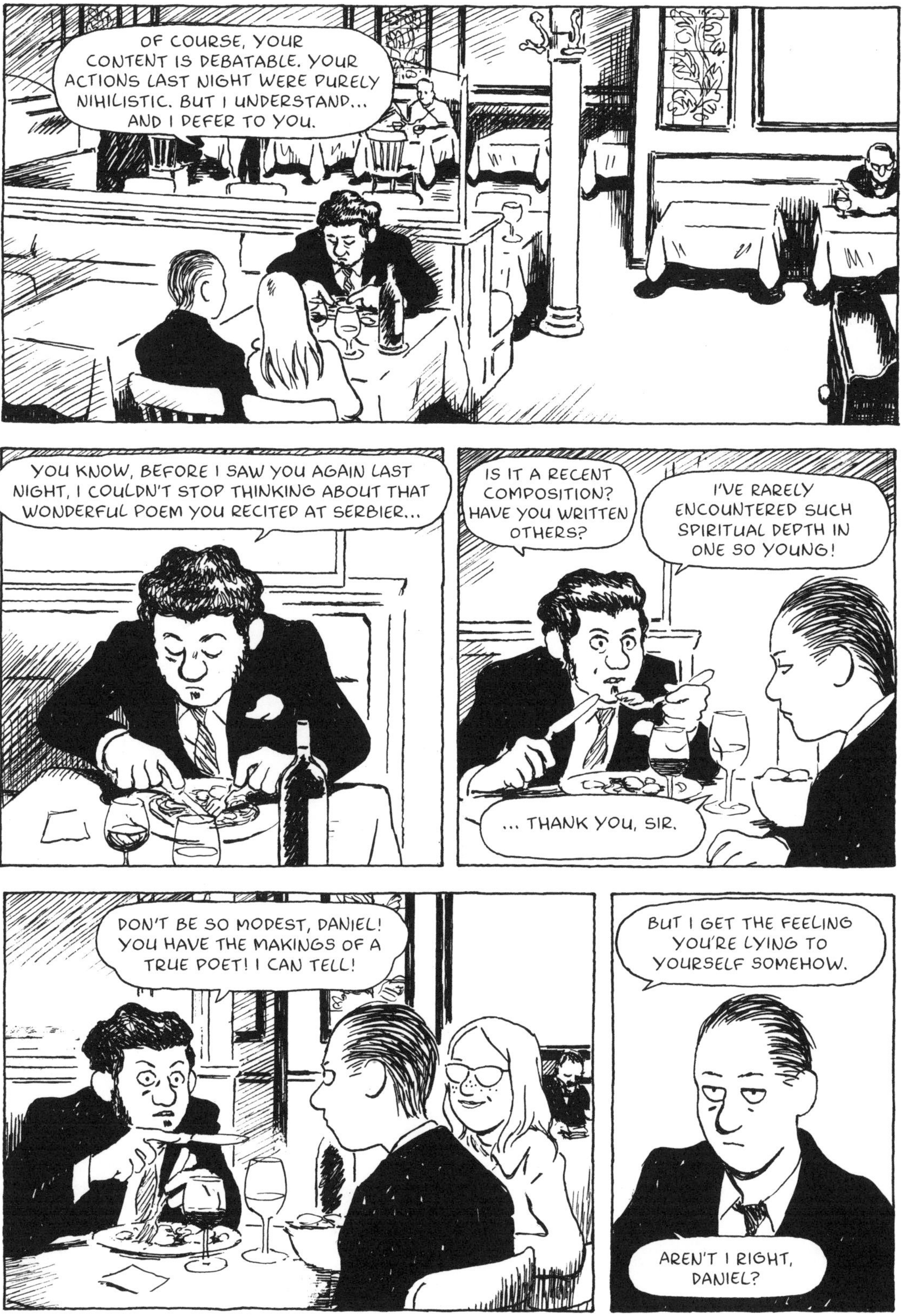
OF COURSE, YOUR CONTENT IS DEBATABLE. YOUR ACTIONS LAST NIGHT WERE PURELY NIHILISTIC. BUT I UNDERSTAND... AND I DEFER TO YOU.
YOU KNOW, BEFORE I SAW YOU AGAIN LAST NIGHT, I COULDN'T STOP THINKING ABOUT THAT WONDERFUL POEM YOU RECITED AT SERBIER...
IS IT A RECENT COMPOSITION? HAVE YOU WRITTEN OTHERS?
I'VE RARELY ENCOUNTERED SUCH SPIRITUAL DEPTH IN ONE SO YOUNG!
... THANK YOU, SIR.
DON'T BE SO MODEST, DANIEL! YOU HAVE THE MAKINGS OF A TRUE POET! I CAN TELL!
BUT I GET THE FEELING YOU'RE LYING TO YOURSELF SOMEHOW.
AREN'T I RIGHT, DANIEL?

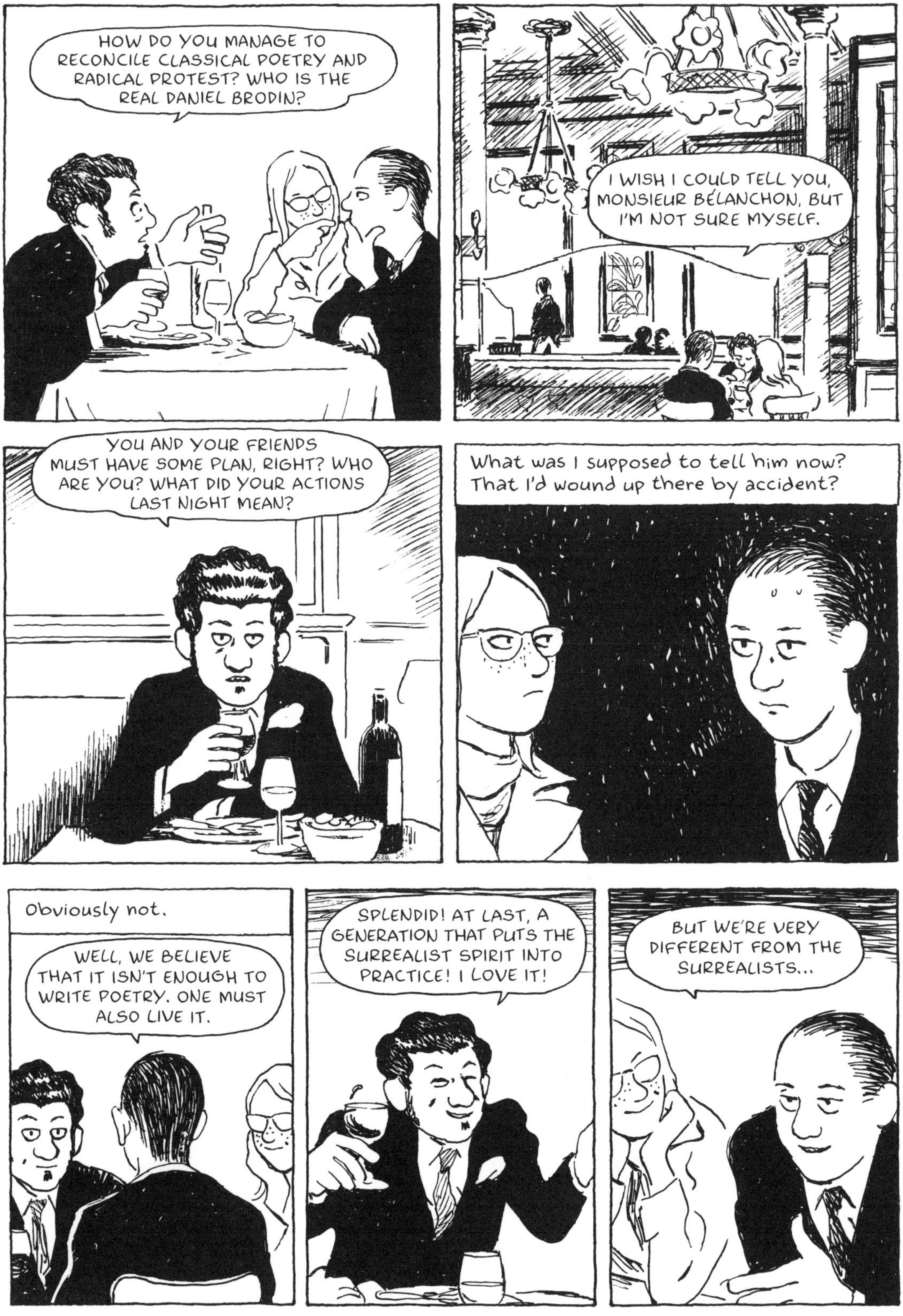
HOW DO YOU MANAGE TO RECONCILE CLASSICAL POETRY AND RADICAL PROTEST? WHO IS THE REAL DANIEL BRODIN?
I WISH I COULD TELL YOU, MONSIEUR BÉLANCHON, BUT I'M NOT SURE MYSELF.
YOU AND YOUR FRIENDS MUST HAVE SOME PLAN, RIGHT? WHO ARE YOU? WHAT DID YOUR ACTIONS LAST NIGHT MEAN?
What was I supposed to tell him now? That I'd wound up there by accident?
Obviously not.
WELL, WE BELIEVE THAT IT ISN'T ENOUGH TO WRITE POETRY. ONE MUST ALSO LIVE IT.
SPLENDID! AT LAST, A GENERATION THAT PUTS THE SURREALIST SPIRIT INTO PRACTICE! I LOVE IT!
BUT WE'RE VERY DIFFERENT FROM THE SURREALISTS...

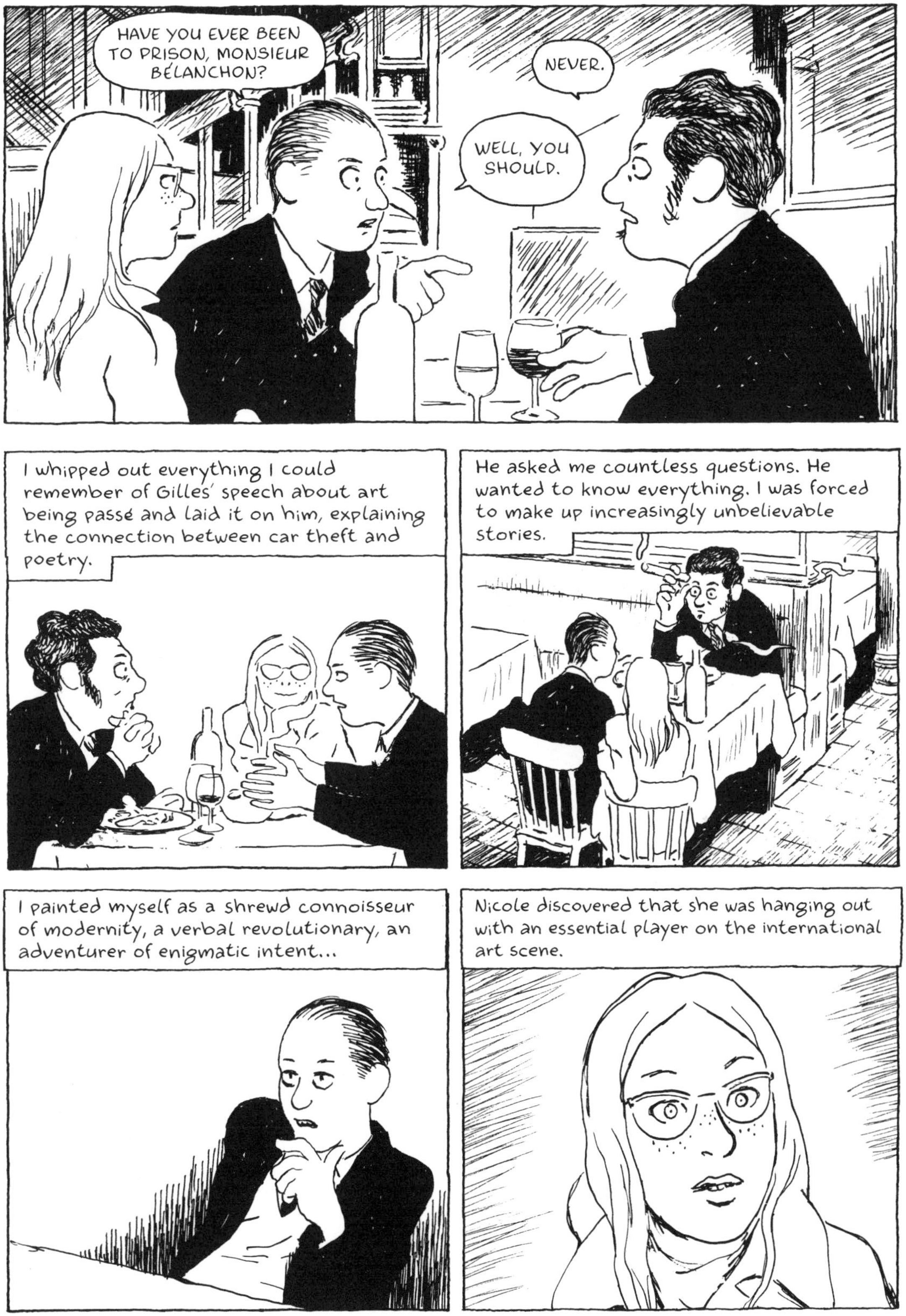
HAVE YOU EVER BEEN TO PRISON, MONSIEUR BÉLANCHON?
NEVER.
WELL, YOU SHOULD.
I whipped out everything I could remember of Gilles' speech about art being passé and laid it on him, explaining the connection between car theft and poetry.
He asked me countless questions. He wanted to know everything. I was forced to make up increasingly unbelievable stories.
I painted myself as a shrewd connoisseur of modernity, a verbal revolutionary, an adventurer of enigmatic intent...
Nicole discovered that she was hanging out with an essential player on the international art scene.

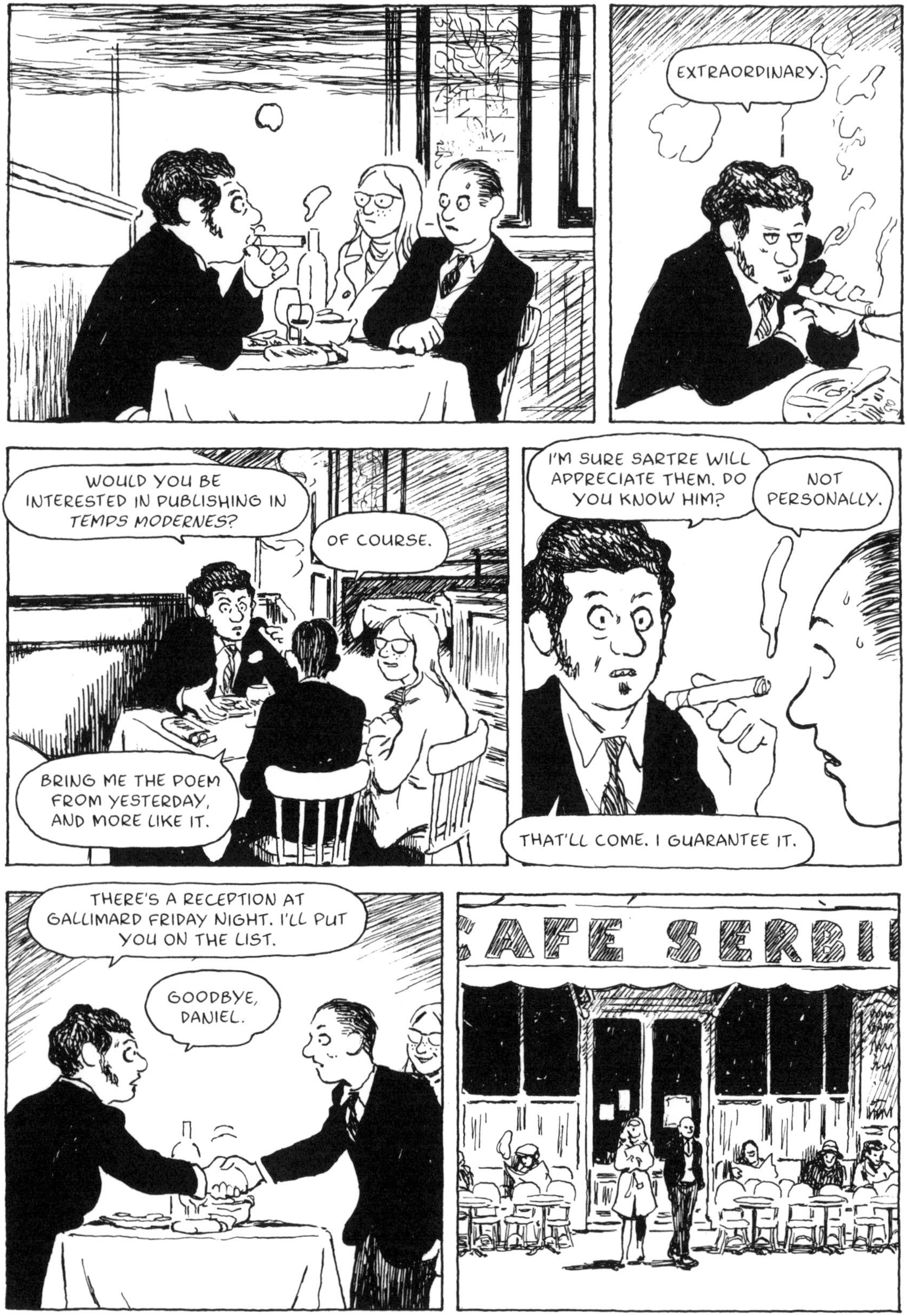
EXTRAORDINARY.
WOULD YOU BE INTERESTED IN PUBLISHING IN *TEMPS MODERNES*?
OF COURSE.
BRING ME THE POEM FROM YESTERDAY, AND MORE LIKE IT.
I'M SURE SARTRE WILL APPRECIATE THEM. DO YOU KNOW HIM?
NOT PERSONALLY.
THAT'LL COME. I GUARANTEE IT.
THERE'S A RECEPTION AT GALLIMARD FRIDAY NIGHT. I'LL PUT YOU ON THE LIST.
GOODBYE, DANIEL.
CAFE SERBI

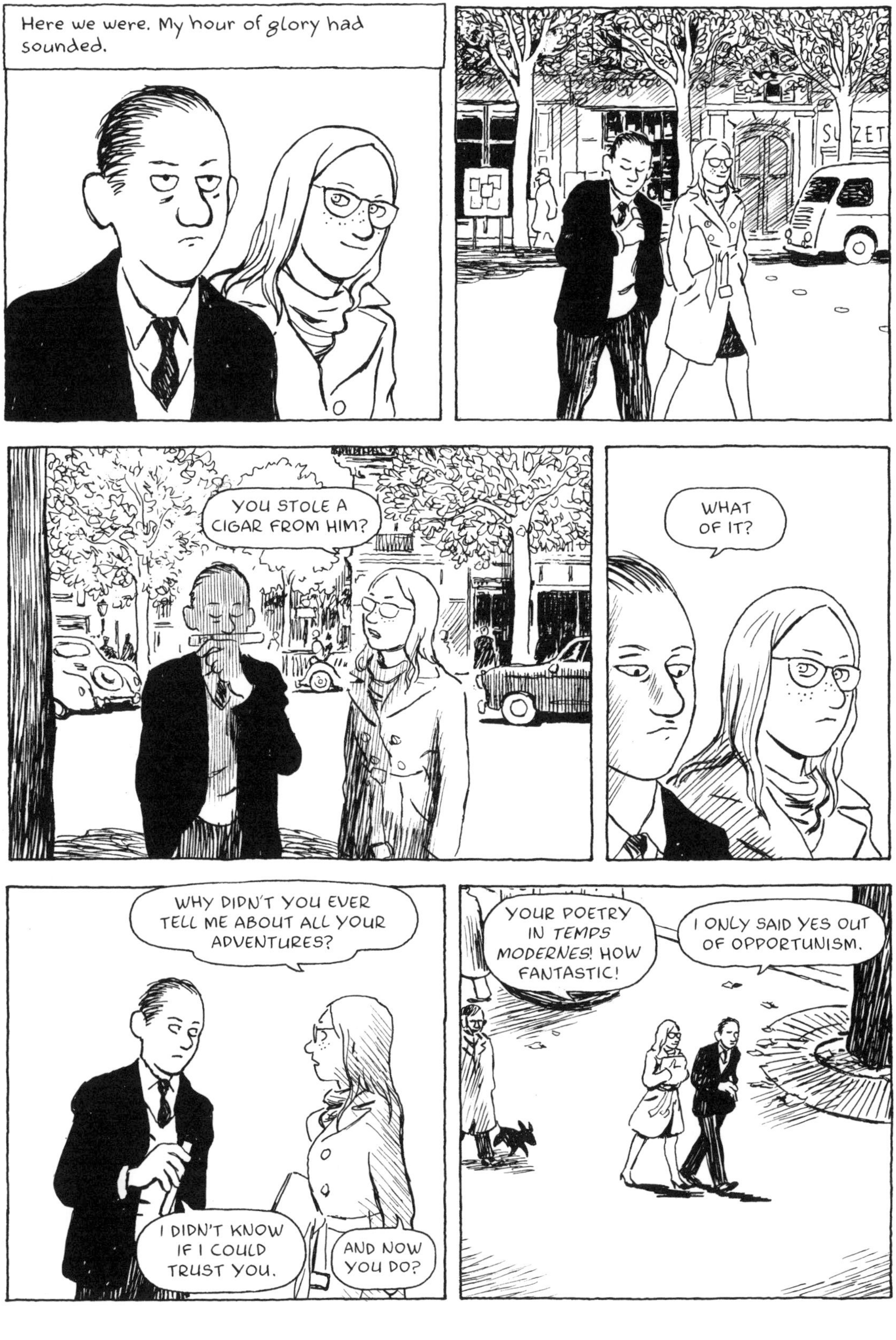
Here we were. My hour of glory had sounded.
SU ZET
YOU STOLE A CIGAR FROM HIM?
WHAT OF IT?
WHY DIDN'T YOU EVER TELL ME ABOUT ALL YOUR ADVENTURES?
I DIDN'T KNOW IF I COULD TRUST YOU.
AND NOW YOU DO?
YOUR POETRY IN *TEMPS MODERNES*! HOW FANTASTIC!
I ONLY SAID YES OUT OF OPPORTUNISM.

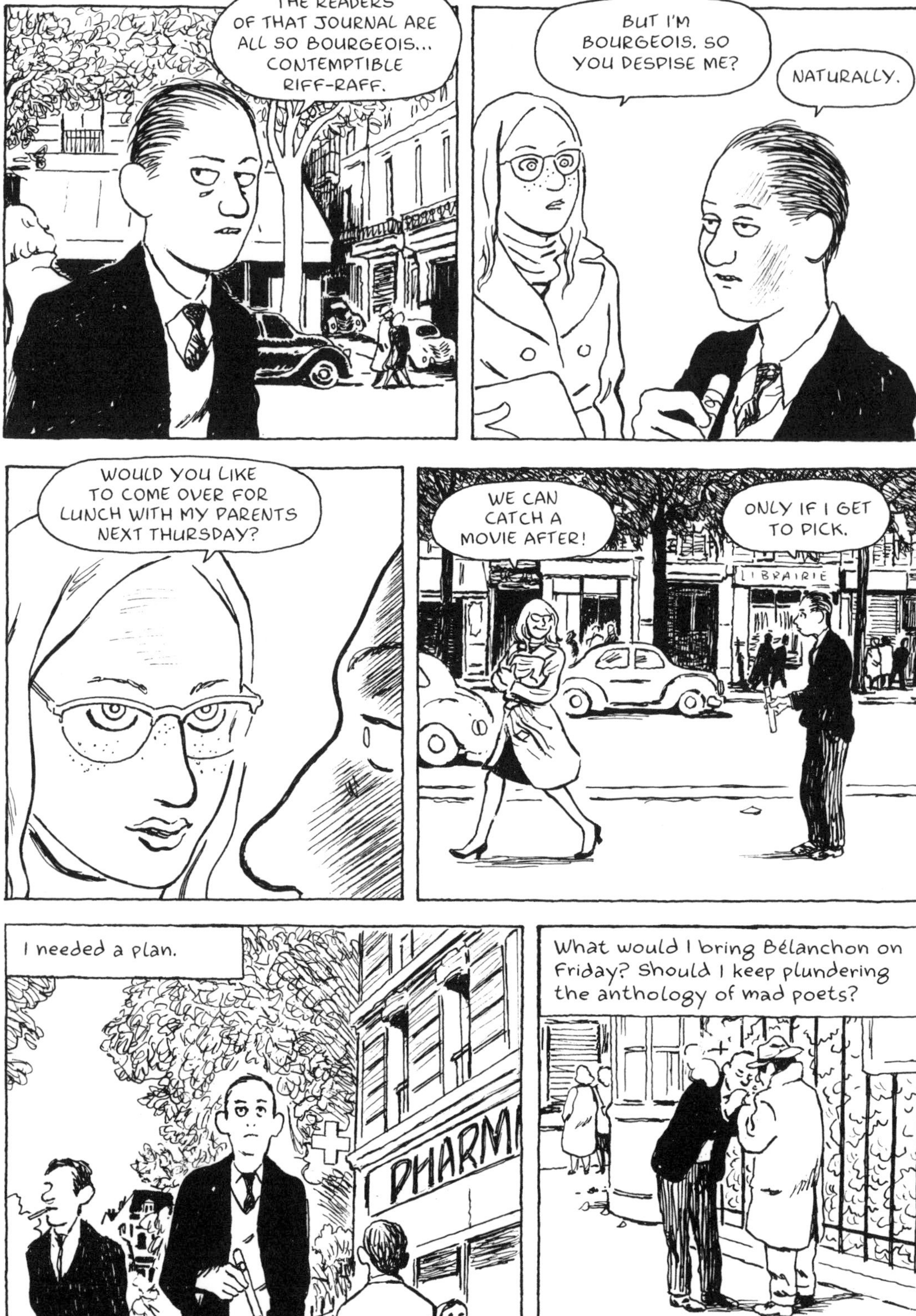
THE READERS OF THAT JOURNAL ARE ALL SO BOURGEOIS... CONTEMPTIBLE RIFF-RAFF.
BUT I'M BOURGEOIS. SO YOU DESPISE ME?
NATURALLY.
WOULD YOU LIKE TO COME OVER FOR LUNCH WITH MY PARENTS NEXT THURSDAY?
WE CAN CATCH A MOVIE AFTER!
ONLY IF I GET TO PICK.
LIBRAIRIE
I needed a plan.
PHARM
What would I bring Bélanchon on Friday? Should I keep plundering the anthology of mad poets?

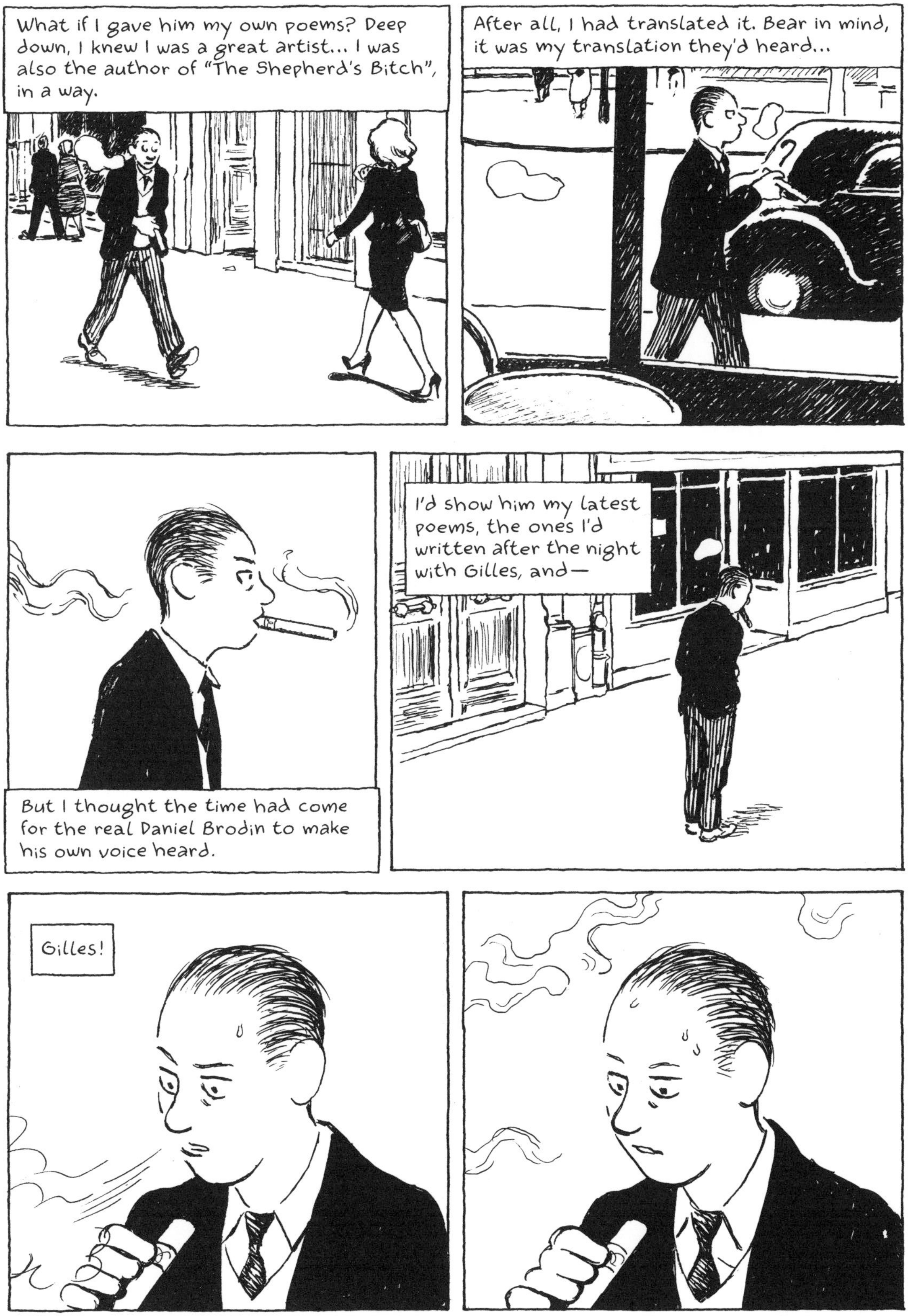

What if I gave him my own poems? Deep down, I knew I was a great artist... I was also the author of "The Shepherd's Bitch", in a way.
After all, I had translated it. Bear in mind, it was my translation they'd heard...
But I thought the time had come for the real Daniel Brodin to make his own voice heard.
I'd show him my latest poems, the ones I'd written after the night with Gilles, and—
Gilles!

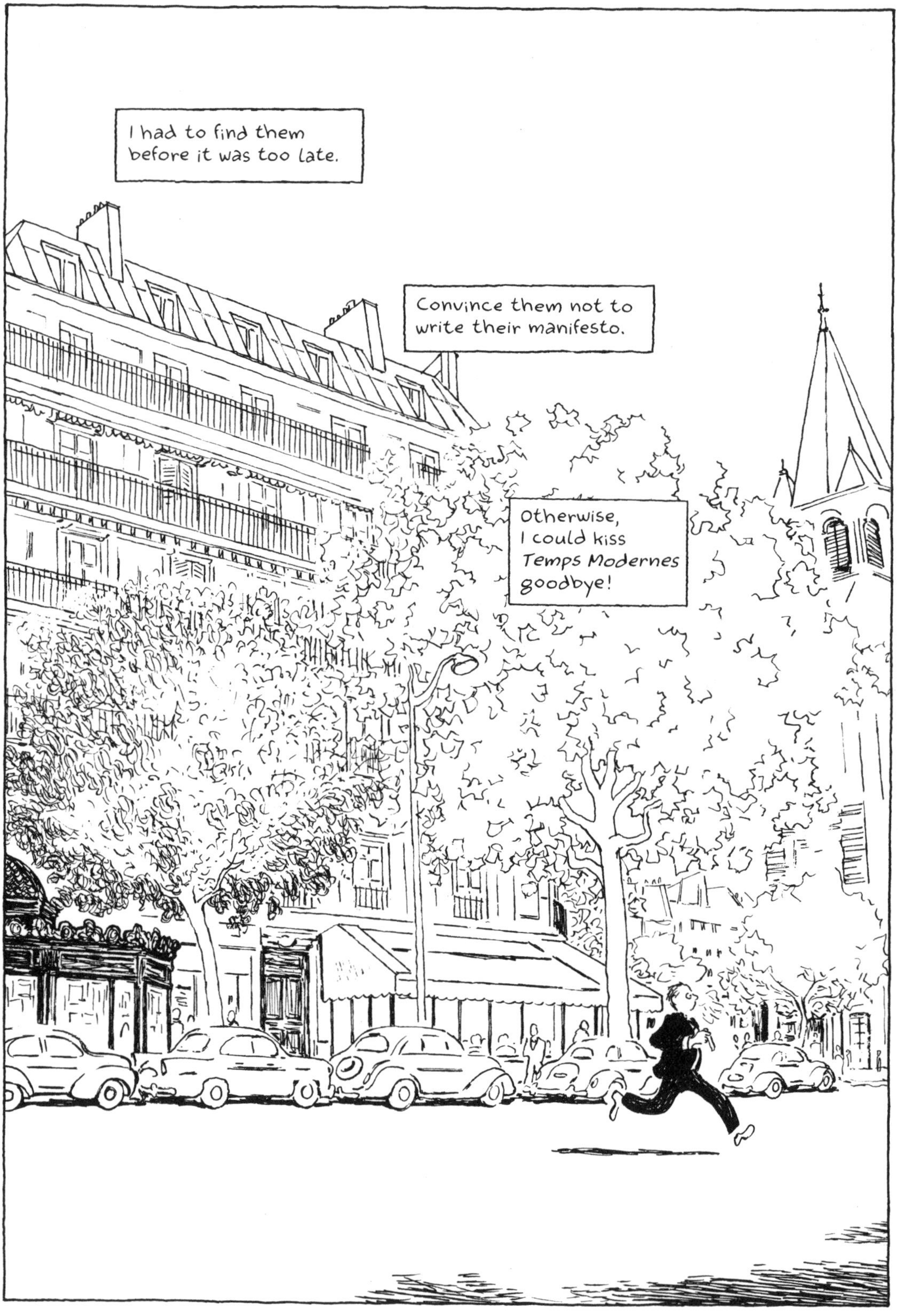
I had to find them before it was too late.
Convince them not to write their manifesto.
Otherwise, I could kiss *Temps Modernes* goodbye!

CHAPTER 4

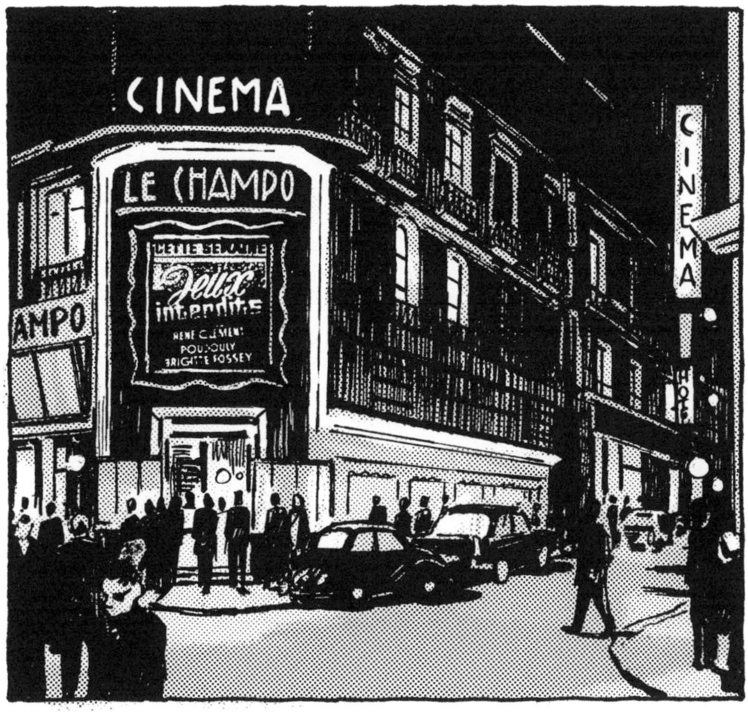
CINEMA
LE CHAMPO
AMPO
CINEMA

"DO YOU LIKE ME, DANIEL?"
Colette F.

His ring was the first thing I noticed about him.

Then his stylish outfit.

And especially, his gold tooth.

"You seem to be devoting yourself to activities that far exceed your abilities," said Mr. C.

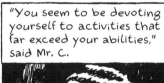

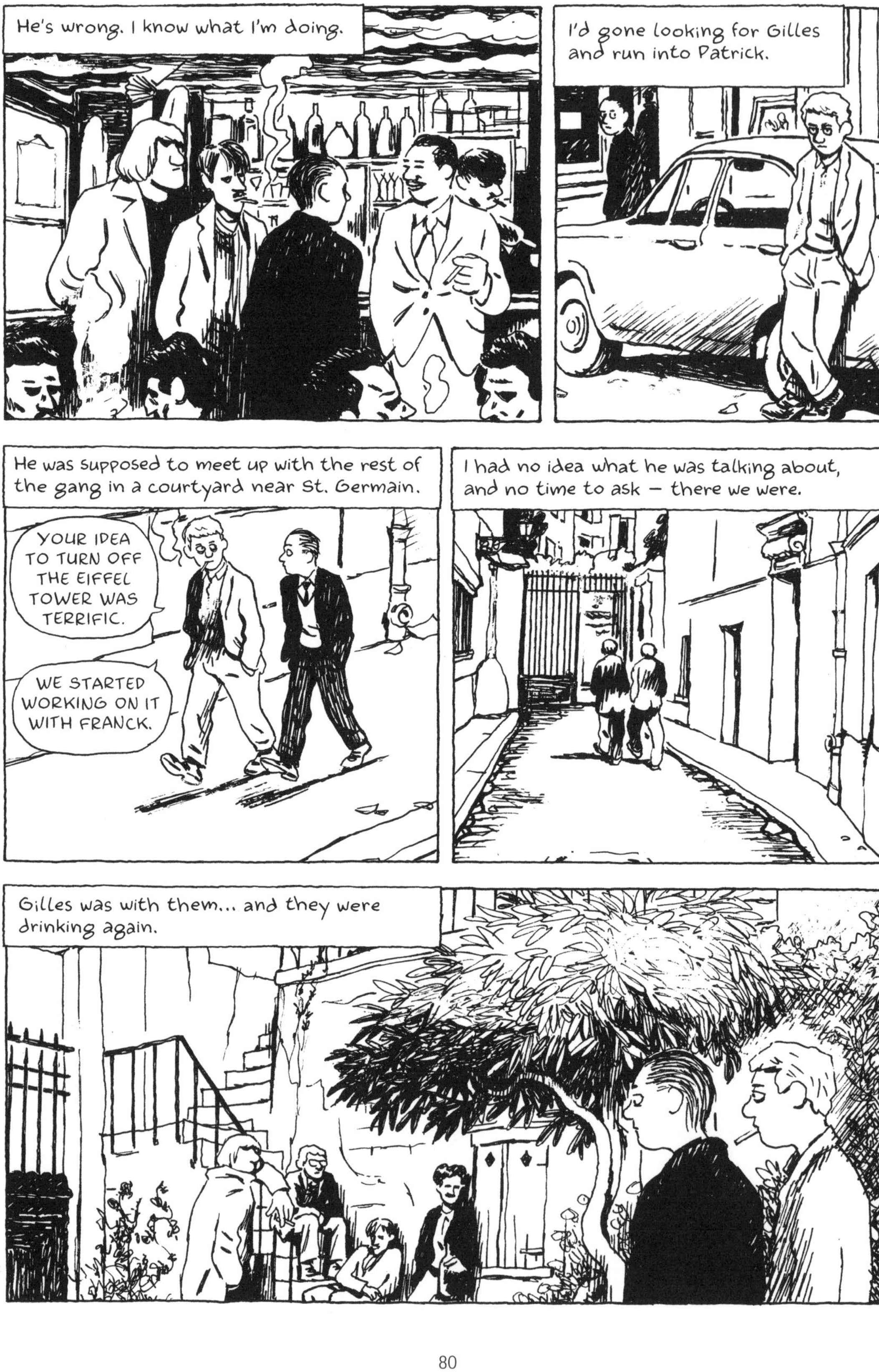
He's wrong. I know what I'm doing.
I'd gone looking for Gilles and run into Patrick.
He was supposed to meet up with the rest of the gang in a courtyard near St. Germain.
YOUR IDEA TO TURN OFF THE EIFFEL TOWER WAS TERRIFIC.
WE STARTED WORKING ON IT WITH FRANCK.
I had no idea what he was talking about, and no time to ask – there we were.
Gilles was with them... and they were drinking again.

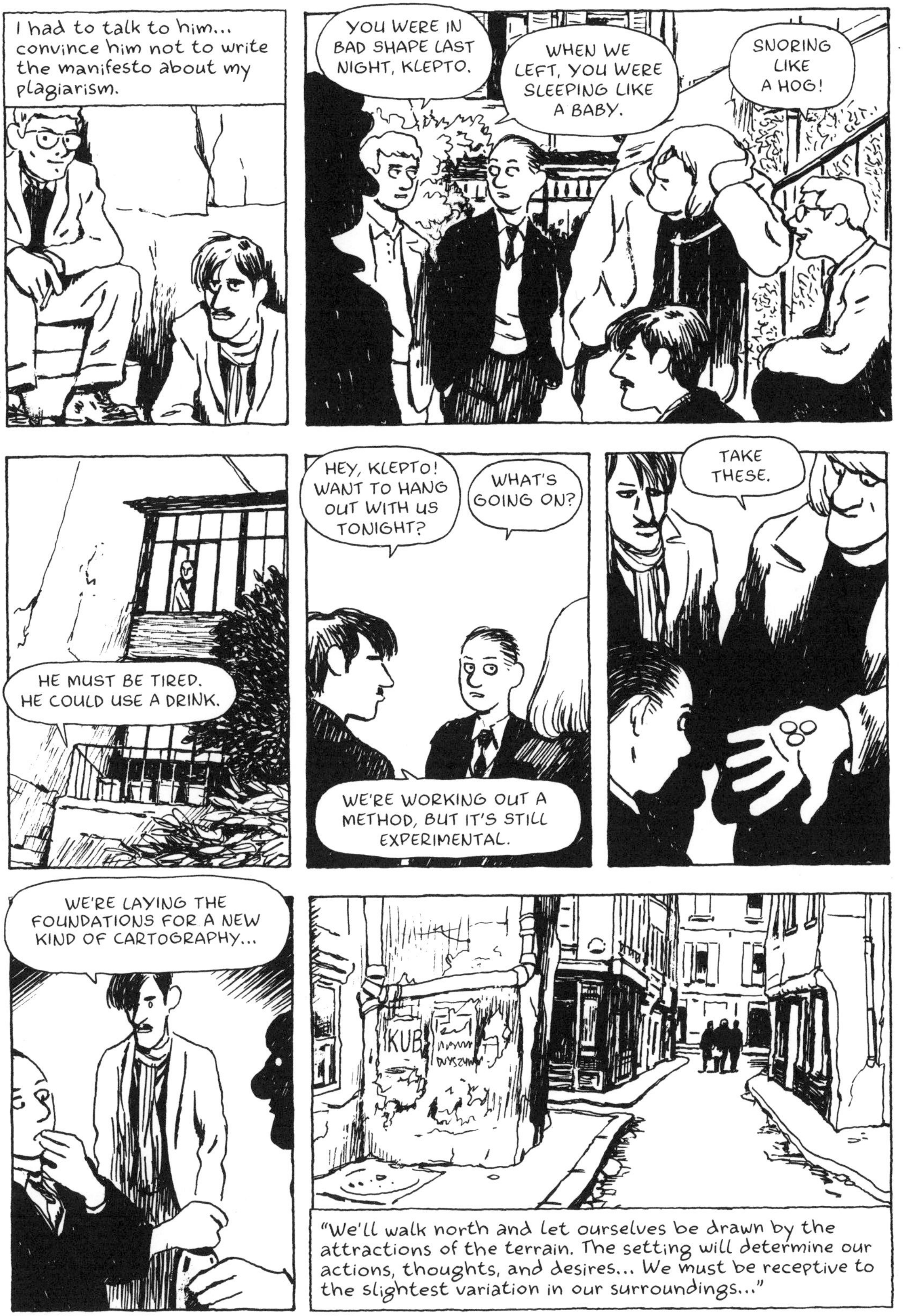
I had to talk to him... convince him not to write the manifesto about my plagiarism.
YOU WERE IN BAD SHAPE LAST NIGHT, KLEPTO.
WHEN WE LEFT, YOU WERE SLEEPING LIKE A BABY.
SNORING LIKE A HOG!
HE MUST BE TIRED. HE COULD USE A DRINK.
HEY, KLEPTO! WANT TO HANG OUT WITH US TONIGHT?
WHAT'S GOING ON?
WE'RE WORKING OUT A METHOD, BUT IT'S STILL EXPERIMENTAL.
TAKE THESE.
WE'RE LAYING THE FOUNDATIONS FOR A NEW KIND OF CARTOGRAPHY...
KUB
"We'll walk north and let ourselves be drawn by the attractions of the terrain. The setting will determine our actions, thoughts, and desires... We must be receptive to the slightest variation in our surroundings..."

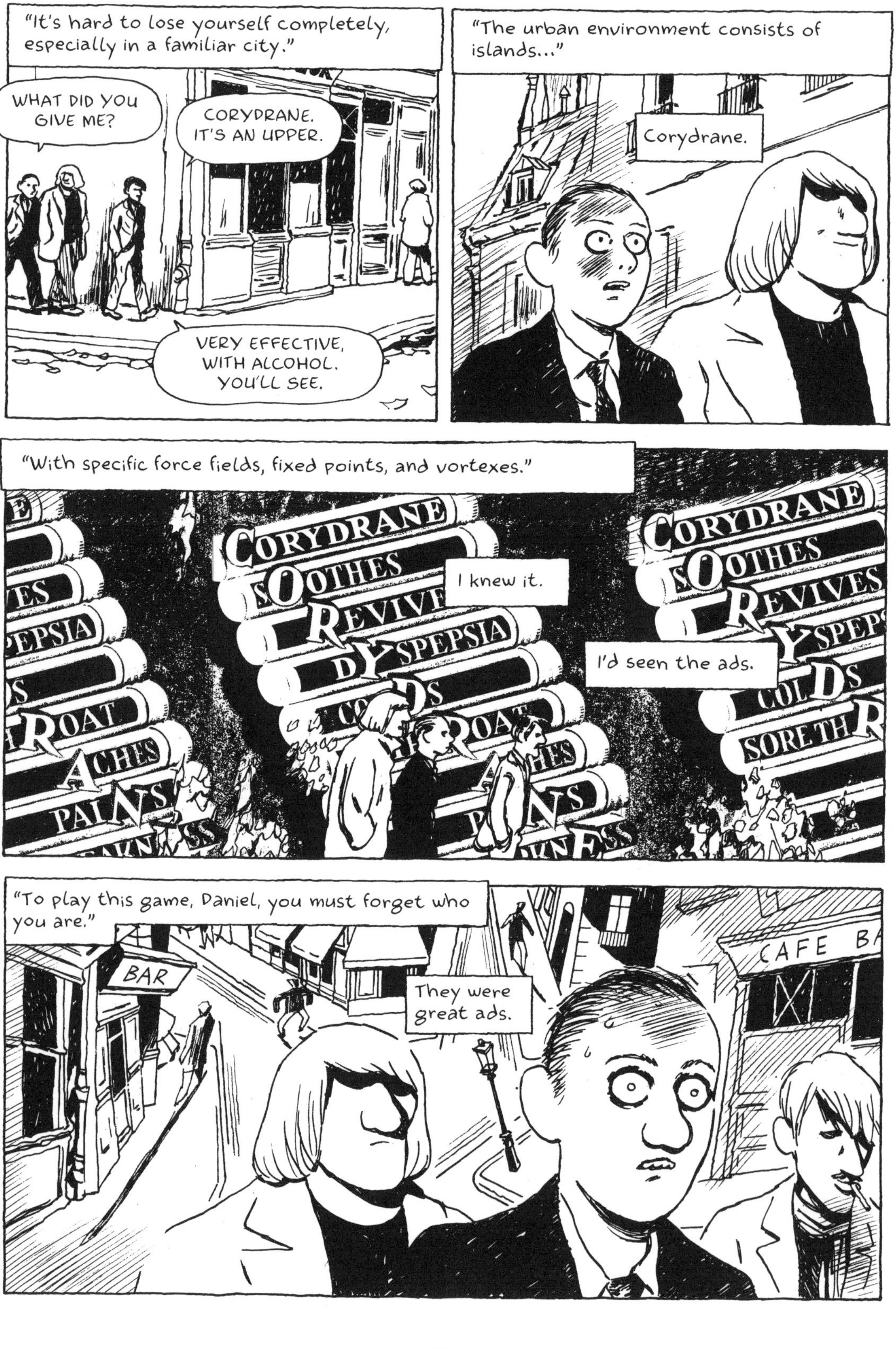
"It's hard to lose yourself completely, especially in a familiar city."
WHAT DID YOU GIVE ME?
CORYDRANE. IT'S AN UPPER.
VERY EFFECTIVE, WITH ALCOHOL. YOU'LL SEE.
"The urban environment consists of islands..."
Corydrane.
"With specific force fields, fixed points, and vortexes."
CORYDRANE
SOOTHES
DYSPEPSIA
I knew it.
CORYDRANE
SOOTHES
REVIVES
COLDS
I'd seen the ads.
"To play this game, Daniel, you must forget who you are."
BAR
CAFE
They were great ads.

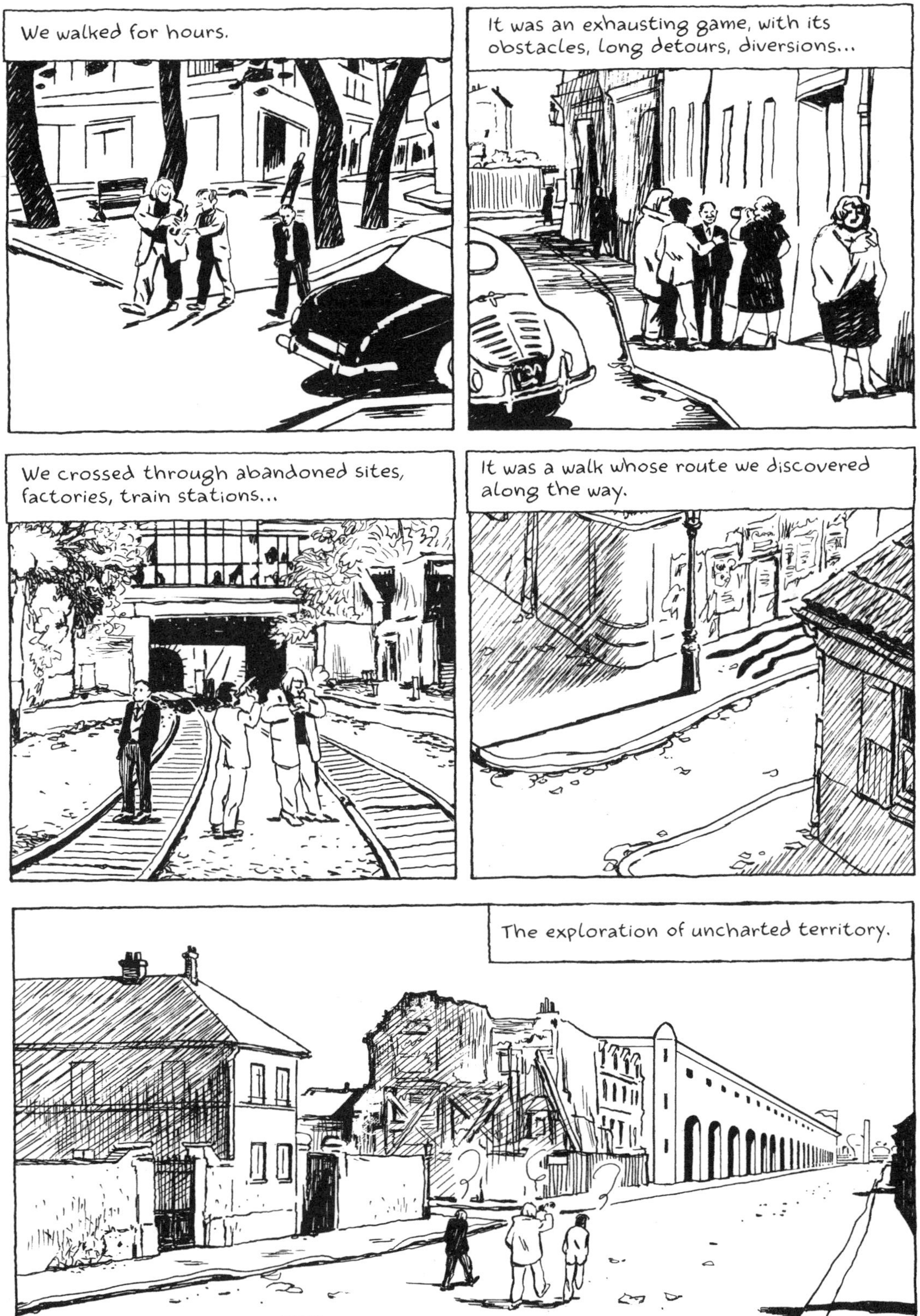
We walked for hours.
It was an exhausting game, with its obstacles, long detours, diversions...
We crossed through abandoned sites, factories, train stations...
It was a walk whose route we discovered along the way.
The exploration of uncharted territory.

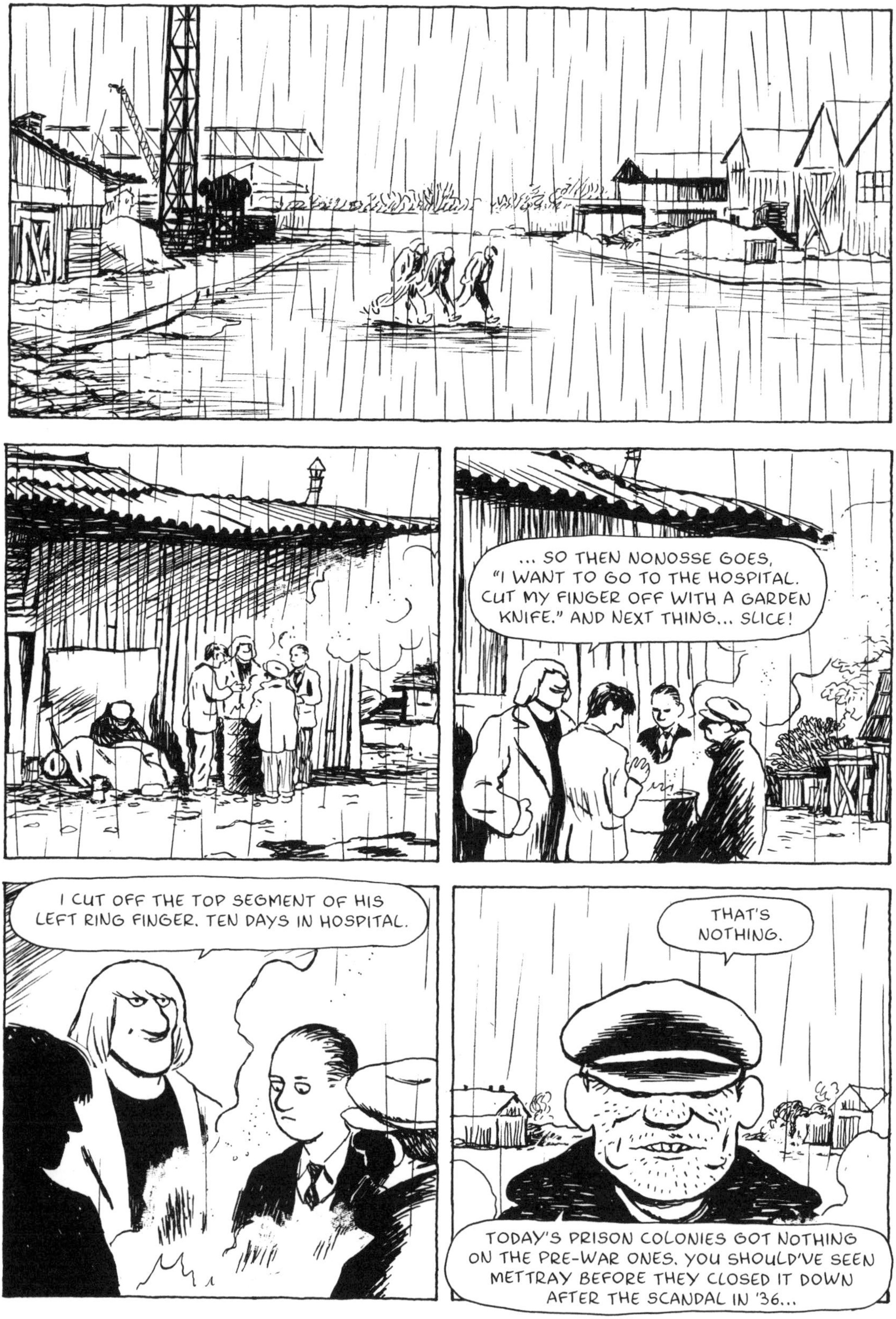
... SO THEN NONOSSE GOES, "I WANT TO GO TO THE HOSPITAL. CUT MY FINGER OFF WITH A GARDEN KNIFE." AND NEXT THING... SLICE!
I CUT OFF THE TOP SEGMENT OF HIS LEFT RING FINGER. TEN DAYS IN HOSPITAL.
THAT'S NOTHING.
TODAY'S PRISON COLONIES GOT NOTHING ON THE PRE-WAR ONES. YOU SHOULD'VE SEEN METTRAY BEFORE THEY CLOSED IT DOWN AFTER THE SCANDAL IN '36...

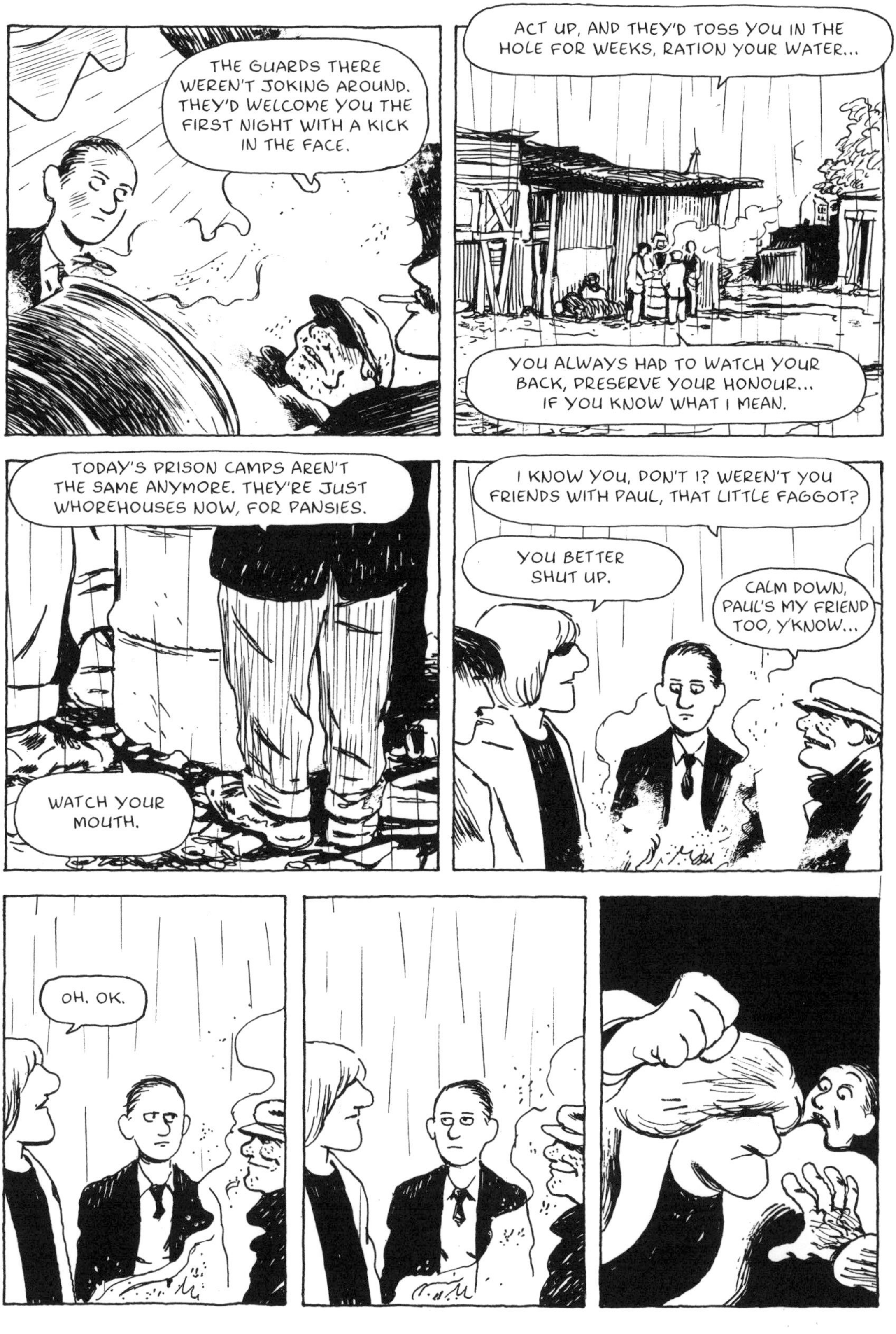
THE GUARDS THERE WEREN'T JOKING AROUND. THEY'D WELCOME YOU THE FIRST NIGHT WITH A KICK IN THE FACE.
ACT UP, AND THEY'D TOSS YOU IN THE HOLE FOR WEEKS, RATION YOUR WATER...
YOU ALWAYS HAD TO WATCH YOUR BACK, PRESERVE YOUR HONOUR... IF YOU KNOW WHAT I MEAN.
TODAY'S PRISON CAMPS AREN'T THE SAME ANYMORE. THEY'RE JUST WHOREHOUSES NOW, FOR PANSIES.
WATCH YOUR MOUTH.
I KNOW YOU, DON'T I? WEREN'T YOU FRIENDS WITH PAUL, THAT LITTLE FAGGOT?
YOU BETTER SHUT UP.
CALM DOWN, PAUL'S MY FRIEND TOO, Y'KNOW...
OH. OK.

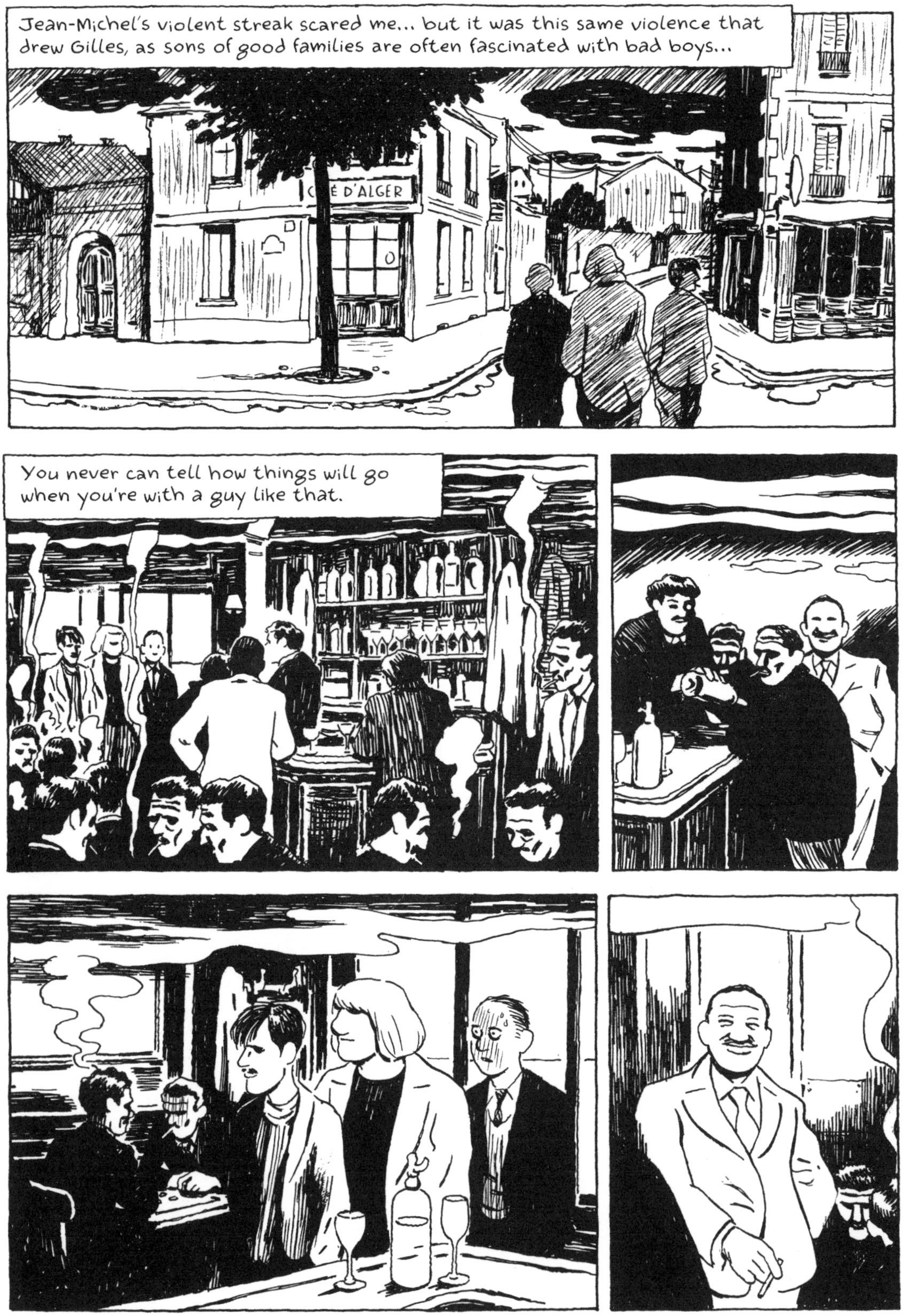
Jean-Michel's violent streak scared me... but it was this same violence that drew Gilles, as sons of good families are often fascinated with bad boys...
You never can tell how things will go when you're with a guy like that.

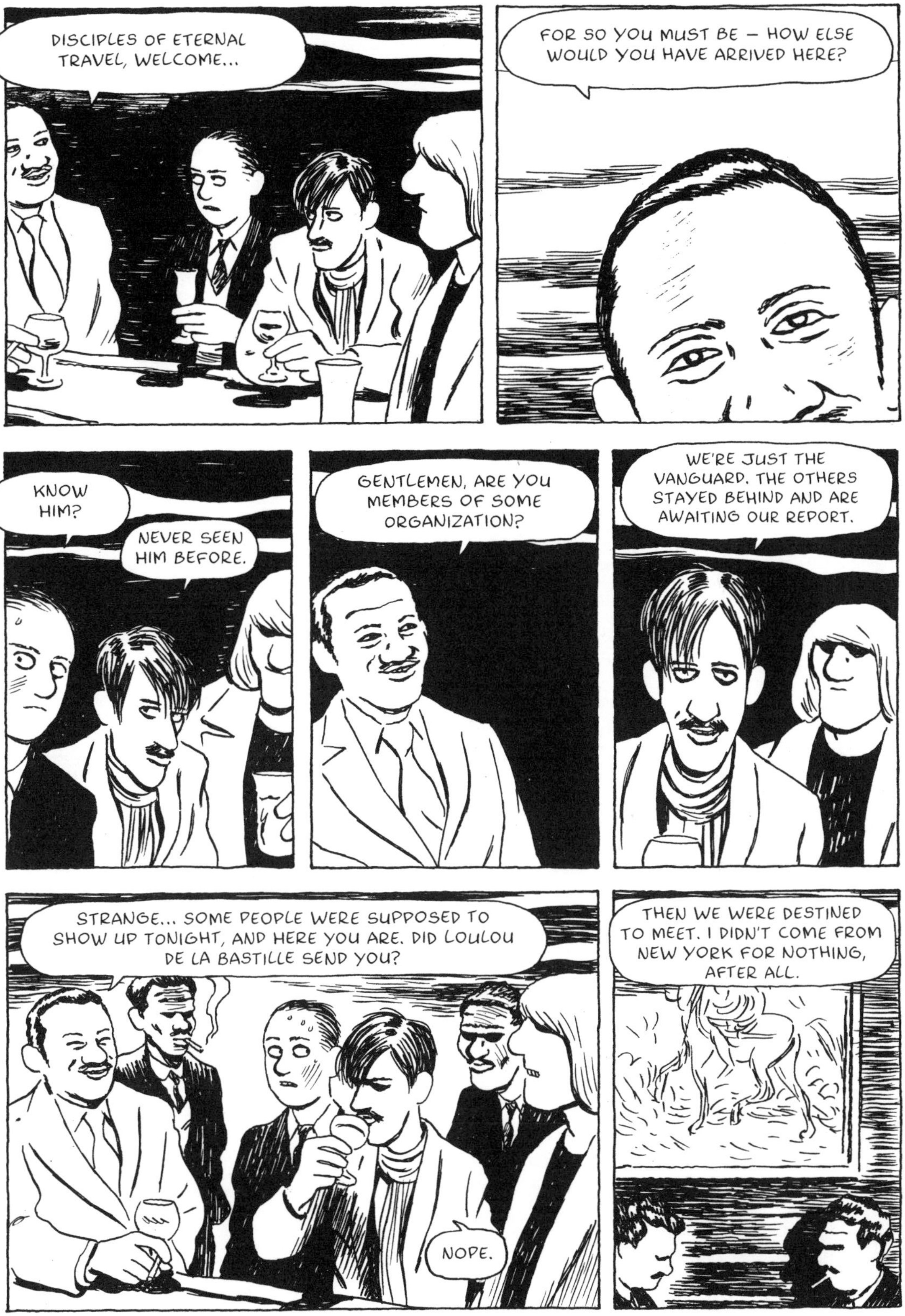
DISCIPLES OF ETERNAL TRAVEL, WELCOME...
FOR SO YOU MUST BE – HOW ELSE WOULD YOU HAVE ARRIVED HERE?
KNOW HIM?
NEVER SEEN HIM BEFORE.
GENTLEMEN, ARE YOU MEMBERS OF SOME ORGANIZATION?
WE'RE JUST THE VANGUARD. THE OTHERS STAYED BEHIND AND ARE AWAITING OUR REPORT.
STRANGE... SOME PEOPLE WERE SUPPOSED TO SHOW UP TONIGHT, AND HERE YOU ARE. DID LOULOU DE LA BASTILLE SEND YOU?
NOPE.
THEN WE WERE DESTINED TO MEET. I DIDN'T COME FROM NEW YORK FOR NOTHING, AFTER ALL.

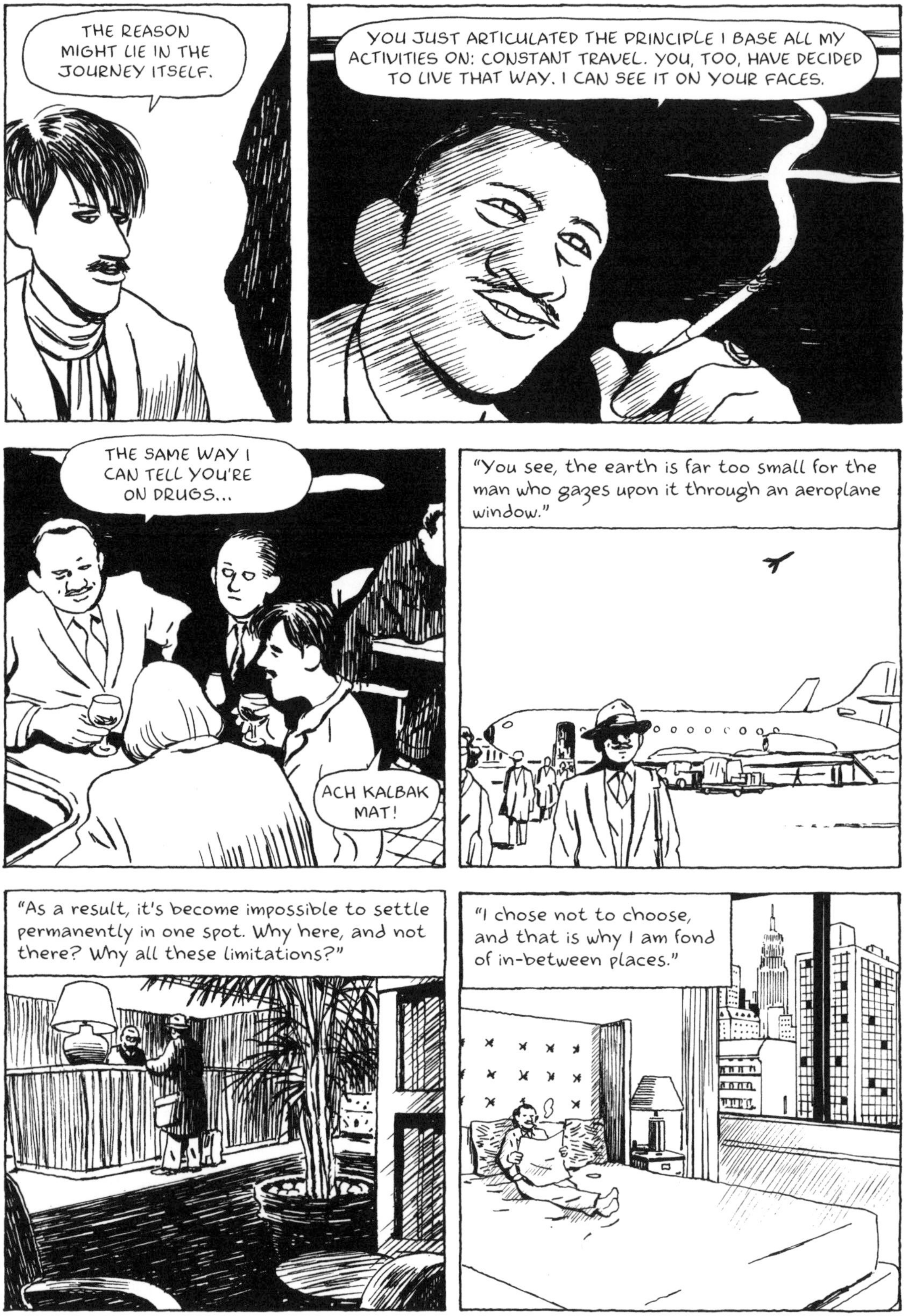
THE REASON MIGHT LIE IN THE JOURNEY ITSELF.
YOU JUST ARTICULATED THE PRINCIPLE I BASE ALL MY ACTIVITIES ON: CONSTANT TRAVEL. YOU, TOO, HAVE DECIDED TO LIVE THAT WAY. I CAN SEE IT ON YOUR FACES.
THE SAME WAY I CAN TELL YOU'RE ON DRUGS...
ACH KALBAK MAT!
"You see, the earth is far too small for the man who gazes upon it through an aeroplane window."
"As a result, it's become impossible to settle permanently in one spot. Why here, and not there? Why all these limitations?"
"I chose not to choose, and that is why I am fond of in-between places."

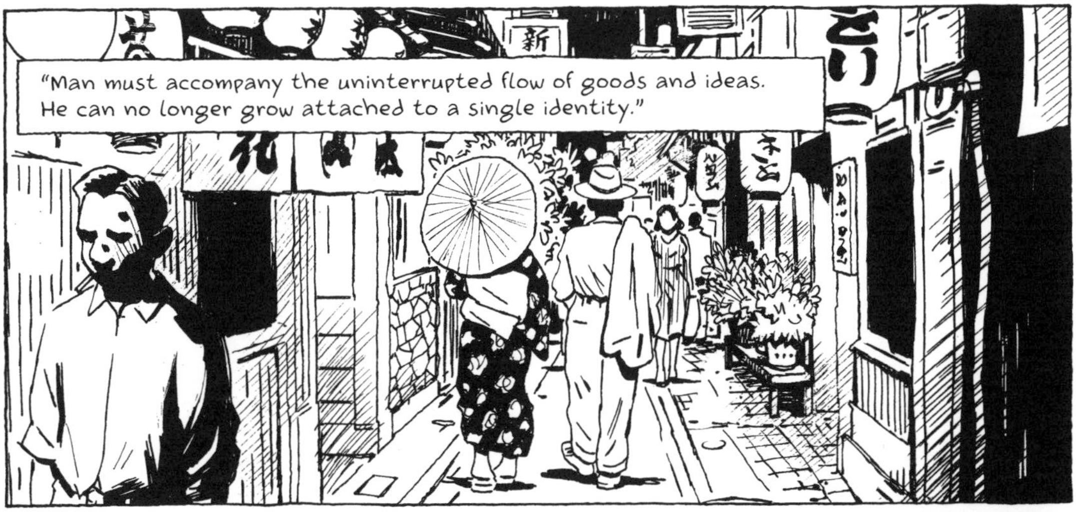
"Man must accompany the uninterrupted flow of goods and ideas. He can no longer grow attached to a single identity."
新

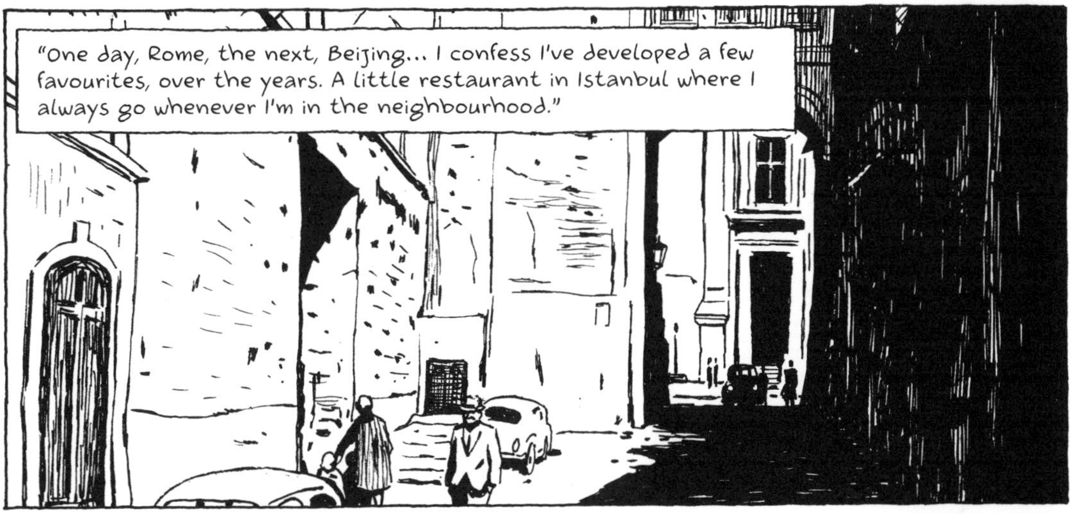
"One day, Rome, the next, Beijing... I confess I've developed a few favourites, over the years. A little restaurant in Istanbul where I always go whenever I'm in the neighbourhood."

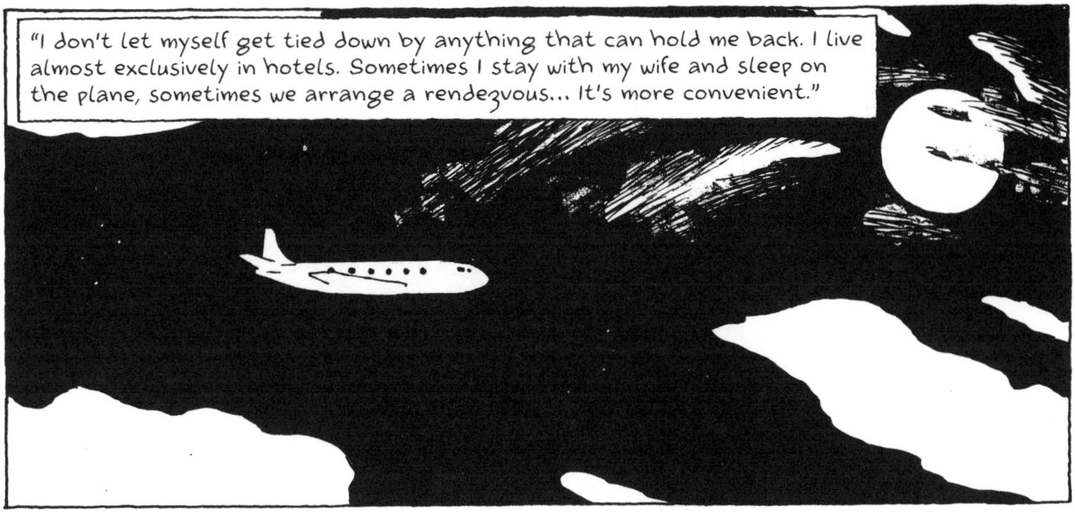
"I don't let myself get tied down by anything that can hold me back. I live almost exclusively in hotels. Sometimes I stay with my wife and sleep on the plane, sometimes we arrange a rendezvous... It's more convenient."

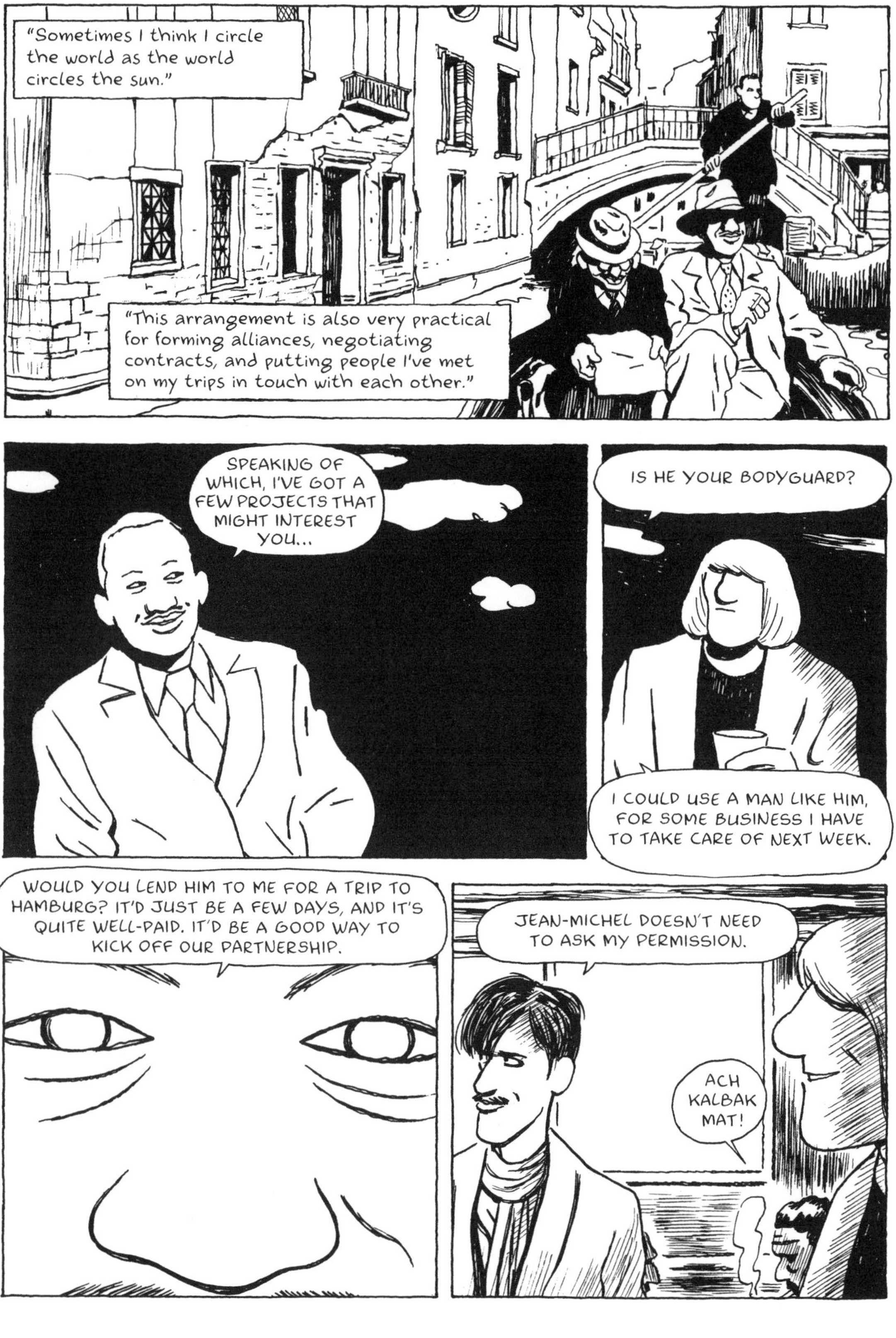

"Sometimes I think I circle the world as the world circles the sun."
"This arrangement is also very practical for forming alliances, negotiating contracts, and putting people I've met on my trips in touch with each other."
SPEAKING OF WHICH, I'VE GOT A FEW PROJECTS THAT MIGHT INTEREST YOU...
IS HE YOUR BODYGUARD?
I COULD USE A MAN LIKE HIM, FOR SOME BUSINESS I HAVE TO TAKE CARE OF NEXT WEEK.
WOULD YOU LEND HIM TO ME FOR A TRIP TO HAMBURG? IT'D JUST BE A FEW DAYS, AND IT'S QUITE WELL-PAID. IT'D BE A GOOD WAY TO KICK OFF OUR PARTNERSHIP.
JEAN-MICHEL DOESN'T NEED TO ASK MY PERMISSION.
ACH KALBAK MAT!

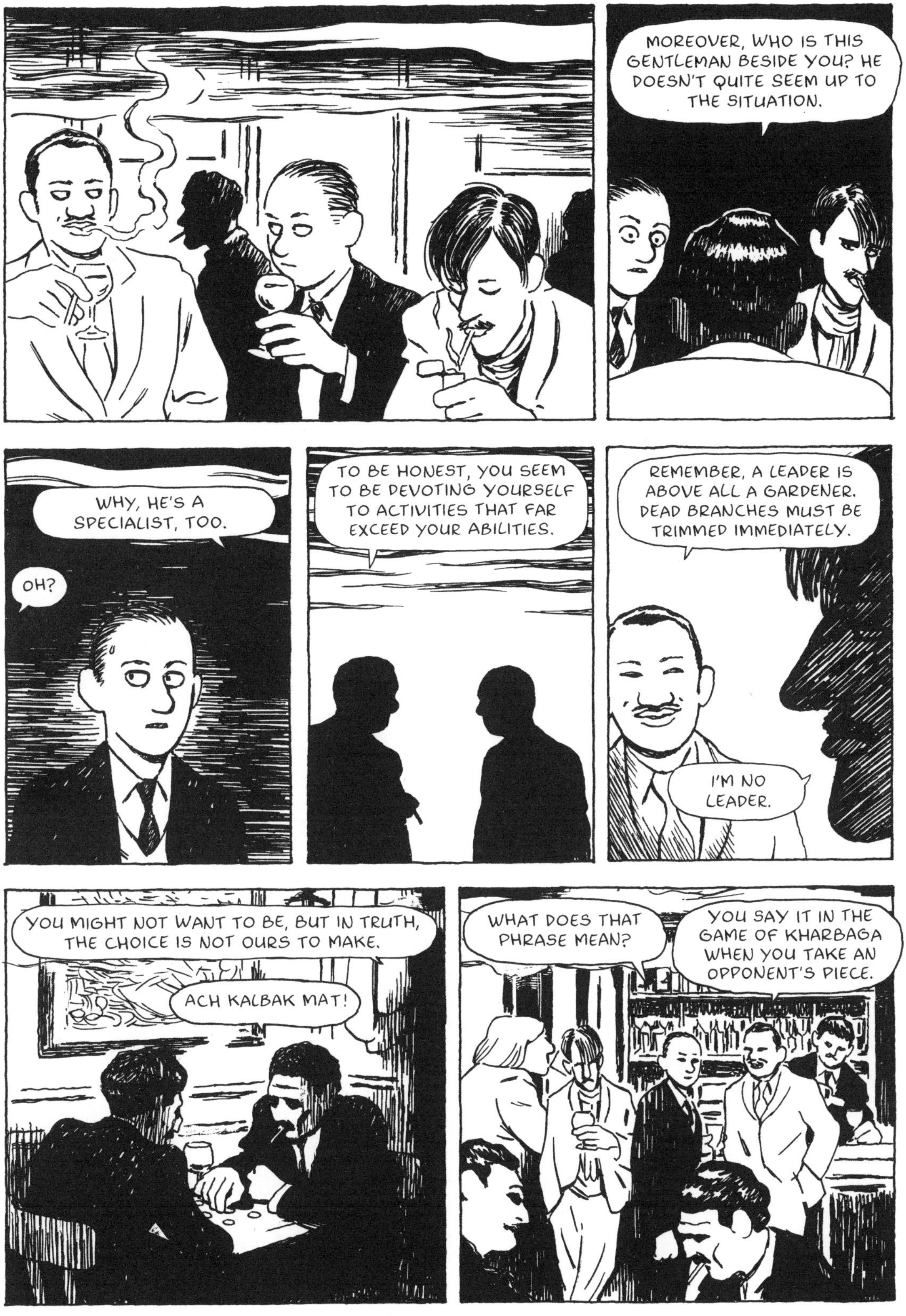
MOREOVER, WHO IS THIS GENTLEMAN BESIDE YOU? HE DOESN'T QUITE SEEM UP TO THE SITUATION.
WHY, HE'S A SPECIALIST, TOO.
OH?
TO BE HONEST, YOU SEEM TO BE DEVOTING YOURSELF TO ACTIVITIES THAT FAR EXCEED YOUR ABILITIES.
REMEMBER, A LEADER IS ABOVE ALL A GARDENER. DEAD BRANCHES MUST BE TRIMMED IMMEDIATELY.
I'M NO LEADER.
YOU MIGHT NOT WANT TO BE, BUT IN TRUTH, THE CHOICE IS NOT OURS TO MAKE.
ACH KALBAK MAT!
WHAT DOES THAT PHRASE MEAN?
YOU SAY IT IN THE GAME OF KHARBAGA WHEN YOU TAKE AN OPPONENT'S PIECE.

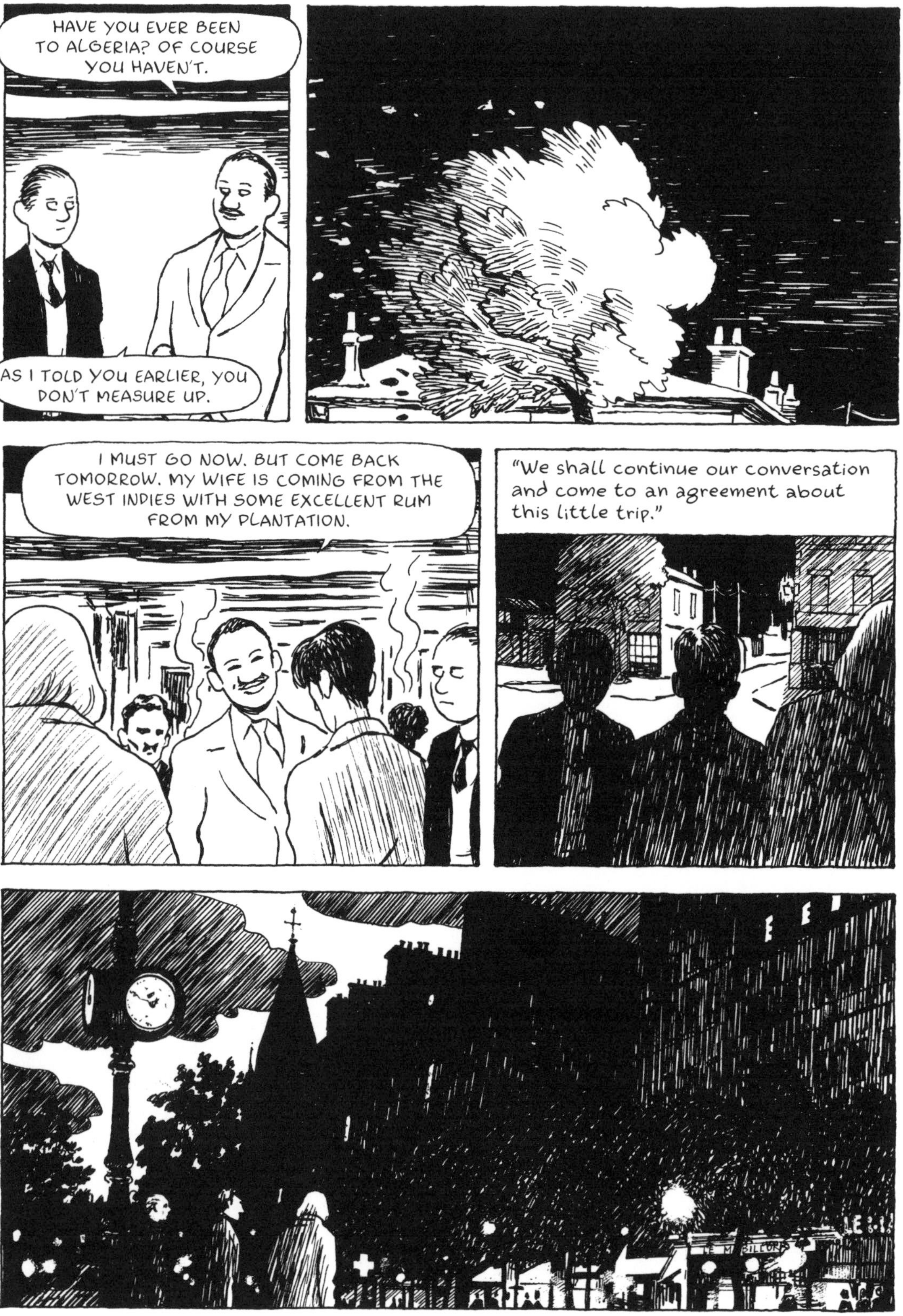
HAVE YOU EVER BEEN TO ALGERIA? OF COURSE YOU HAVEN'T.
AS I TOLD YOU EARLIER, YOU DON'T MEASURE UP.
I MUST GO NOW. BUT COME BACK TOMORROW. MY WIFE IS COMING FROM THE WEST INDIES WITH SOME EXCELLENT RUM FROM MY PLANTATION.
"We shall continue our conversation and come to an agreement about this little trip."

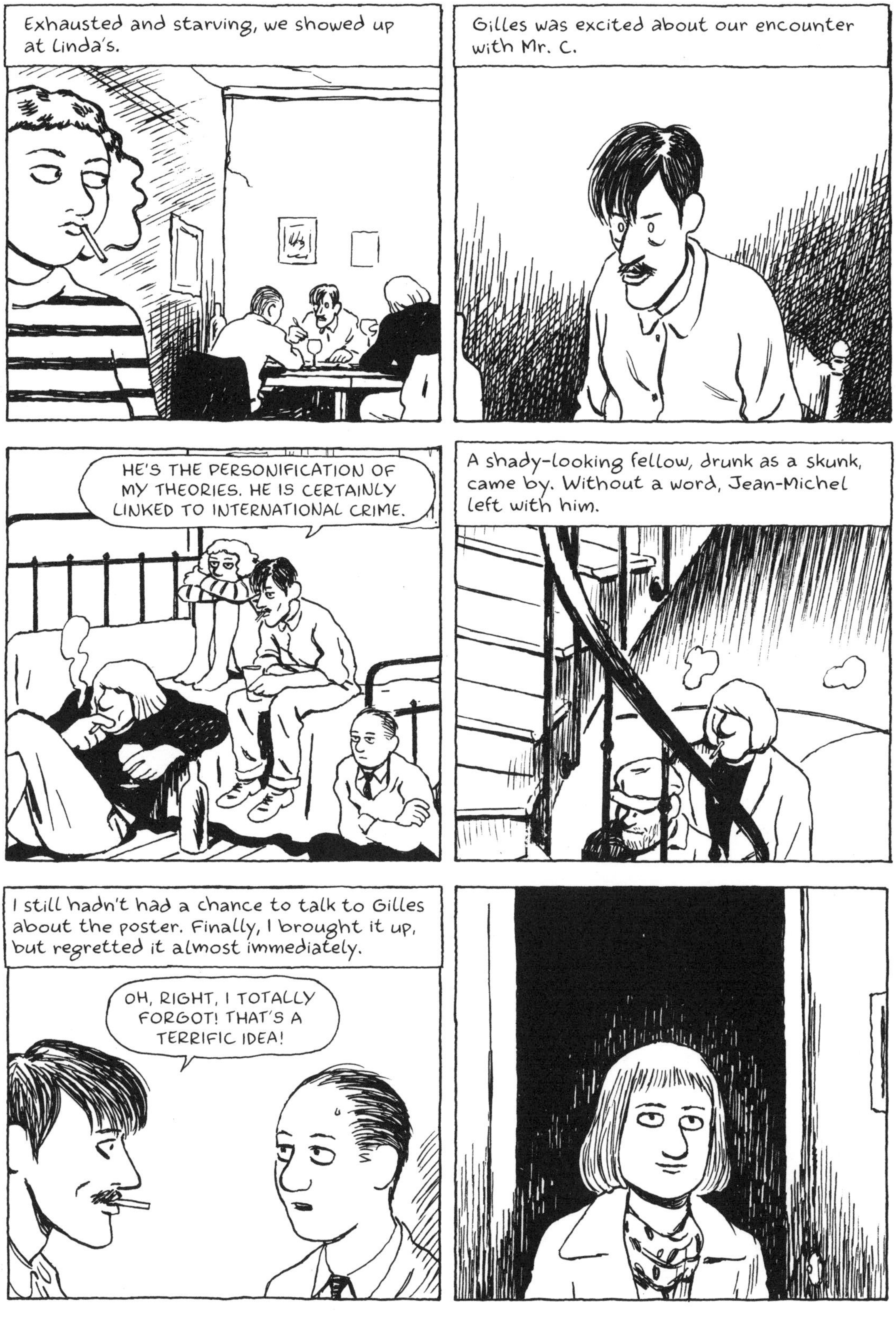
Exhausted and starving, we showed up at Linda's.
Gilles was excited about our encounter with Mr. C.
HE'S THE PERSONIFICATION OF MY THEORIES. HE IS CERTAINLY LINKED TO INTERNATIONAL CRIME.
A shady-looking fellow, drunk as a skunk, came by. Without a word, Jean-Michel left with him.
I still hadn't had a chance to talk to Gilles about the poster. Finally, I brought it up, but regretted it almost immediately.
OH, RIGHT, I TOTALLY FORGOT! THAT'S A TERRIFIC IDEA!

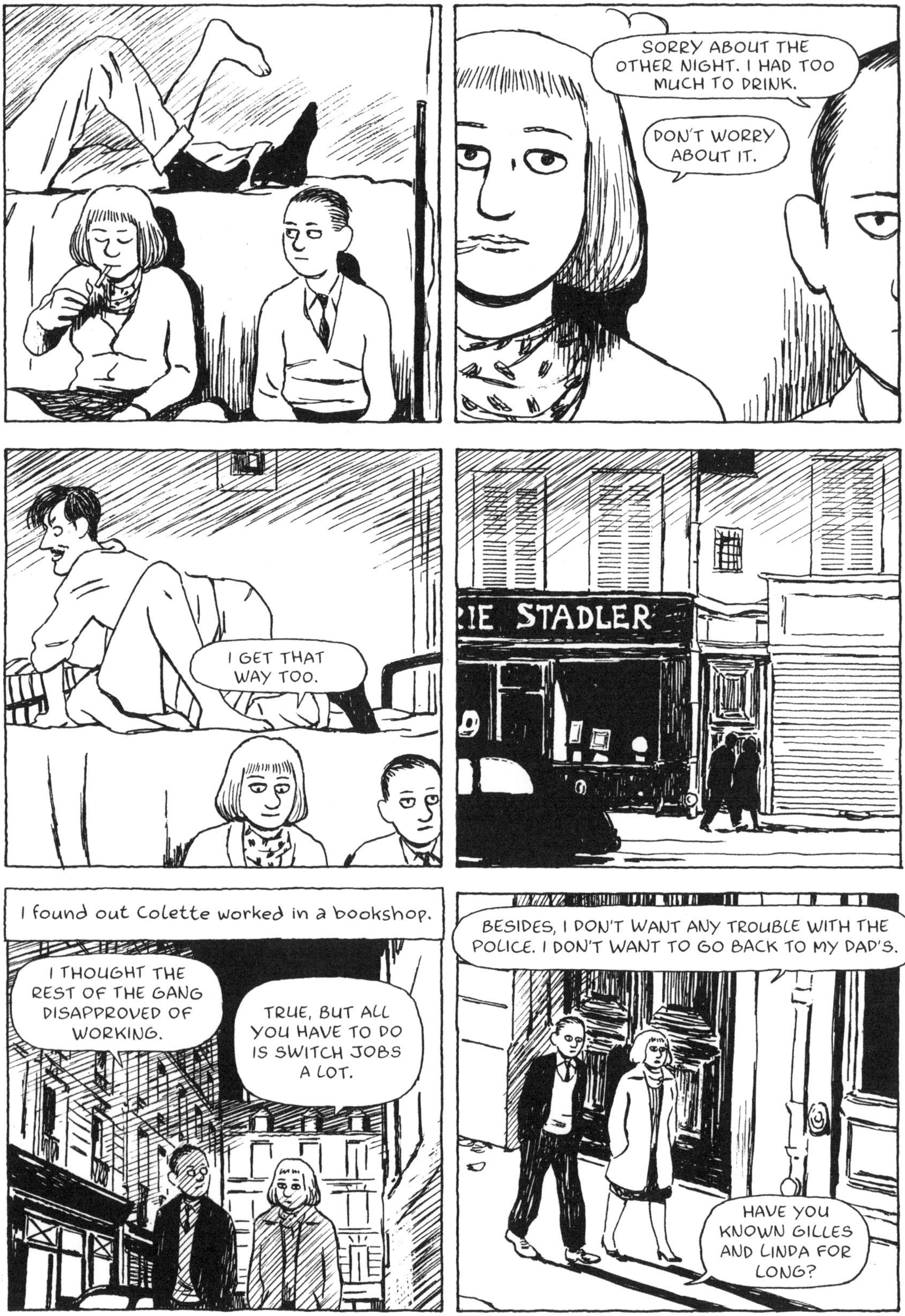
SORRY ABOUT THE OTHER NIGHT. I HAD TOO MUCH TO DRINK.
DON'T WORRY ABOUT IT.
I GET THAT WAY TOO.
RIE STADLER
I found out Colette worked in a bookshop.
I THOUGHT THE REST OF THE GANG DISAPPROVED OF WORKING.
TRUE, BUT ALL YOU HAVE TO DO IS SWITCH JOBS A LOT.
BESIDES, I DON'T WANT ANY TROUBLE WITH THE POLICE. I DON'T WANT TO GO BACK TO MY DAD'S.
HAVE YOU KNOWN GILLES AND LINDA FOR LONG?

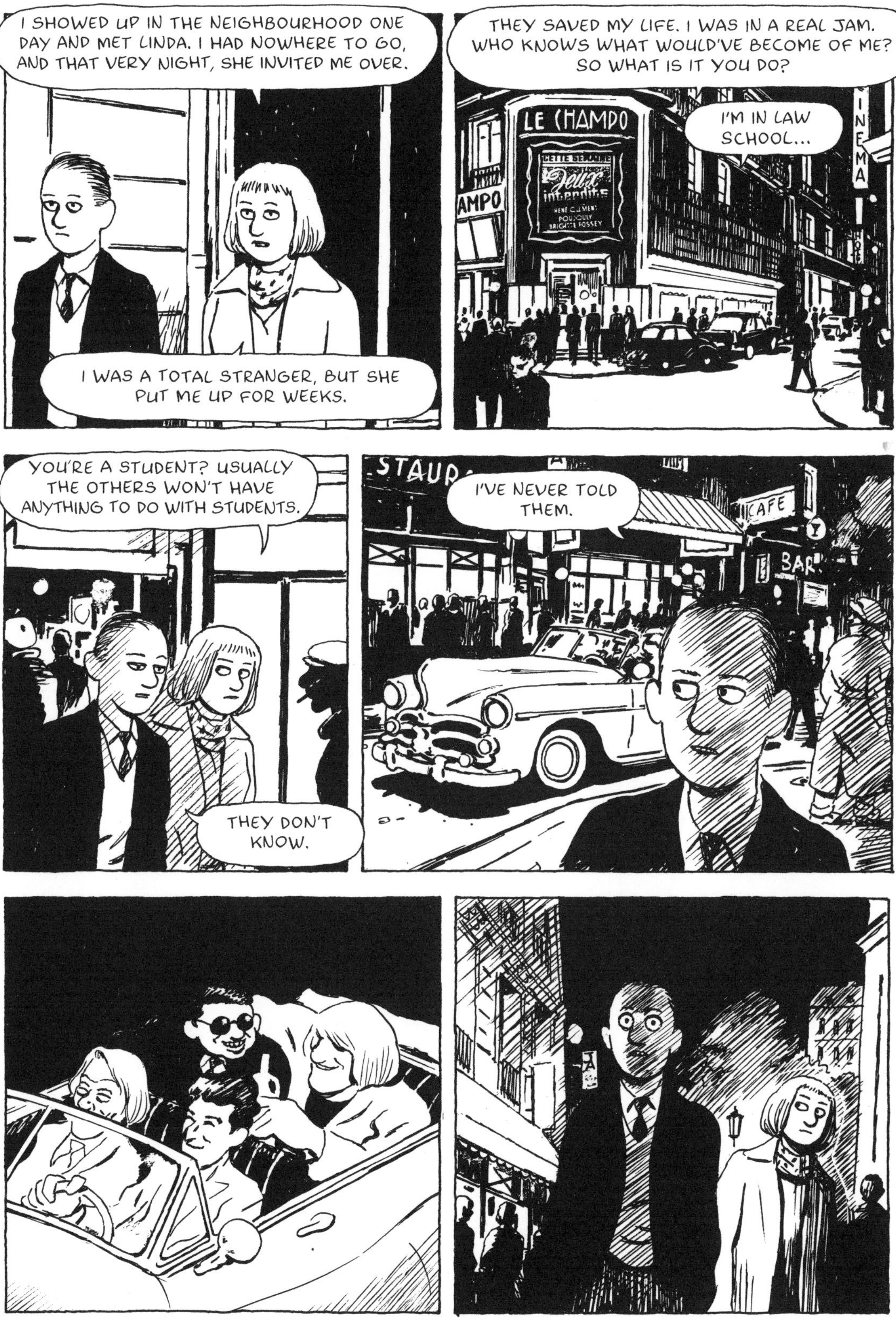
I SHOWED UP IN THE NEIGHBOURHOOD ONE DAY AND MET LINDA. I HAD NOWHERE TO GO, AND THAT VERY NIGHT, SHE INVITED ME OVER.
I WAS A TOTAL STRANGER, BUT SHE PUT ME UP FOR WEEKS.
THEY SAVED MY LIFE. I WAS IN A REAL JAM. WHO KNOWS WHAT WOULD'VE BECOME OF ME? SO WHAT IS IT YOU DO?
LE CHAMPO
AMPO
I'M IN LAW SCHOOL...
YOU'RE A STUDENT? USUALLY THE OTHERS WON'T HAVE ANYTHING TO DO WITH STUDENTS.
THEY DON'T KNOW.
I'VE NEVER TOLD THEM.
CAFE
BAR

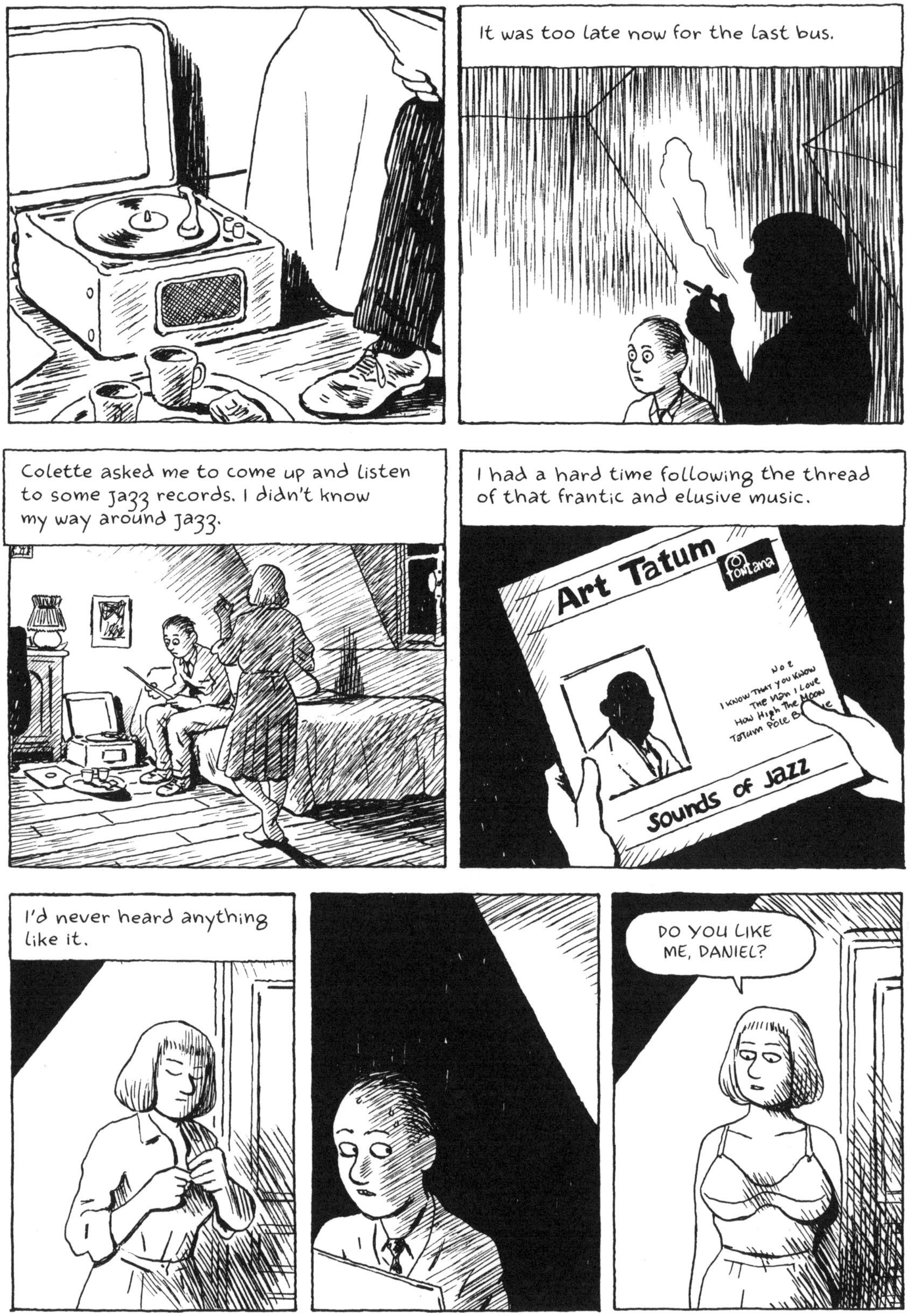
It was too late now for the last bus.
Colette asked me to come up and listen to some jazz records. I didn't know my way around jazz.
I had a hard time following the thread of that frantic and elusive music.
Art Tatum
Fontana
No 2
I KNOW THAT YOU KNOW
The Man I Love
How High The Moon
Sounds of Jazz
I'd never heard anything like it.
DO YOU LIKE ME, DANIEL?

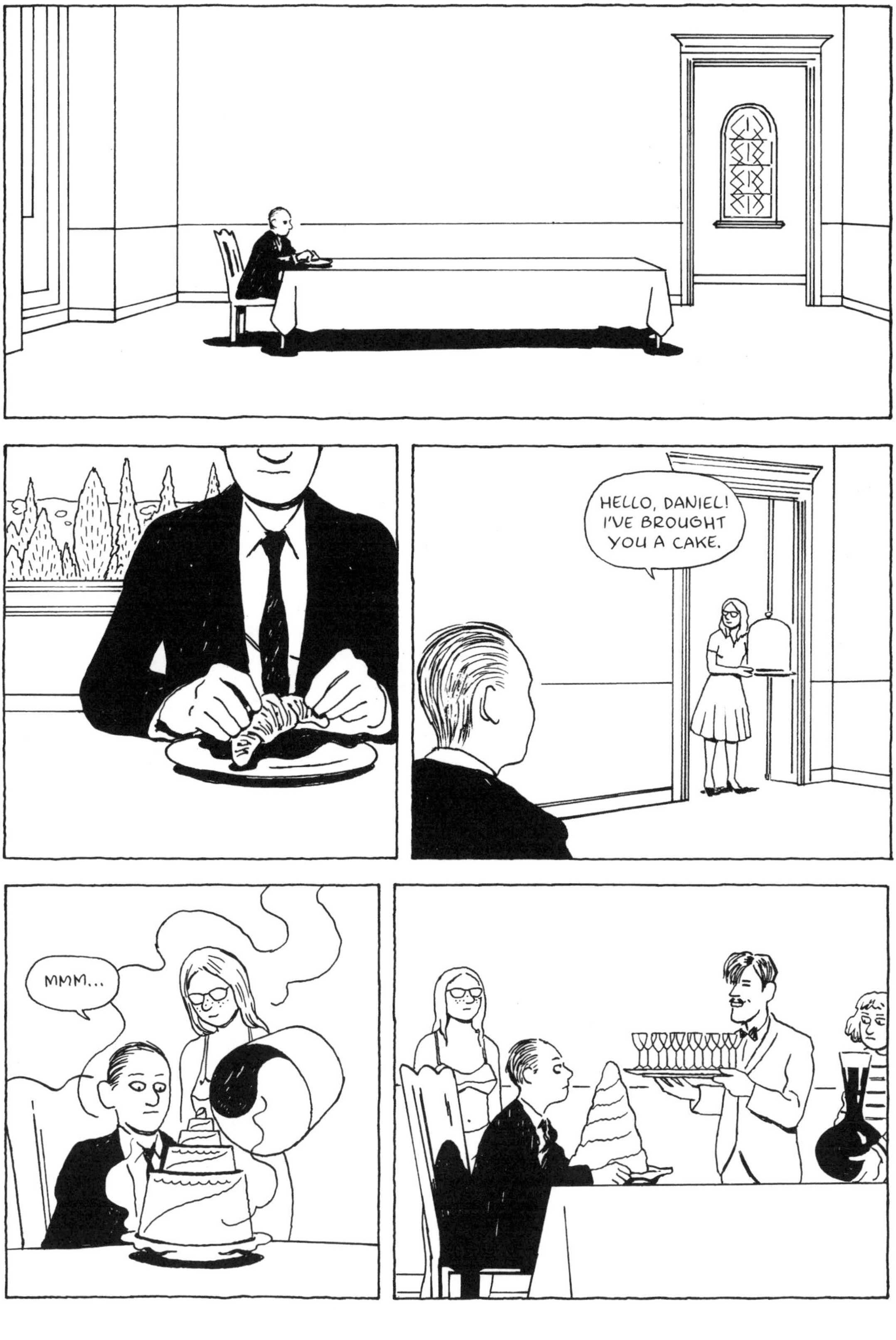
HELLO, DANIEL! I'VE BROUGHT YOU A CAKE.
MMM...

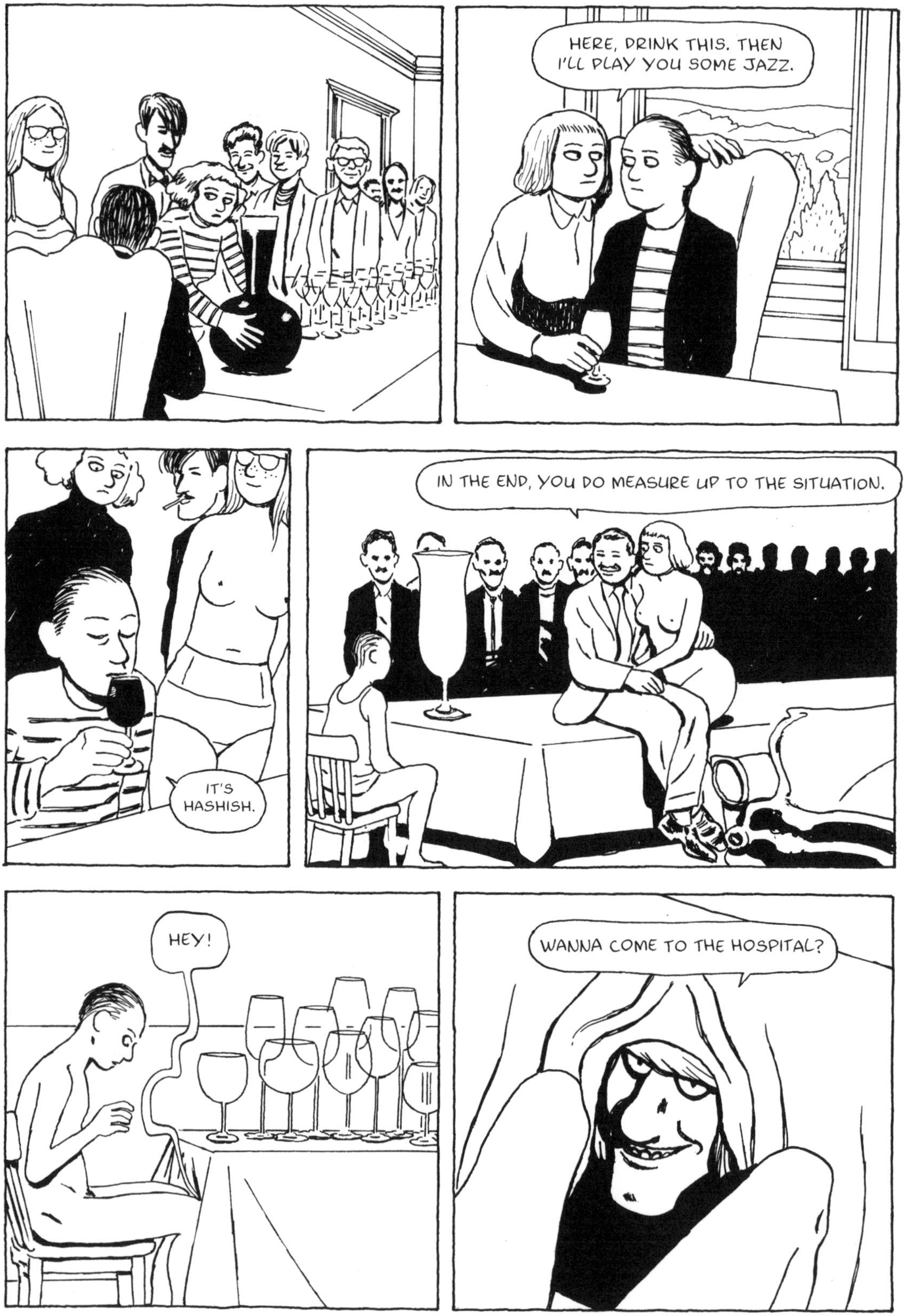
HERE, DRINK THIS. THEN I'LL PLAY YOU SOME JAZZ.
IT'S HASHISH.
IN THE END, YOU DO MEASURE UP TO THE SITUATION.
HEY!
WANNA COME TO THE HOSPITAL?

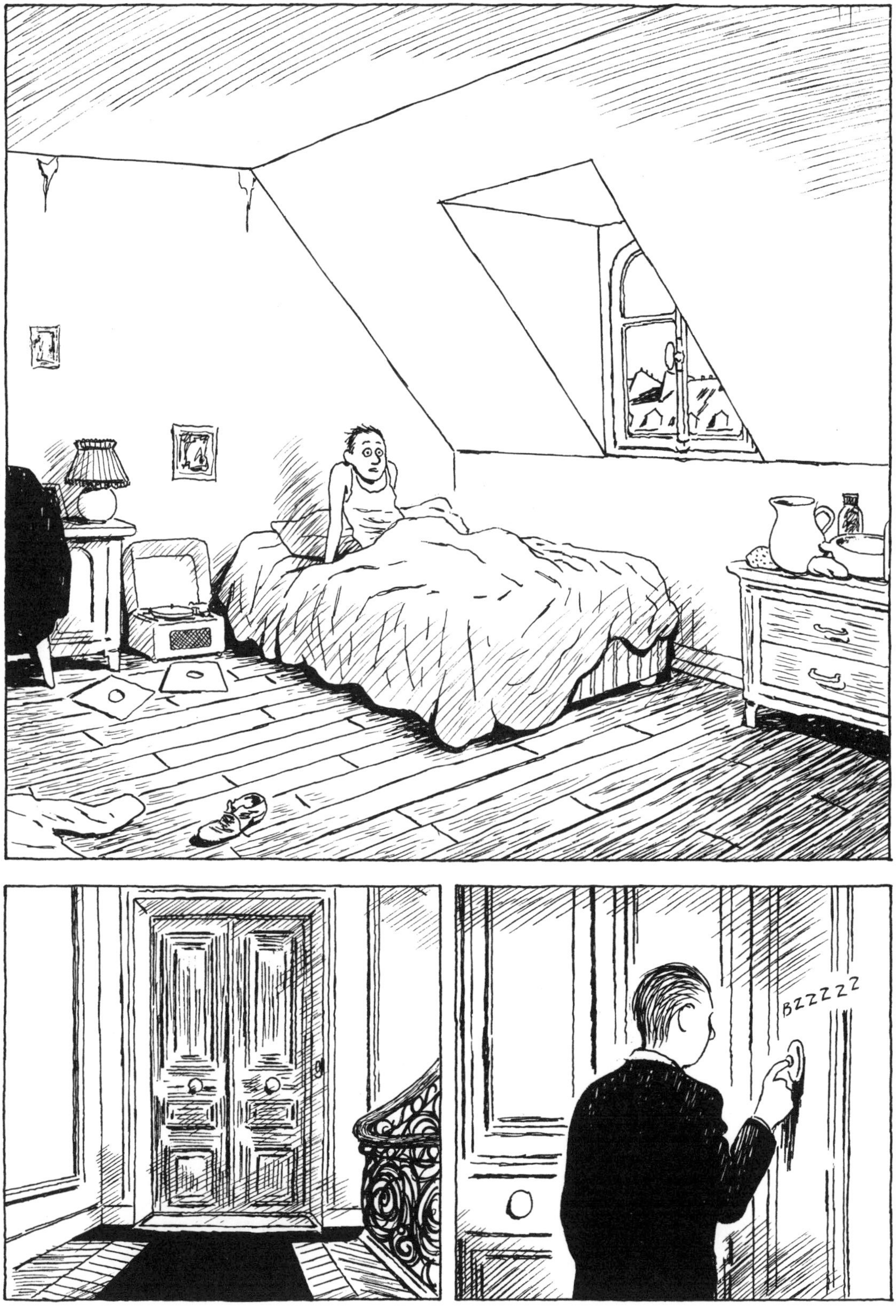
BZZZZZ

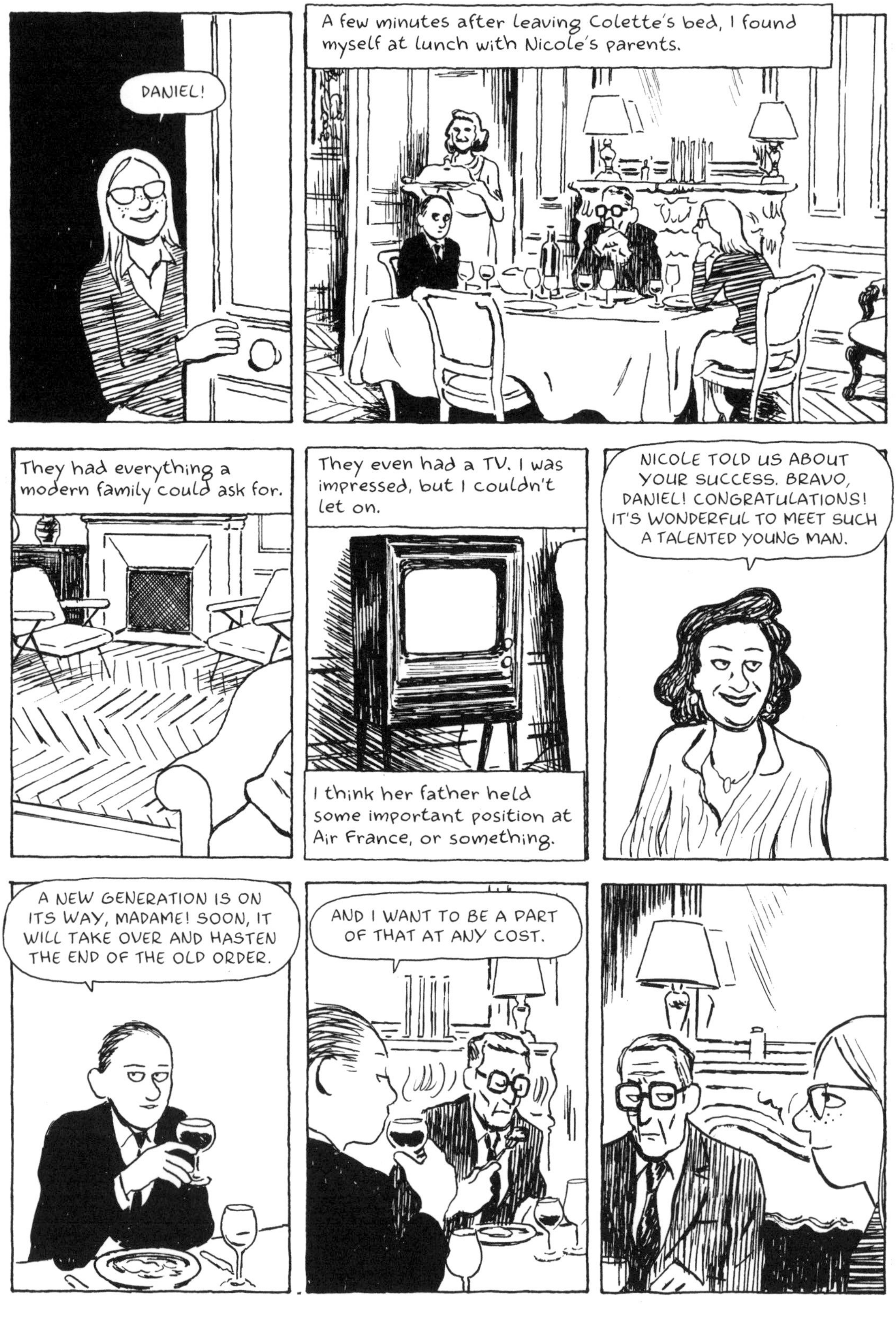
DANIEL!
A few minutes after leaving Colette's bed, I found myself at lunch with Nicole's parents.
They had everything a modern family could ask for.
They even had a TV. I was impressed, but I couldn't let on.
I think her father held some important position at Air France, or something.
NICOLE TOLD US ABOUT YOUR SUCCESS. BRAVO, DANIEL! CONGRATULATIONS! IT'S WONDERFUL TO MEET SUCH A TALENTED YOUNG MAN.
A NEW GENERATION IS ON ITS WAY, MADAME! SOON, IT WILL TAKE OVER AND HASTEN THE END OF THE OLD ORDER.
AND I WANT TO BE A PART OF THAT AT ANY COST.

DANIEL, HAVE YOU ALREADY PICKED WHICH POEMS YOU'RE SENDING TO *TEMPS MODERNES*?

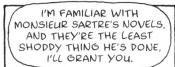
I'LL FIGURE IT OUT TOMORROW. SEE WHAT I'M INSPIRED TO DO IN THE MOMENT.

I, FOR ONE, FIND THAT JOURNAL'S REPUTATION HIGHLY OVERRATED, AND MONSIEUR SARTRE TO BE A MAN OF DUBIOUS MORALITY. EXISTENTIALISM IS STRICTLY FOR DUPES.

PAPA DOESN'T APPRECIATE AVANT-GARDE LITERATURE.

I'M FAMILIAR WITH MONSIEUR SARTRE'S NOVELS, AND THEY'RE THE LEAST SHODDY THING HE'S DONE, I'LL GRANT YOU.

HOW CAN ONE CALL ONESELF A COMMUNIST AND YET LOITER ABOUT IN BISTROS WITH THAT PACK OF SOCIALITES KNOWN AS "EXISTENTIALISTS"? CAN YOU EXPLAIN THAT TO ME, MONSIEUR BRODIN?

I AGREE WITH YOU COMPLETELY, MONSIEUR LEFEBVRE. I'D RATHER DIE THAN HANG AROUND THE CELLARS OF ST. GERMAIN.

IF YOU ASK ME, THERE'S NO DIFFERENCE BETWEEN THE CROWD AT LE TABOU AND DE GAULLE'S RIGHT-WING BUNCH.

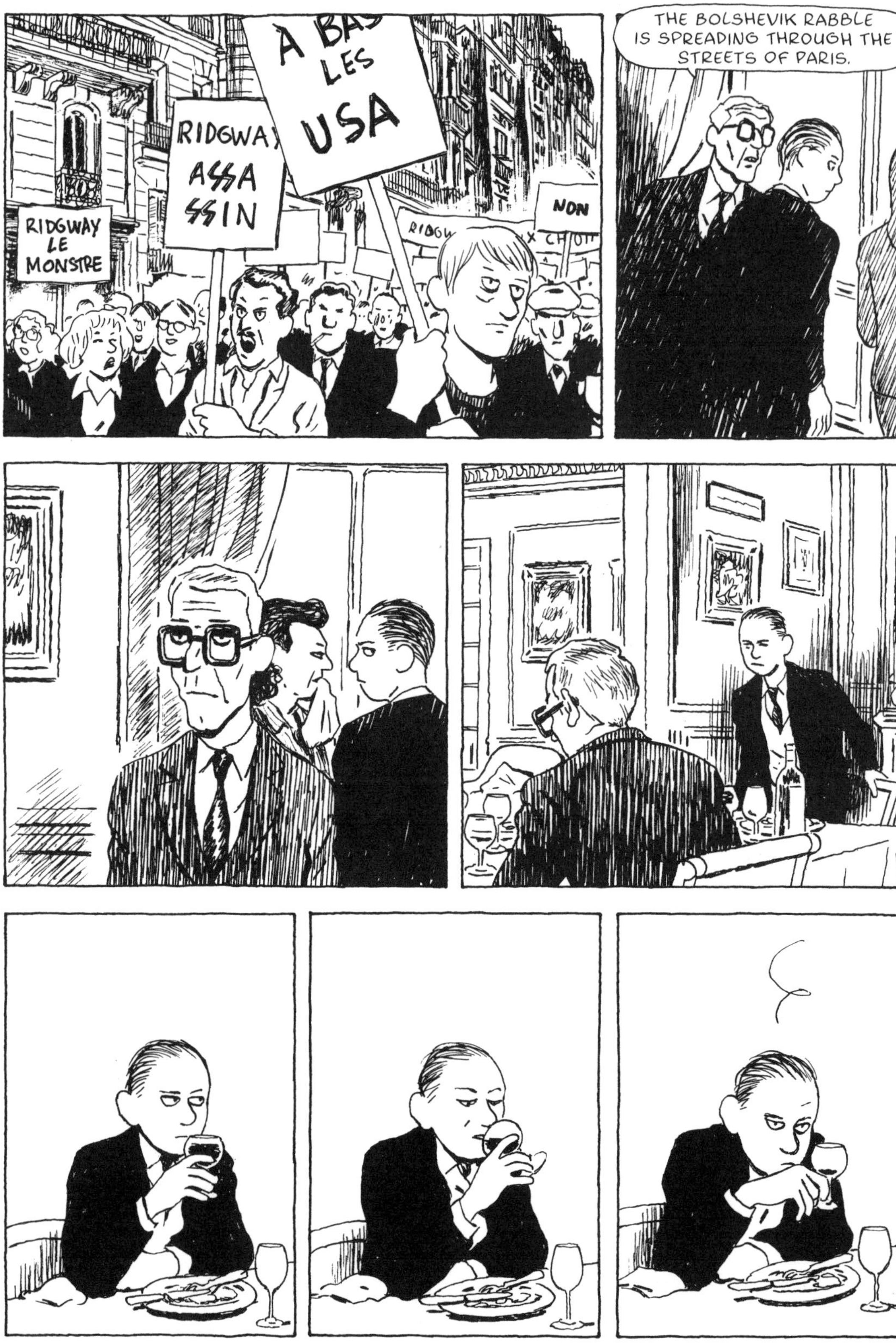
RIDGWAY LE MONSTRE
NON
THE BOLSHEVIK RABBLE IS SPREADING THROUGH THE STREETS OF PARIS.

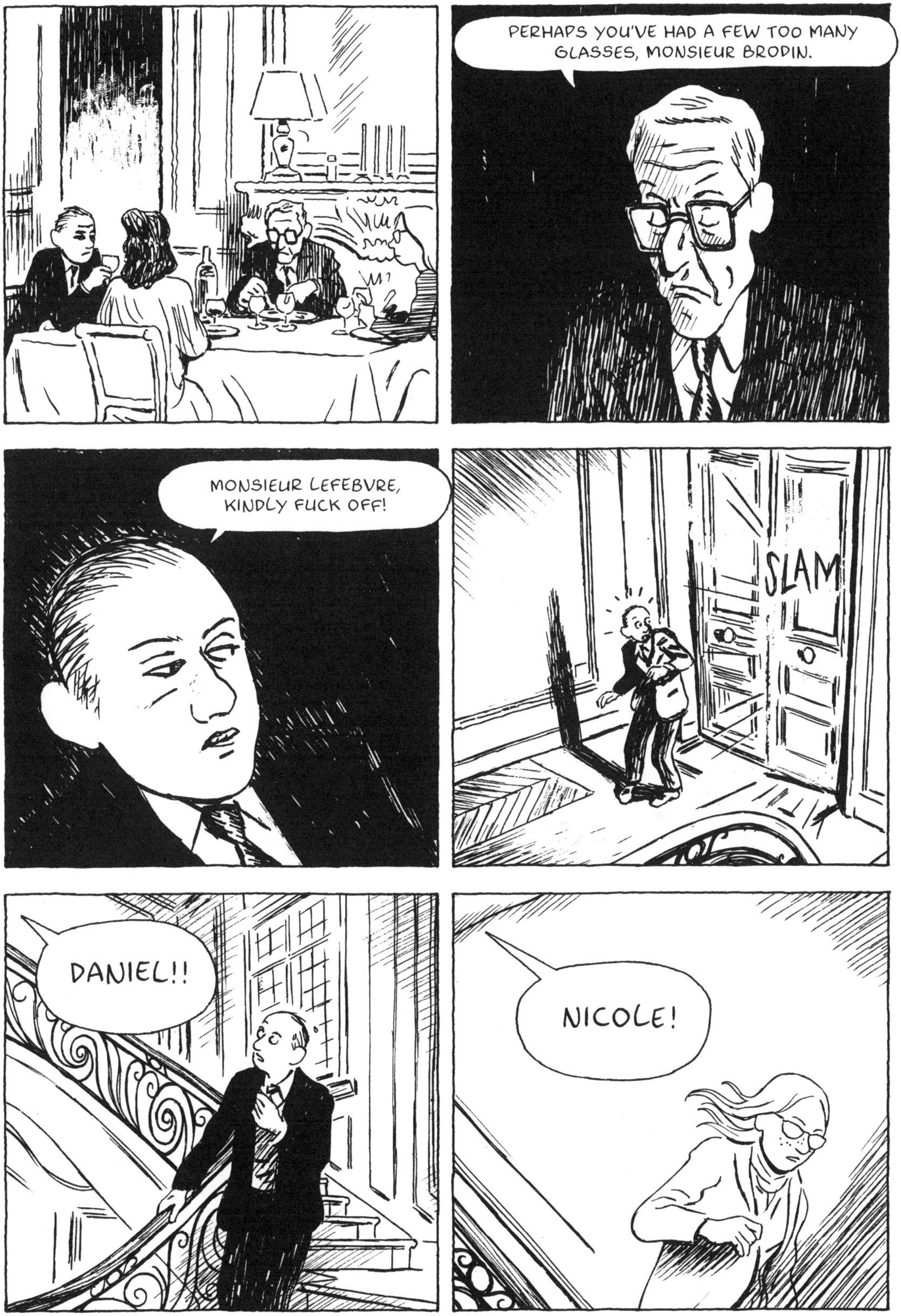
PERHAPS YOU'VE HAD A FEW TOO MANY GLASSES, MONSIEUR BRODIN.
MONSIEUR LEFEBVRE, KINDLY FUCK OFF!
SLAM
DANIEL!!
NICOLE!

I'M COMING WITH YOU!

NICOLE! GET BACK HERE AT ONCE!

ARE WE DEMONSTRATING?

NO, WE'RE GOING TO THE MOVIES.

Nicole decided not to go back home. As if I didn't have enough on my plate already...

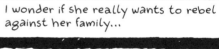
I wonder if she really wants to rebel against her family...

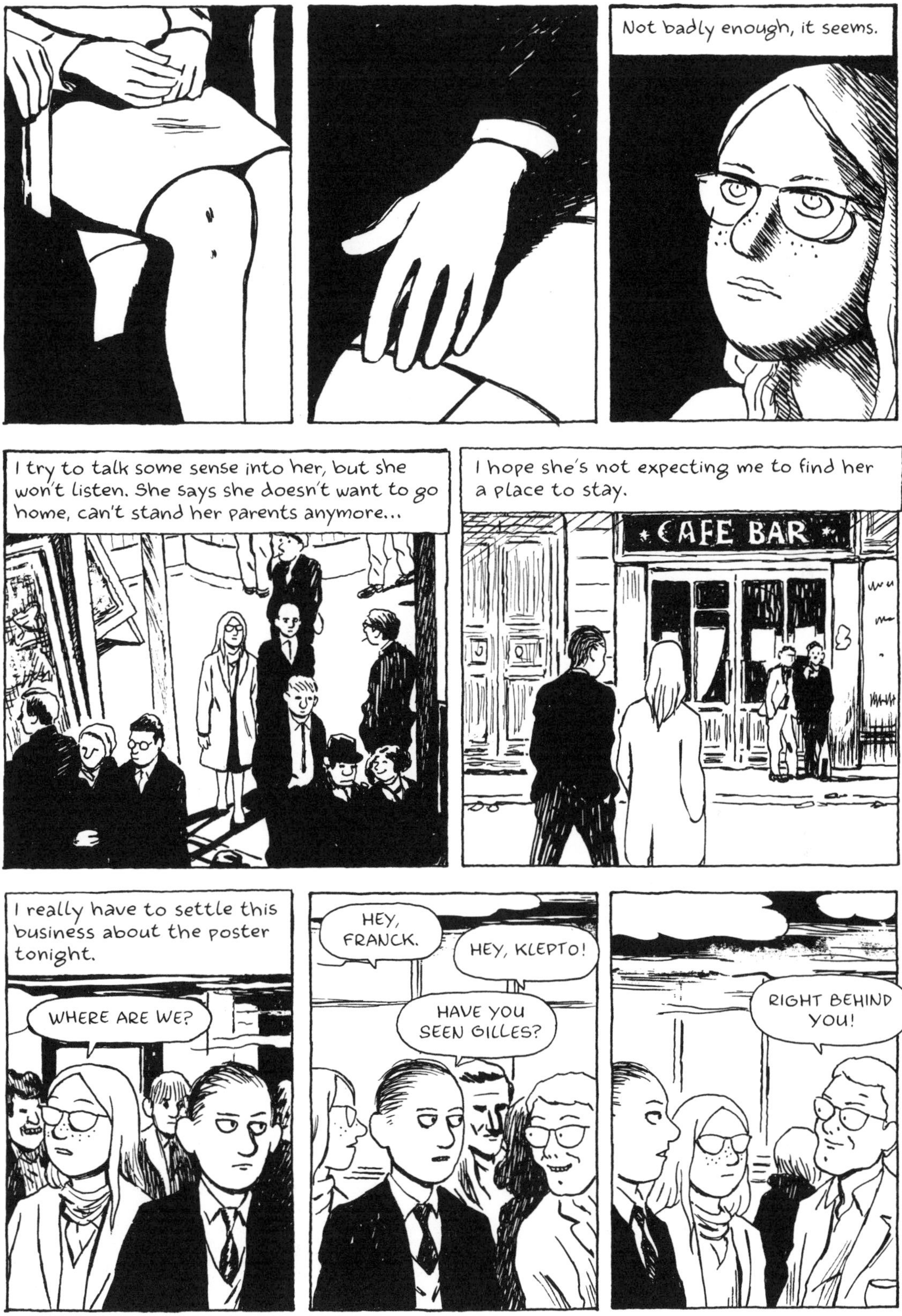
Not badly enough, it seems.
I try to talk some sense into her, but she won't listen. She says she doesn't want to go home, can't stand her parents anymore...
I hope she's not expecting me to find her a place to stay.
CAFE BAR
I really have to settle this business about the poster tonight.
WHERE ARE WE?
HEY, FRANCK.
HEY, KLEPTO!
HAVE YOU SEEN GILLES?
RIGHT BEHIND YOU!

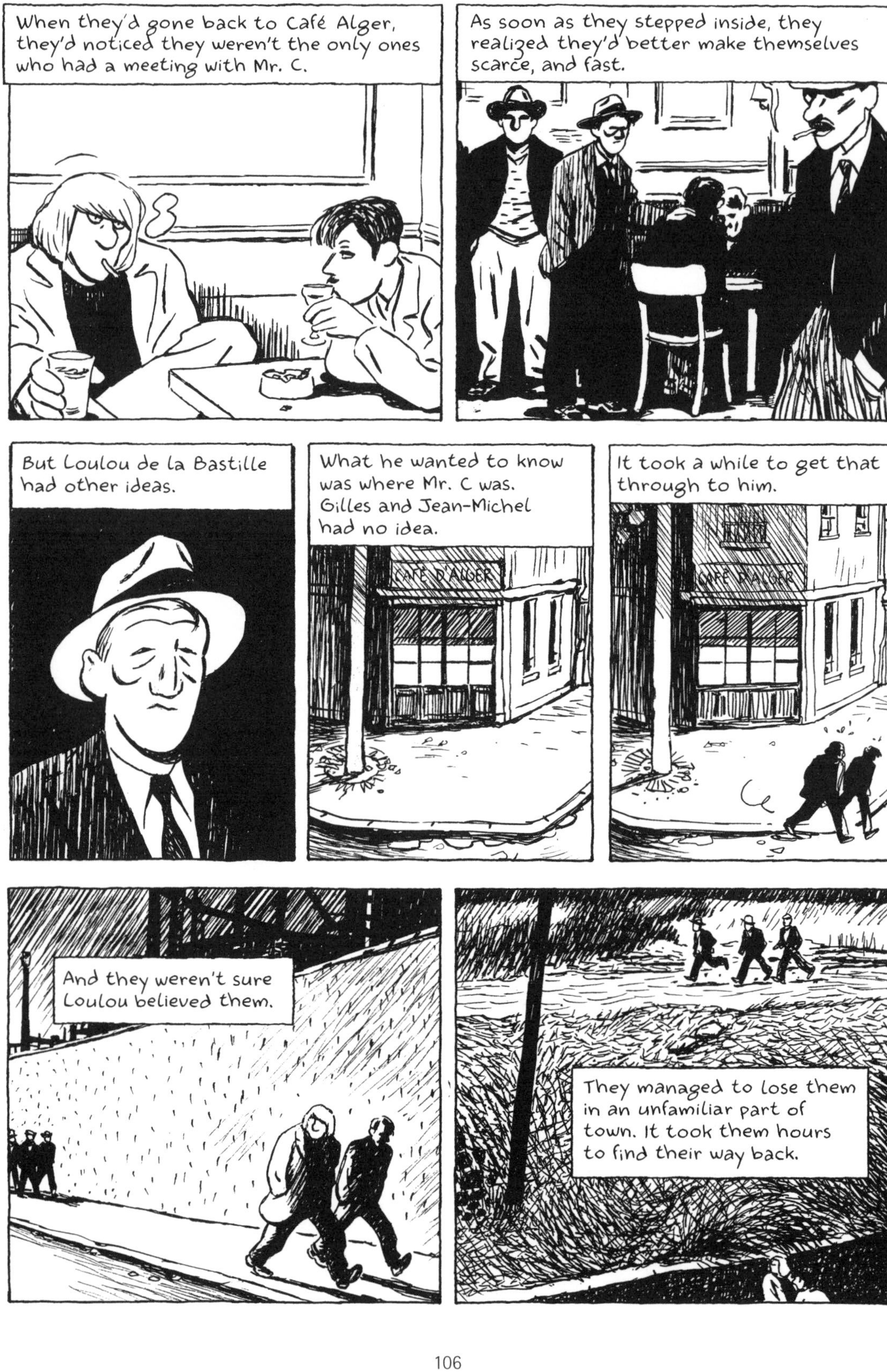
When they'd gone back to Café Alger, they'd noticed they weren't the only ones who had a meeting with Mr. C.
As soon as they stepped inside, they realized they'd better make themselves scarce, and fast.
But Loulou de la Bastille had other ideas.
What he wanted to know was where Mr. C was. Gilles and Jean-Michel had no idea.
CAFÉ D'ALGER
It took a while to get that through to him.
CAFÉ D'ALGER
And they weren't sure Loulou believed them.
They managed to lose them in an unfamiliar part of town. It took them hours to find their way back.

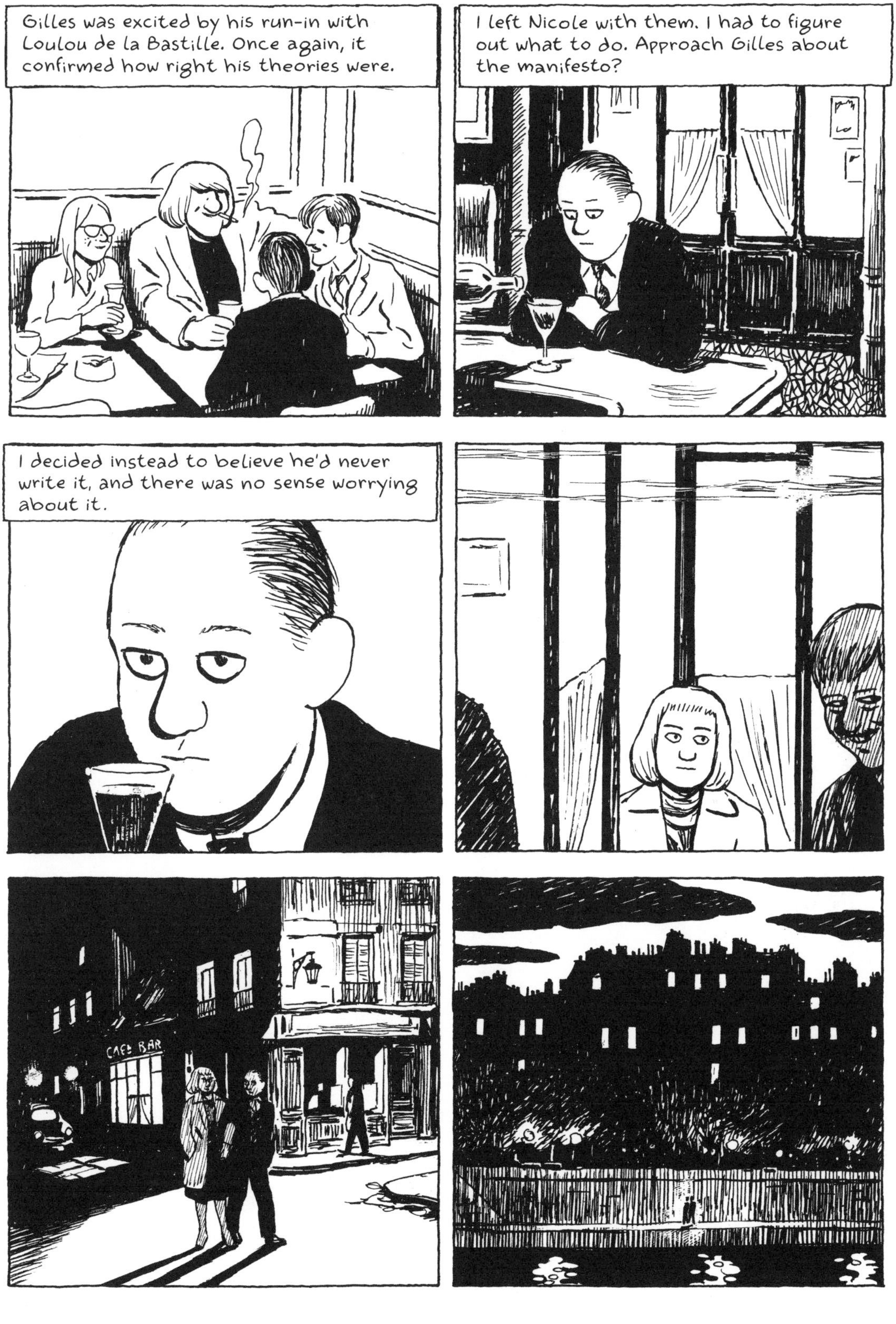
Gilles was excited by his run-in with Loulou de la Bastille. Once again, it confirmed how right his theories were.
I left Nicole with them. I had to figure out what to do. Approach Gilles about the manifesto?
I decided instead to believe he'd never write it, and there was no sense worrying about it.
CAFE BAR

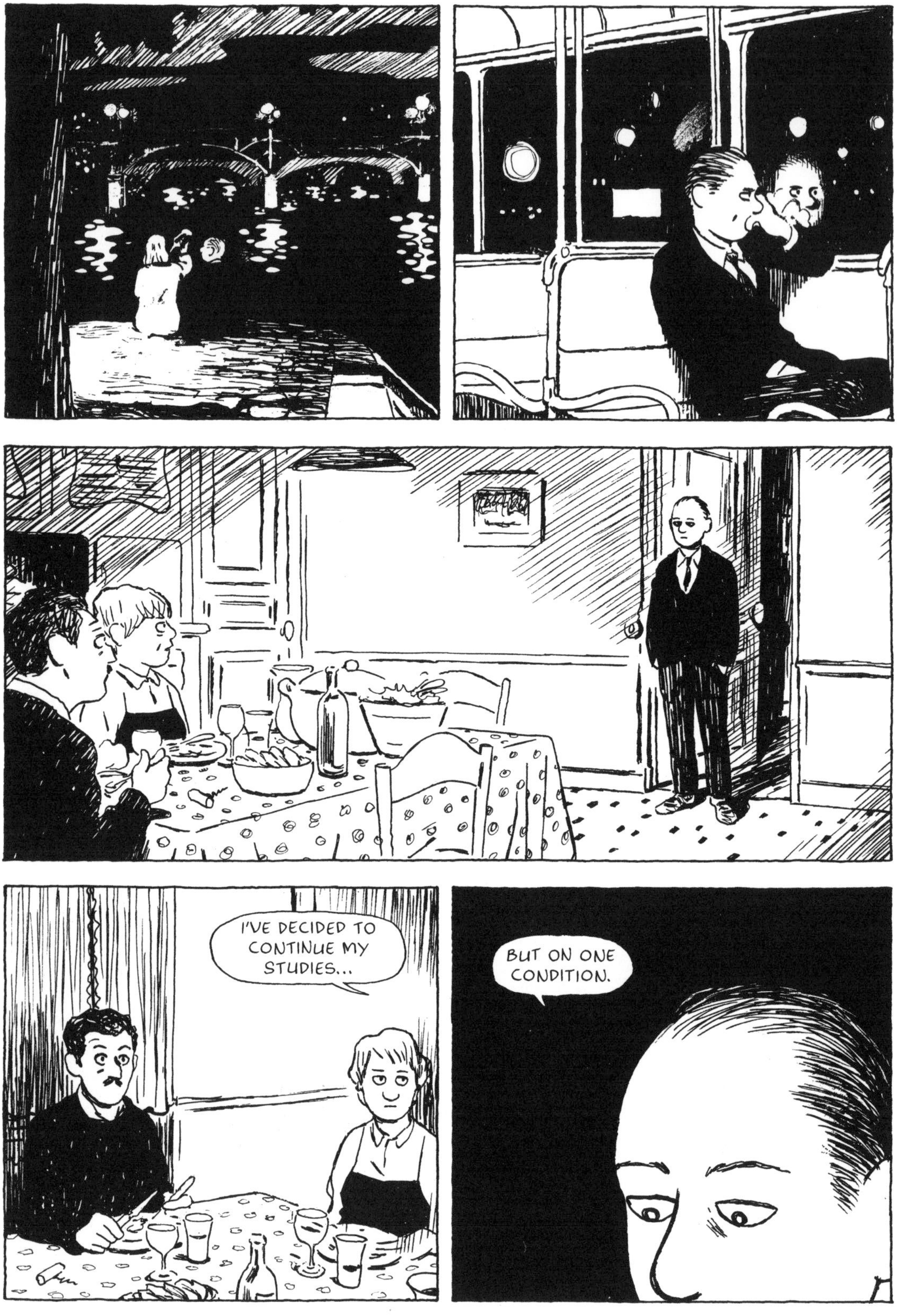
I'VE DECIDED TO CONTINUE MY STUDIES...
BUT ON ONE CONDITION.

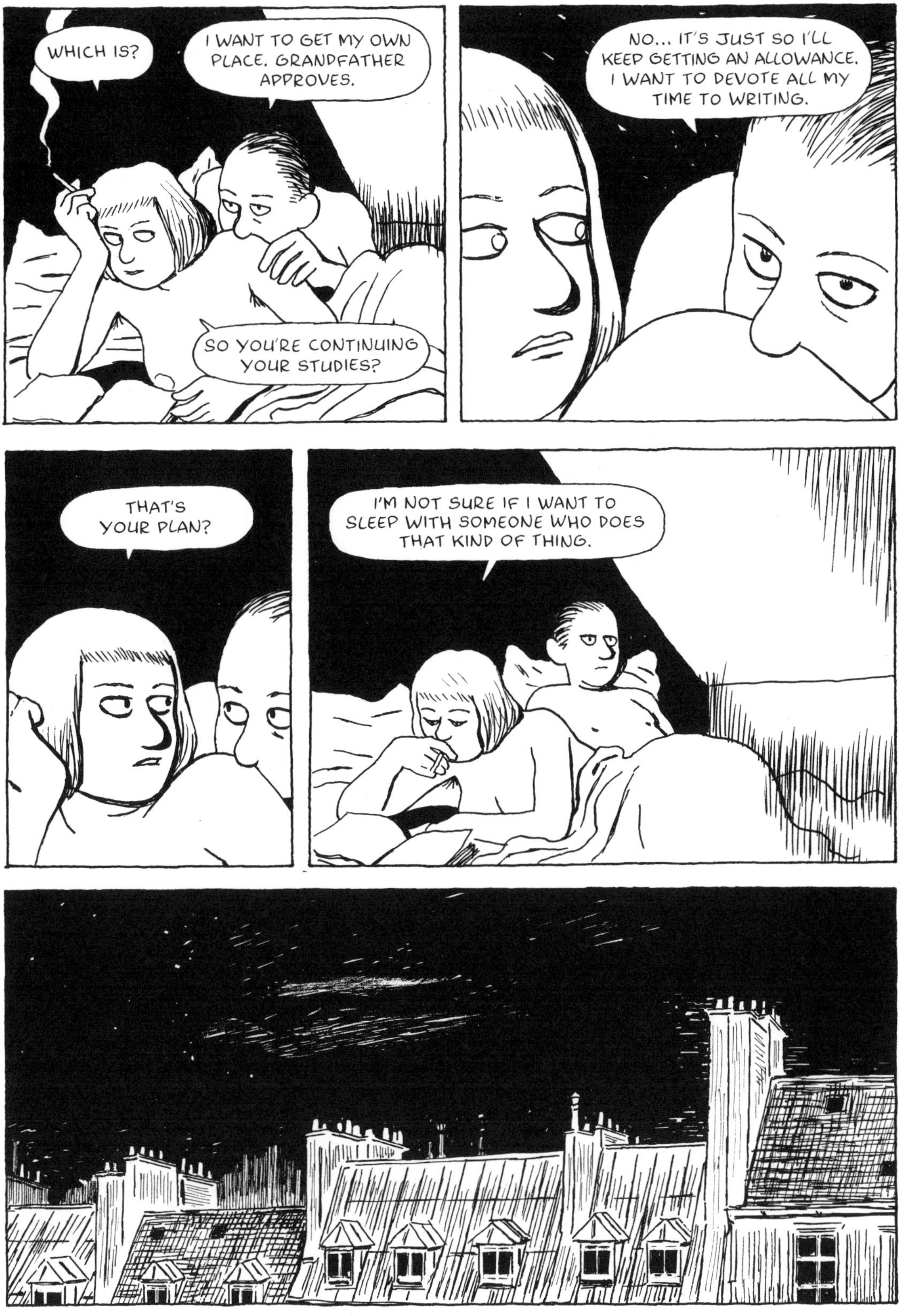
WHICH IS?
I WANT TO GET MY OWN PLACE. GRANDFATHER APPROVES.
SO YOU'RE CONTINUING YOUR STUDIES?
NO... IT'S JUST SO I'LL KEEP GETTING AN ALLOWANCE. I WANT TO DEVOTE ALL MY TIME TO WRITING.
THAT'S YOUR PLAN?
I'M NOT SURE IF I WANT TO SLEEP WITH SOMEONE WHO DOES THAT KIND OF THING.

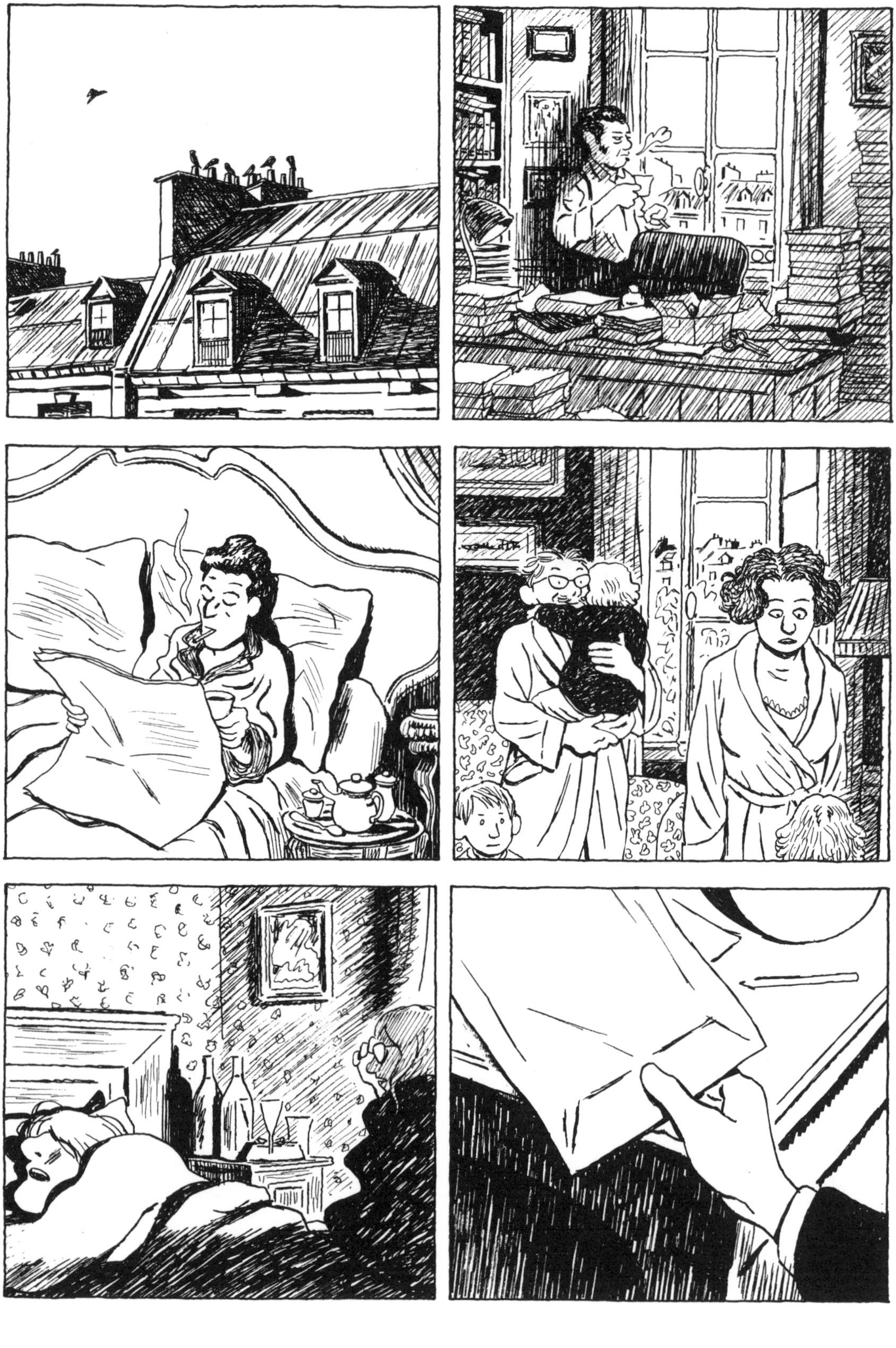

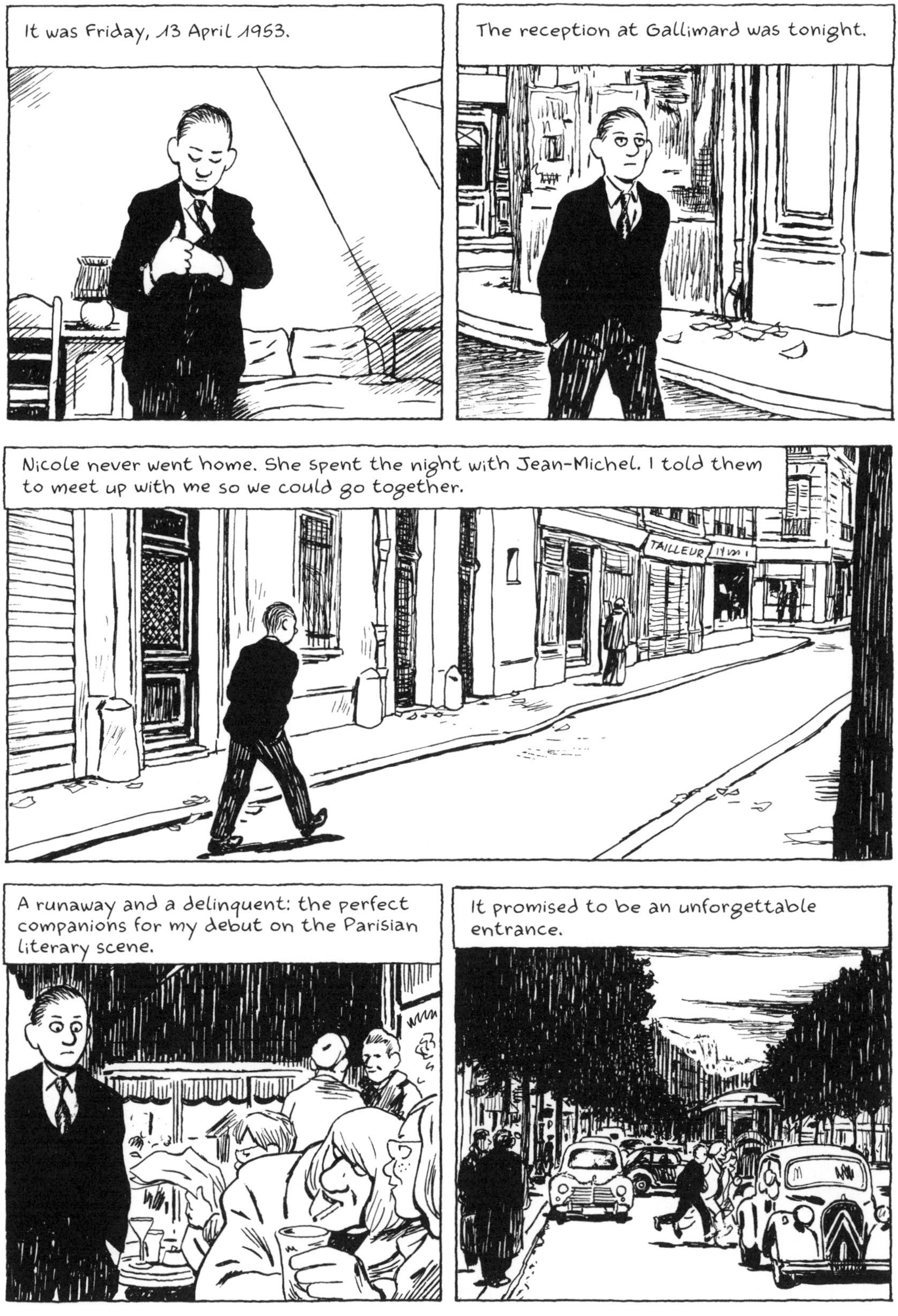
It was Friday, 13 April 1953.
The reception at Gallimard was tonight.
Nicole never went home. She spent the night with Jean-Michel. I told them to meet up with me so we could go together.
TAILLEUR
A runaway and a delinquent: the perfect companions for my debut on the Parisian literary scene.
It promised to be an unforgettable entrance.

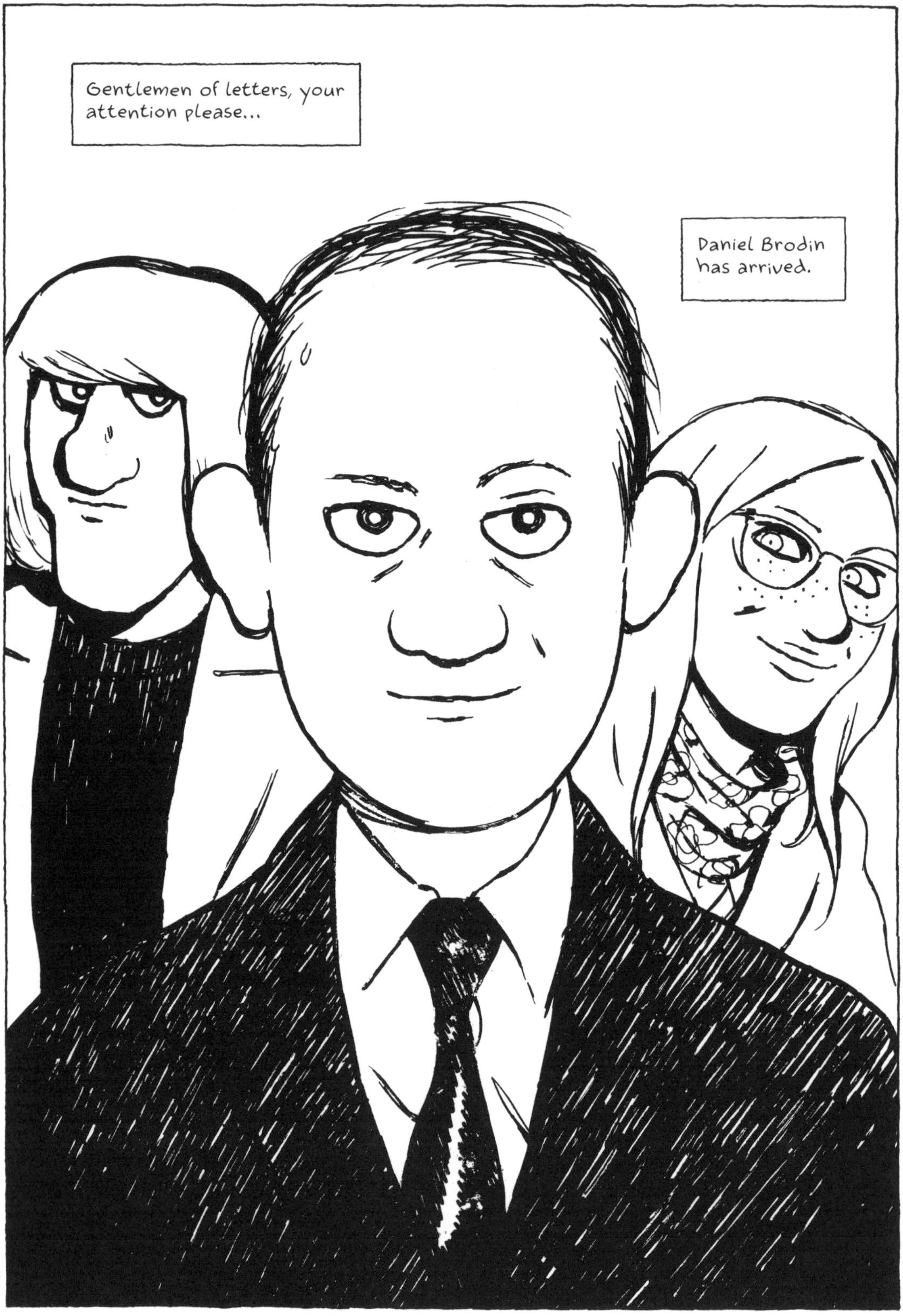
Gentlemen of letters, your attention please...
Daniel Brodin has arrived.

C H A P T E R 5

"POETRY IS FOR SUCKERS."
Jean-Michel A.

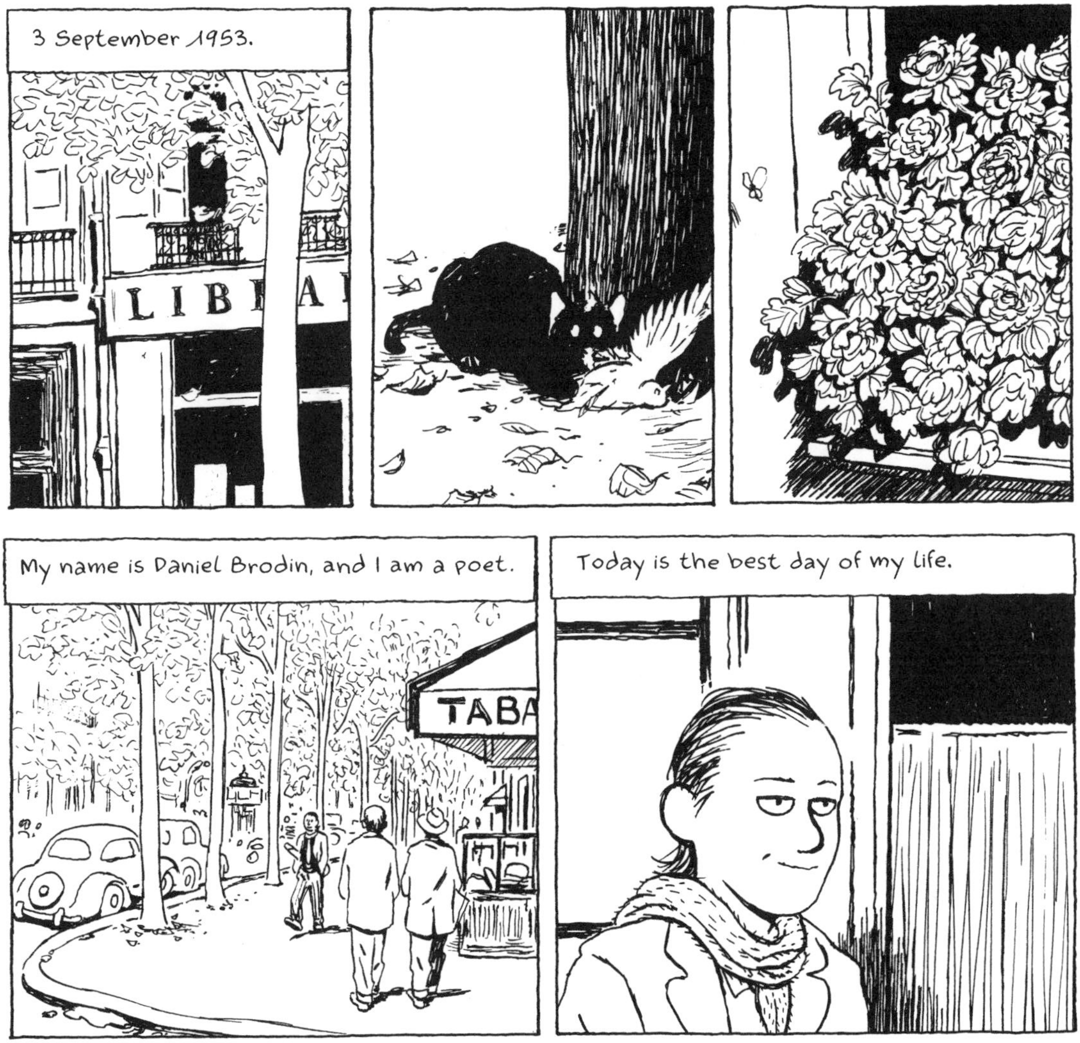
3 September 1953.
LIBRA
My name is Daniel Brodin, and I am a poet.
TABA
Today is the best day of my life.

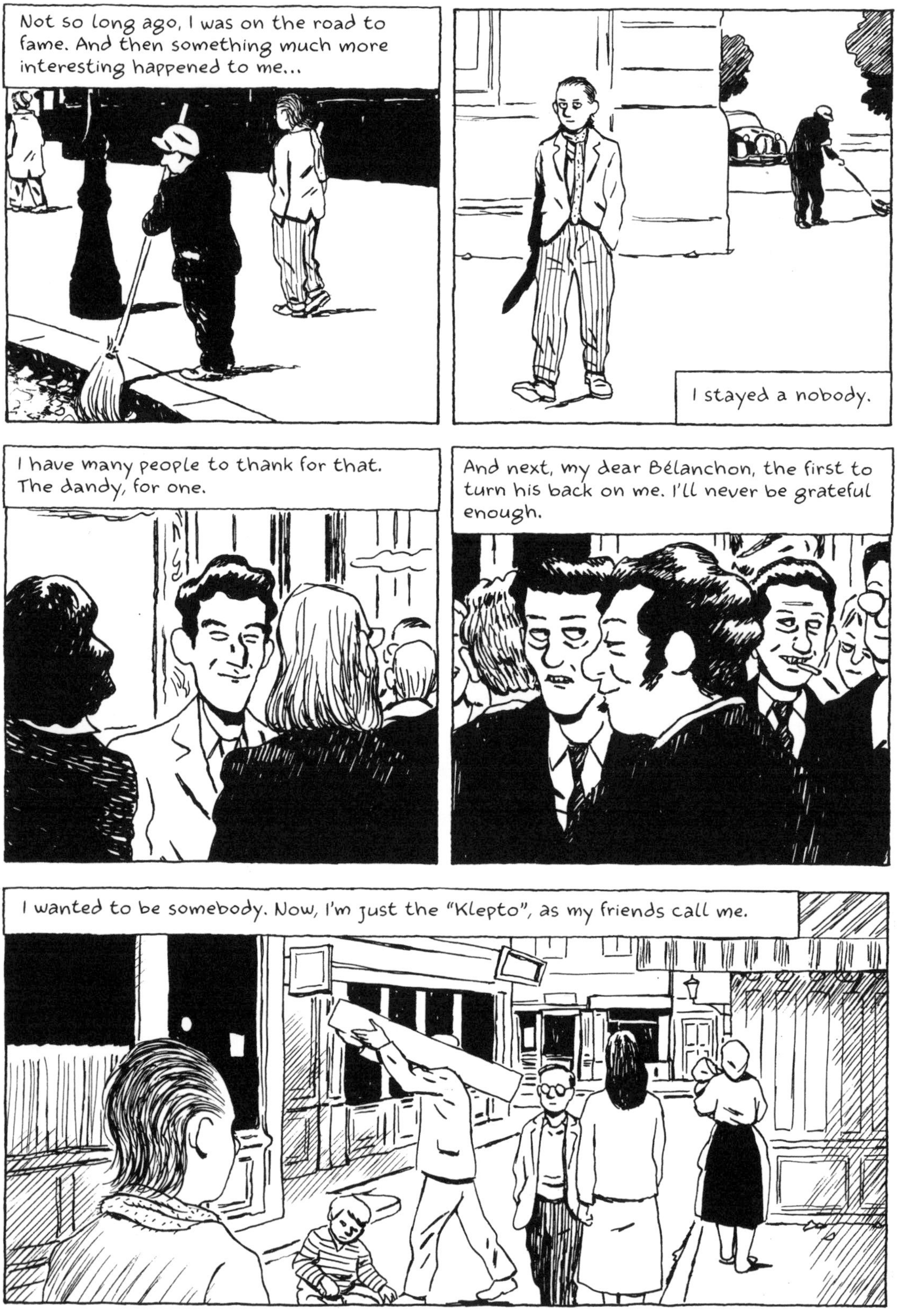
Not so long ago, I was on the road to fame. And then something much more interesting happened to me...
I stayed a nobody.
I have many people to thank for that. The dandy, for one.
And next, my dear Bélanchon, the first to turn his back on me. I'll never be grateful enough.
I wanted to be somebody. Now, I'm just the "Klepto", as my friends call me.

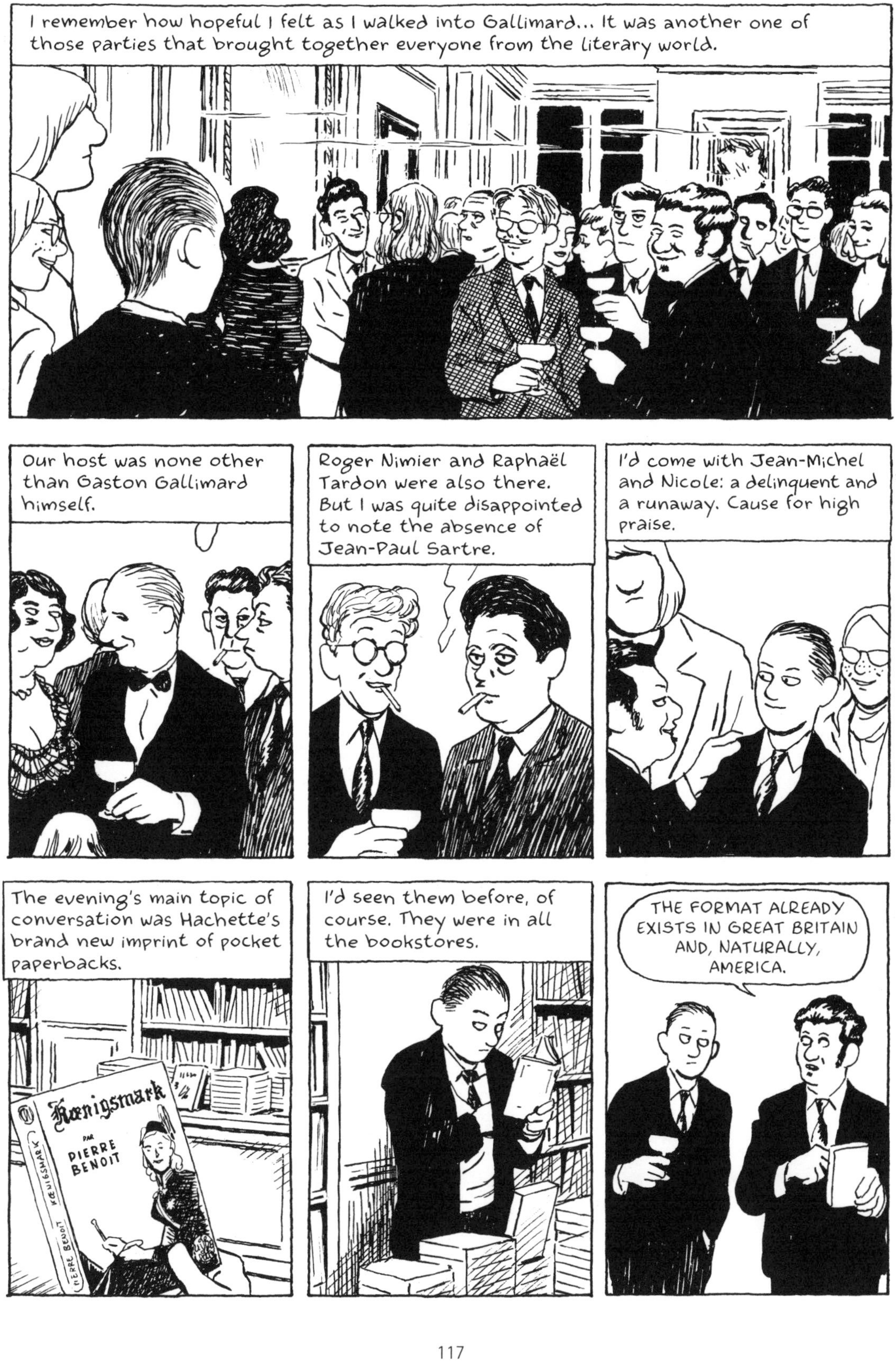

I remember how hopeful I felt as I walked into Gallimard... It was another one of those parties that brought together everyone from the literary world.
Our host was none other than Gaston Gallimard himself.
Roger Nimier and Raphaël Tardon were also there. But I was quite disappointed to note the absence of Jean-Paul Sartre.
I'd come with Jean-Michel and Nicole: a delinquent and a runaway. Cause for high praise.
The evening's main topic of conversation was Hachette's brand new imprint of pocket paperbacks.
Kœnigsmark
PAR
PIERRE BENOIT
I'd seen them before, of course. They were in all the bookstores.
THE FORMAT ALREADY EXISTS IN GREAT BRITAIN AND, NATURALLY, AMERICA.

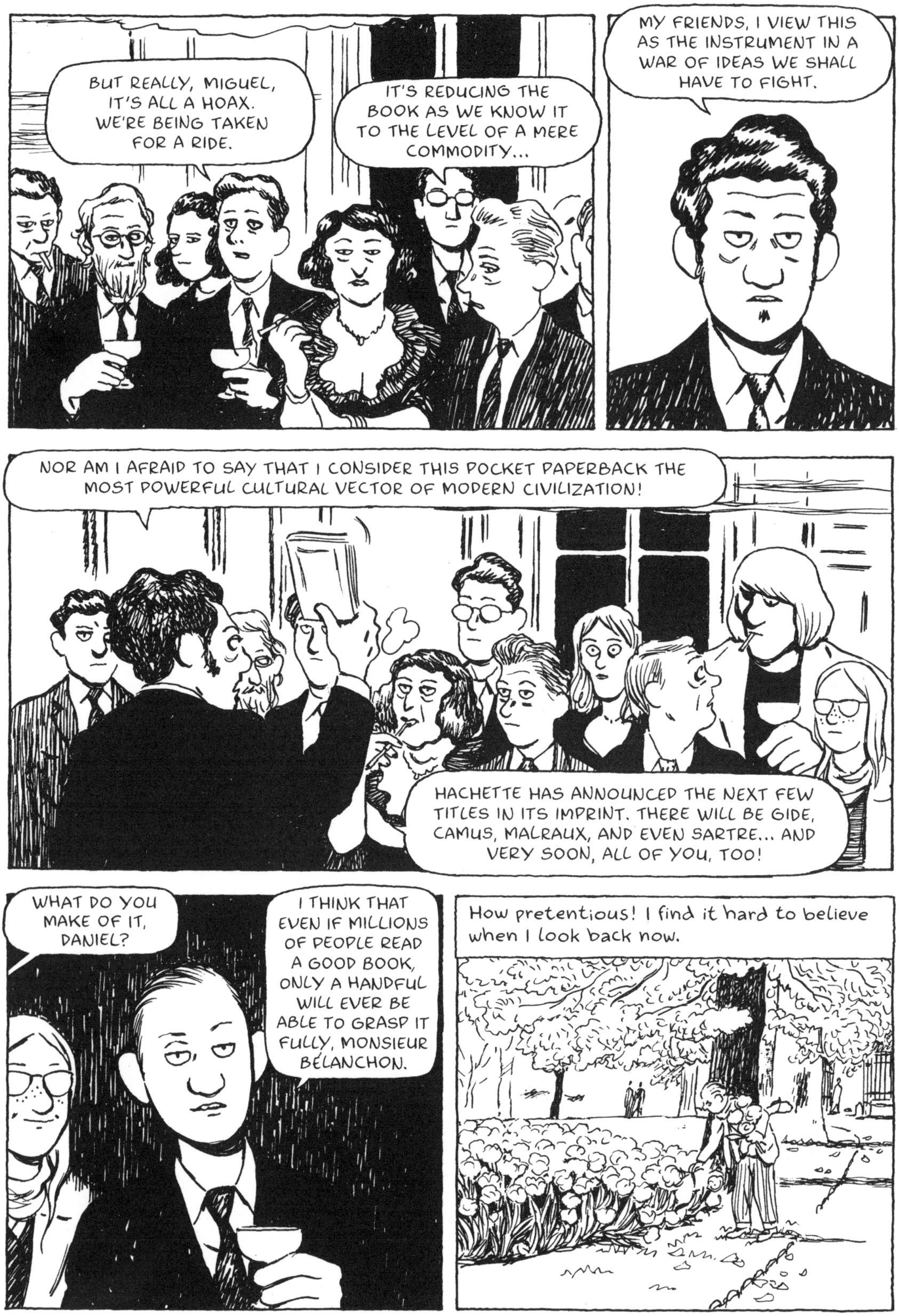
BUT REALLY, MIGUEL, IT'S ALL A HOAX. WE'RE BEING TAKEN FOR A RIDE.
IT'S REDUCING THE BOOK AS WE KNOW IT TO THE LEVEL OF A MERE COMMODITY...
MY FRIENDS, I VIEW THIS AS THE INSTRUMENT IN A WAR OF IDEAS WE SHALL HAVE TO FIGHT.
NOR AM I AFRAID TO SAY THAT I CONSIDER THIS POCKET PAPERBACK THE MOST POWERFUL CULTURAL VECTOR OF MODERN CIVILIZATION!
HACHETTE HAS ANNOUNCED THE NEXT FEW TITLES IN ITS IMPRINT. THERE WILL BE GIDE, CAMUS, MALRAUX, AND EVEN SARTRE... AND VERY SOON, ALL OF YOU, TOO!
WHAT DO YOU MAKE OF IT, DANIEL?
I THINK THAT EVEN IF MILLIONS OF PEOPLE READ A GOOD BOOK, ONLY A HANDFUL WILL EVER BE ABLE TO GRASP IT FULLY, MONSIEUR BÉLANCHON.
How pretentious! I find it hard to believe when I look back now.

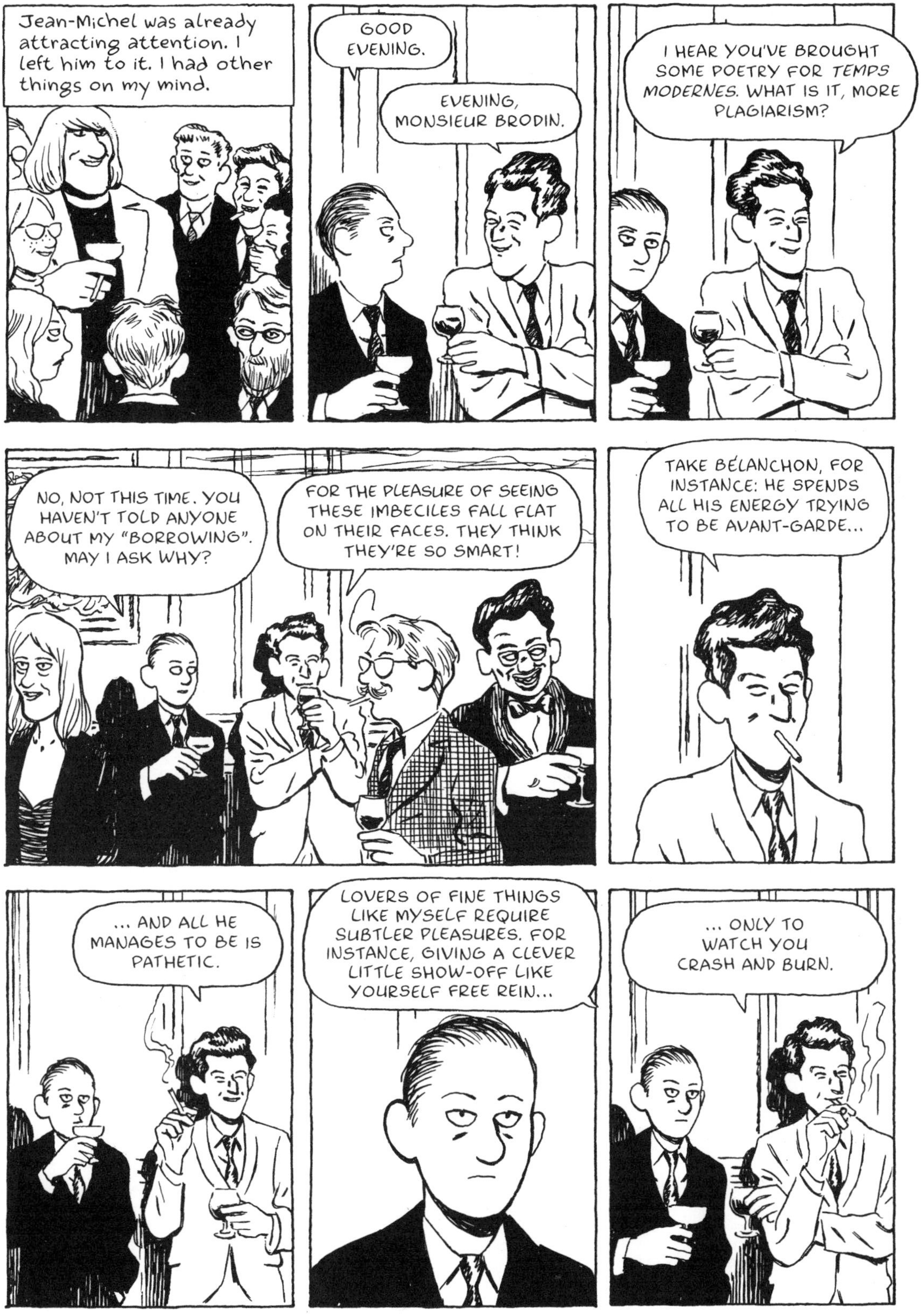
Jean-Michel was already attracting attention. I left him to it. I had other things on my mind.
GOOD EVENING.
EVENING, MONSIEUR BRODIN.
I HEAR YOU'VE BROUGHT SOME POETRY FOR *TEMPS MODERNES*. WHAT IS IT, MORE PLAGIARISM?
NO, NOT THIS TIME. YOU HAVEN'T TOLD ANYONE ABOUT MY "BORROWING". MAY I ASK WHY?
FOR THE PLEASURE OF SEEING THESE IMBECILES FALL FLAT ON THEIR FACES. THEY THINK THEY'RE SO SMART!
TAKE BÉLANCHON, FOR INSTANCE: HE SPENDS ALL HIS ENERGY TRYING TO BE AVANT-GARDE...
... AND ALL HE MANAGES TO BE IS PATHETIC.
LOVERS OF FINE THINGS LIKE MYSELF REQUIRE SUBTLER PLEASURES. FOR INSTANCE, GIVING A CLEVER LITTLE SHOW-OFF LIKE YOURSELF FREE REIN...
... ONLY TO WATCH YOU CRASH AND BURN.

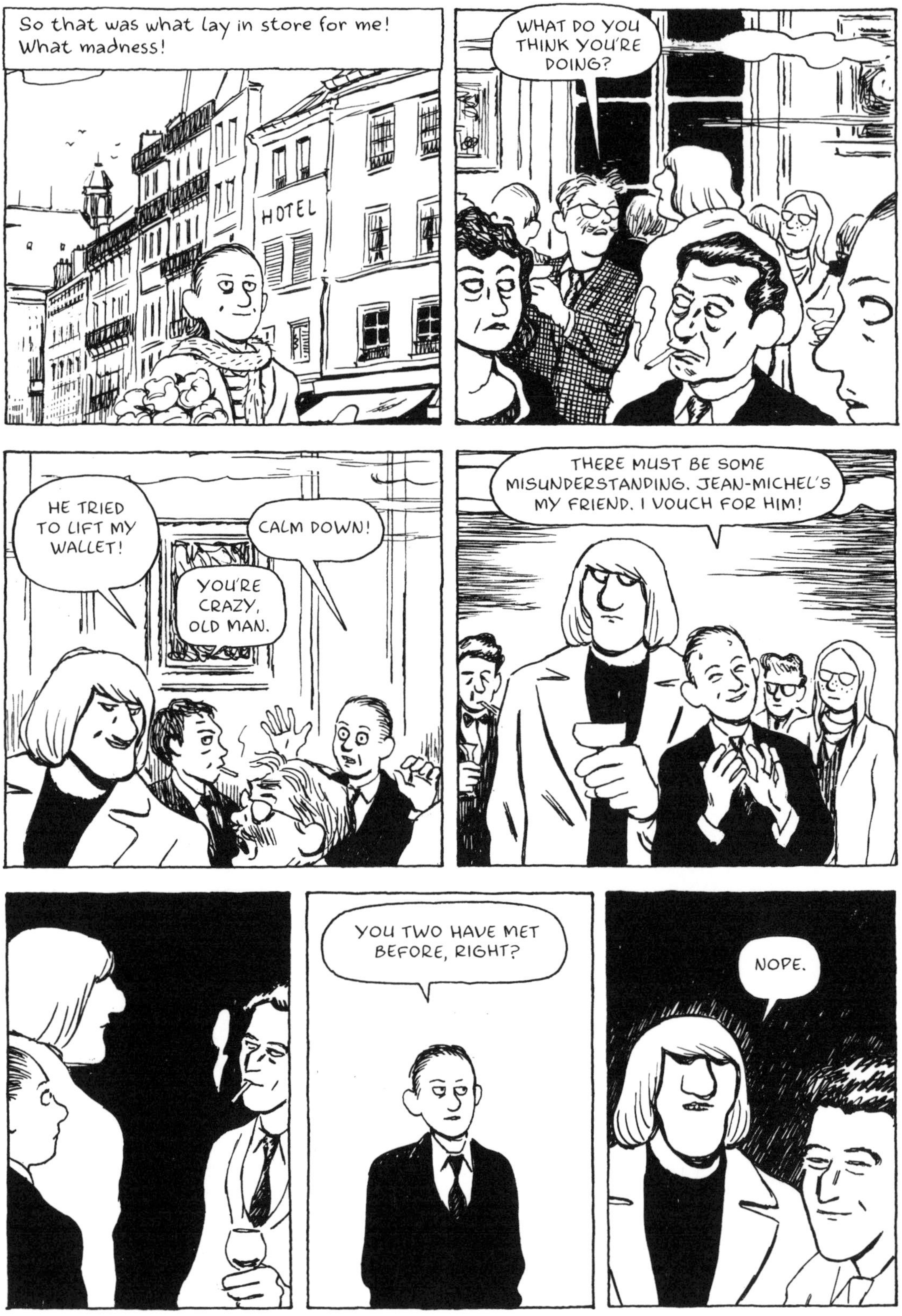
So that was what lay in store for me! What madness!
HOTEL
WHAT DO YOU THINK YOU'RE DOING?
HE TRIED TO LIFT MY WALLET!
CALM DOWN!
YOU'RE CRAZY, OLD MAN.
THERE MUST BE SOME MISUNDERSTANDING. JEAN-MICHEL'S MY FRIEND. I VOUCH FOR HIM!
YOU TWO HAVE MET BEFORE, RIGHT?
NOPE.

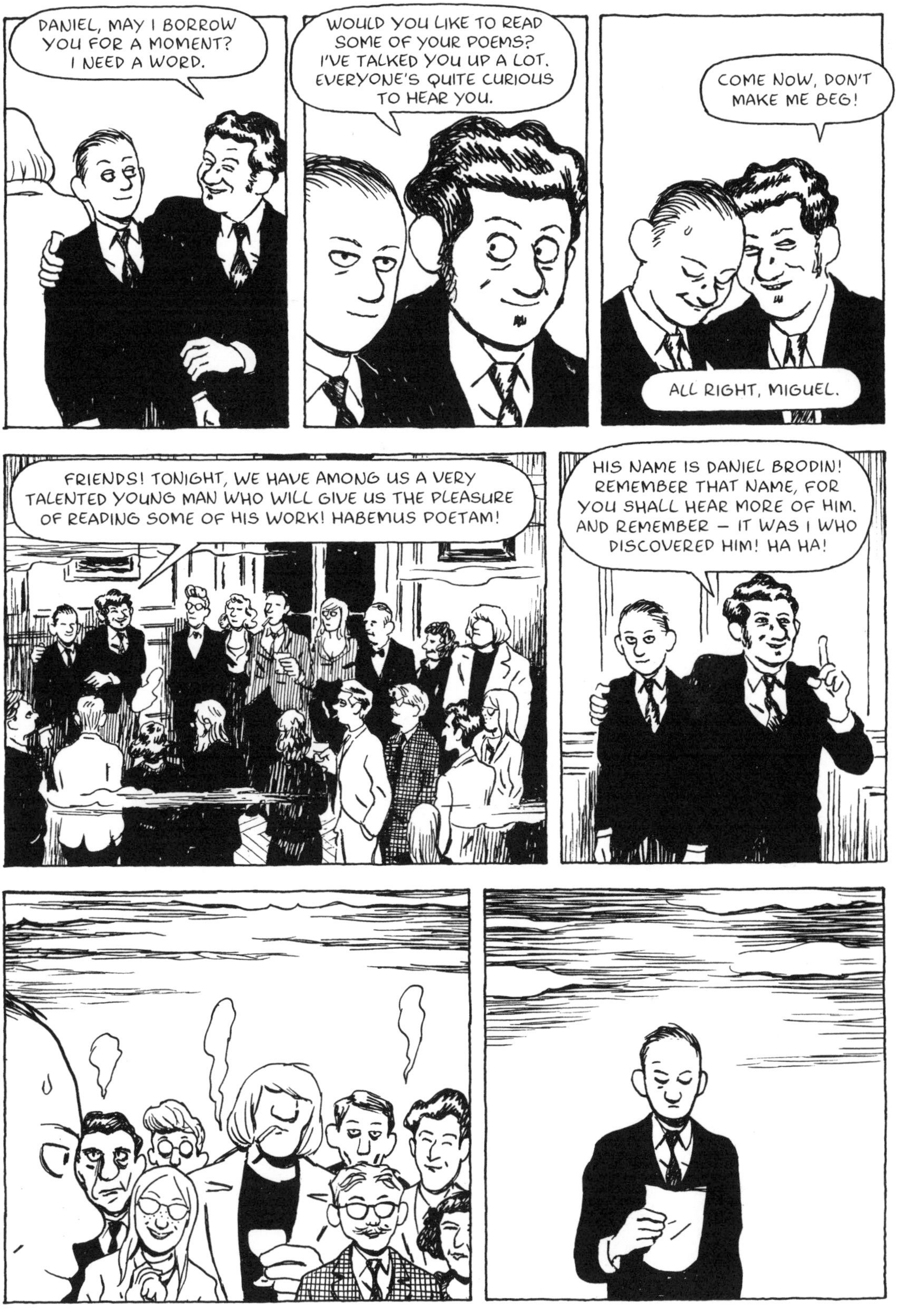
DANIEL, MAY I BORROW YOU FOR A MOMENT? I NEED A WORD.
WOULD YOU LIKE TO READ SOME OF YOUR POEMS? I'VE TALKED YOU UP A LOT. EVERYONE'S QUITE CURIOUS TO HEAR YOU.
COME NOW, DON'T MAKE ME BEG!
ALL RIGHT, MIGUEL.
FRIENDS! TONIGHT, WE HAVE AMONG US A VERY TALENTED YOUNG MAN WHO WILL GIVE US THE PLEASURE OF READING SOME OF HIS WORK! HABEMUS POETAM!
HIS NAME IS DANIEL BRODIN! REMEMBER THAT NAME, FOR YOU SHALL HEAR MORE OF HIM. AND REMEMBER – IT WAS I WHO DISCOVERED HIM! HA HA!

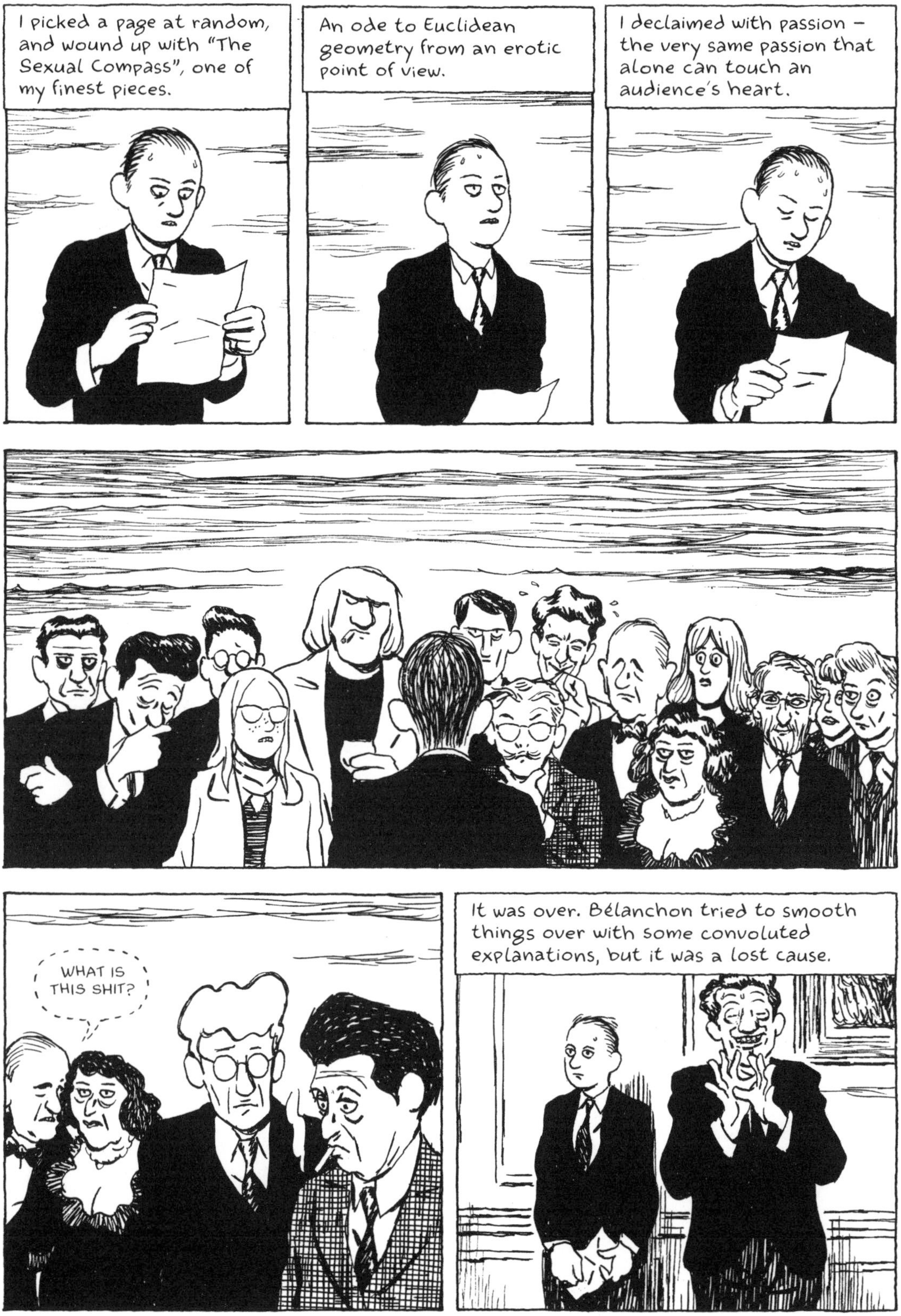
I picked a page at random, and wound up with "The Sexual Compass", one of my finest pieces.
An ode to Euclidean geometry from an erotic point of view.
I declaimed with passion – the very same passion that alone can touch an audience's heart.
WHAT IS THIS SHIT?
It was over. Bélanchon tried to smooth things over with some convoluted explanations, but it was a lost cause.

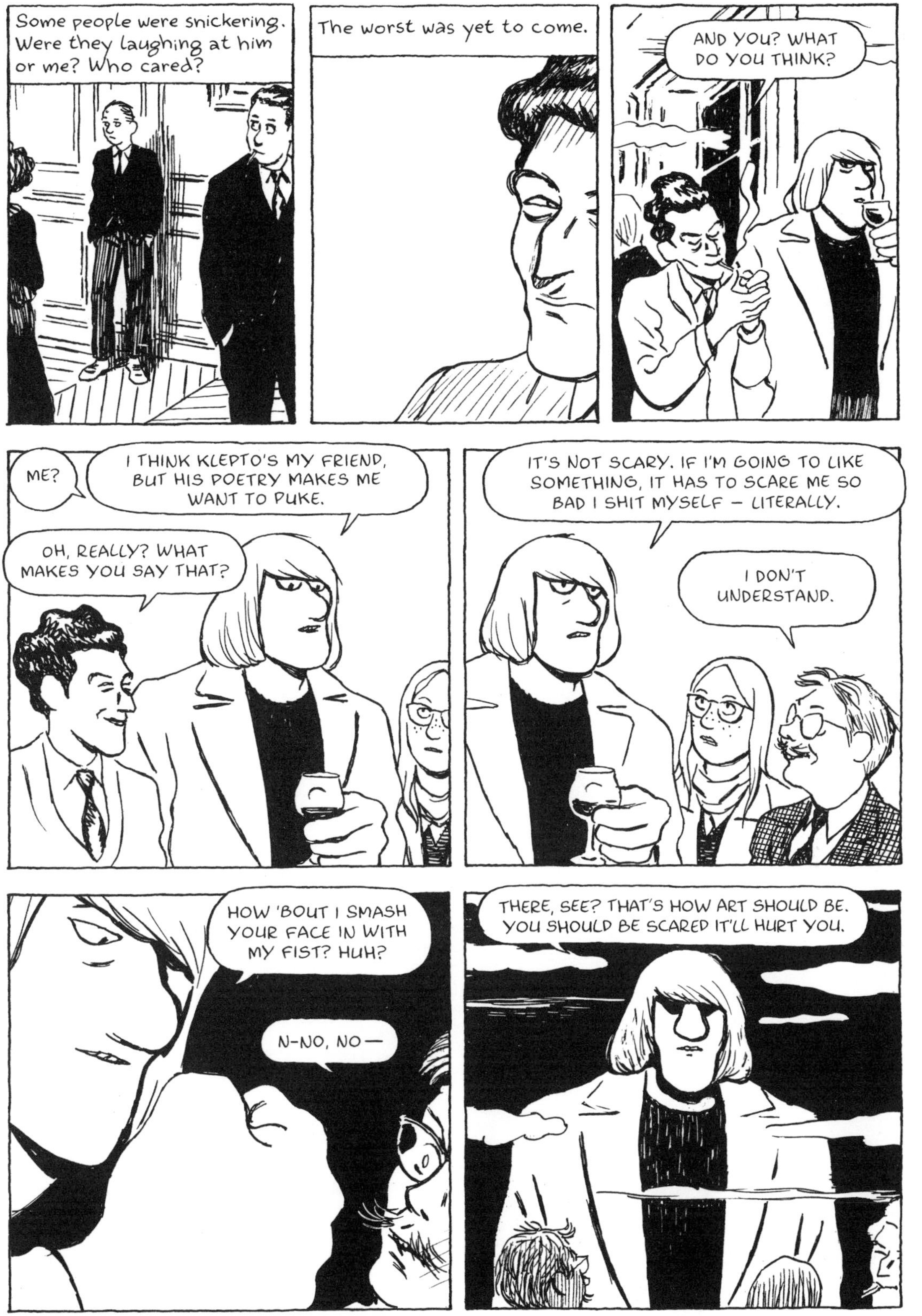
Some people were snickering. Were they laughing at him or me? Who cared?
The worst was yet to come.
AND YOU? WHAT DO YOU THINK?
ME?
I THINK KLEPTO'S MY FRIEND, BUT HIS POETRY MAKES ME WANT TO PUKE.
OH, REALLY? WHAT MAKES YOU SAY THAT?
IT'S NOT SCARY. IF I'M GOING TO LIKE SOMETHING, IT HAS TO SCARE ME SO BAD I SHIT MYSELF – LITERALLY.
I DON'T UNDERSTAND.
HOW 'BOUT I SMASH YOUR FACE IN WITH MY FIST? HUH?
N-NO, NO—
THERE, SEE? THAT'S HOW ART SHOULD BE. YOU SHOULD BE SCARED IT'LL HURT YOU.

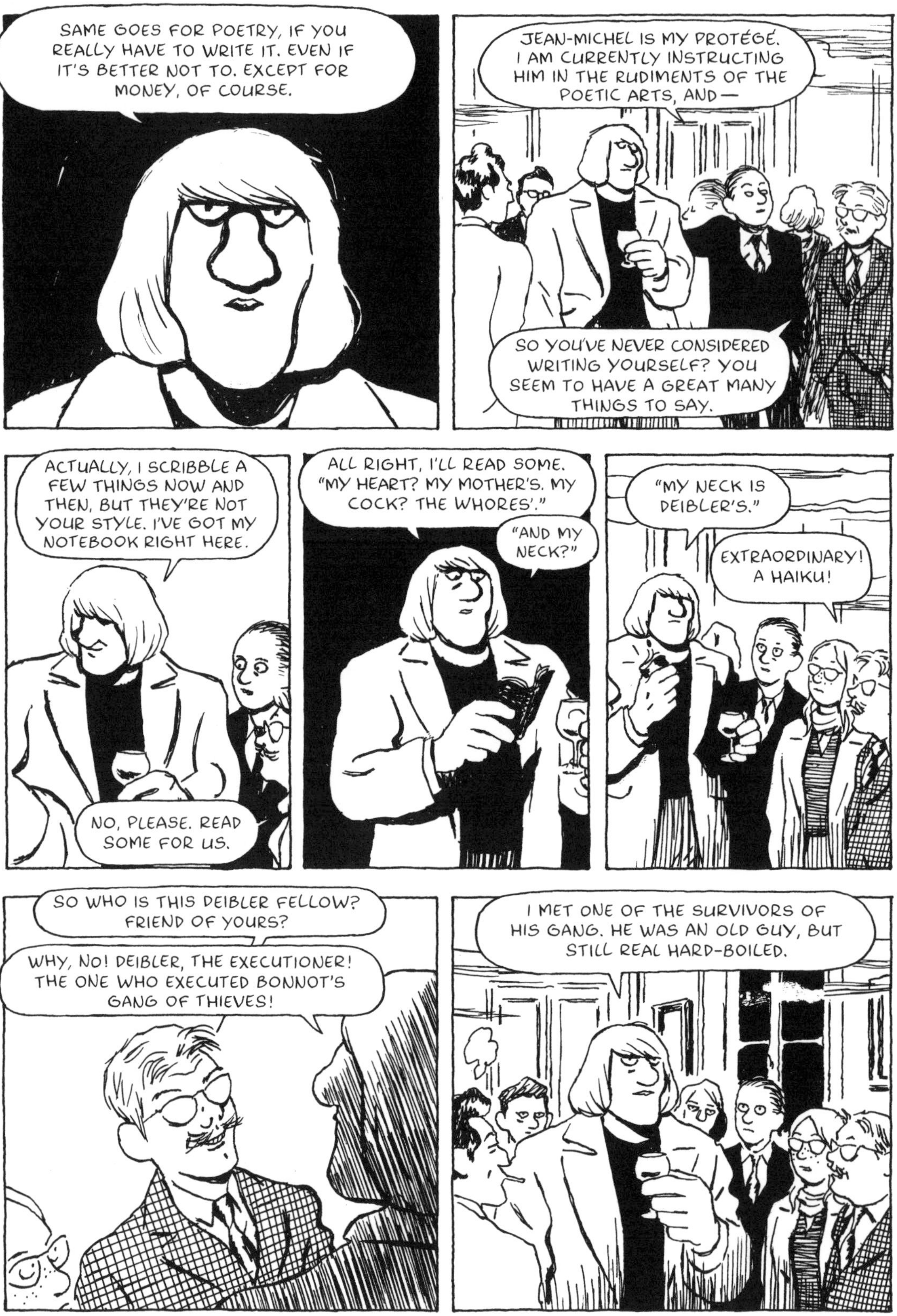
SAME GOES FOR POETRY, IF YOU REALLY HAVE TO WRITE IT. EVEN IF IT'S BETTER NOT TO. EXCEPT FOR MONEY, OF COURSE.
JEAN-MICHEL IS MY PROTÉGÉ. I AM CURRENTLY INSTRUCTING HIM IN THE RUDIMENTS OF THE POETIC ARTS, AND—
SO YOU'VE NEVER CONSIDERED WRITING YOURSELF? YOU SEEM TO HAVE A GREAT MANY THINGS TO SAY.
ACTUALLY, I SCRIBBLE A FEW THINGS NOW AND THEN, BUT THEY'RE NOT YOUR STYLE. I'VE GOT MY NOTEBOOK RIGHT HERE.
NO, PLEASE. READ SOME FOR US.
ALL RIGHT, I'LL READ SOME. "MY HEART? MY MOTHER'S. MY COCK? THE WHORES'."
"AND MY NECK?"
"MY NECK IS DEIBLER'S."
EXTRAORDINARY! A HAIKU!
SO WHO IS THIS DEIBLER FELLOW? FRIEND OF YOURS?
WHY, NO! DEIBLER, THE EXECUTIONER! THE ONE WHO EXECUTED BONNOT'S GANG OF THIEVES!
I MET ONE OF THE SURVIVORS OF HIS GANG. HE WAS AN OLD GUY, BUT STILL REAL HARD-BOILED.

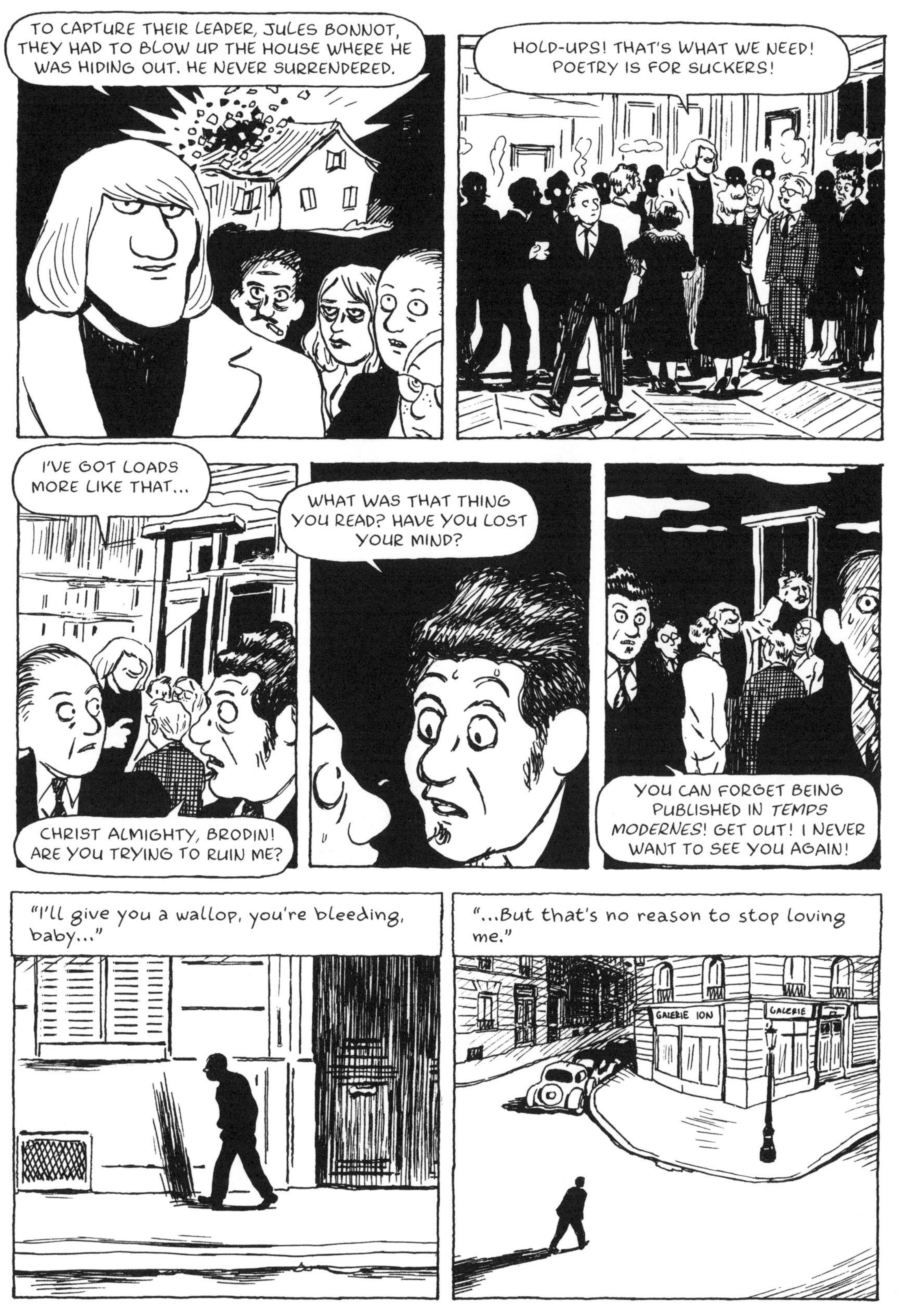
TO CAPTURE THEIR LEADER, JULES BONNOT, THEY HAD TO BLOW UP THE HOUSE WHERE HE WAS HIDING OUT. HE NEVER SURRENDERED.
HOLD-UPS! THAT'S WHAT WE NEED! POETRY IS FOR SUCKERS!
I'VE GOT LOADS MORE LIKE THAT...
CHRIST ALMIGHTY, BRODIN! ARE YOU TRYING TO RUIN ME?
WHAT WAS THAT THING YOU READ? HAVE YOU LOST YOUR MIND?
YOU CAN FORGET BEING PUBLISHED IN *TEMPS MODERNES*! GET OUT! I NEVER WANT TO SEE YOU AGAIN!
"I'll give you a wallop, you're bleeding, baby..."
"...But that's no reason to stop loving me."
GALERIE ION
GALERIE

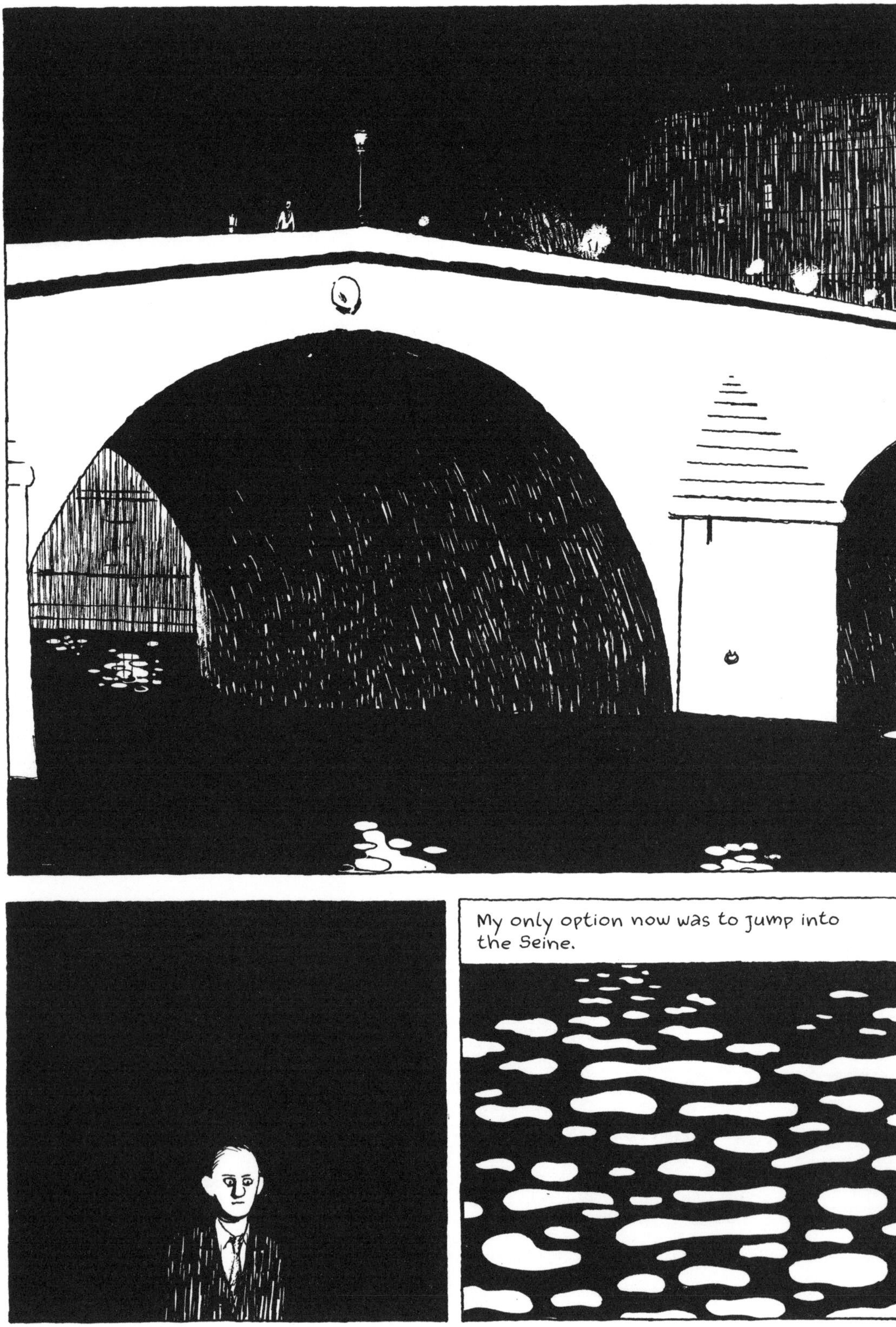
My only option now was to jump into the Seine.

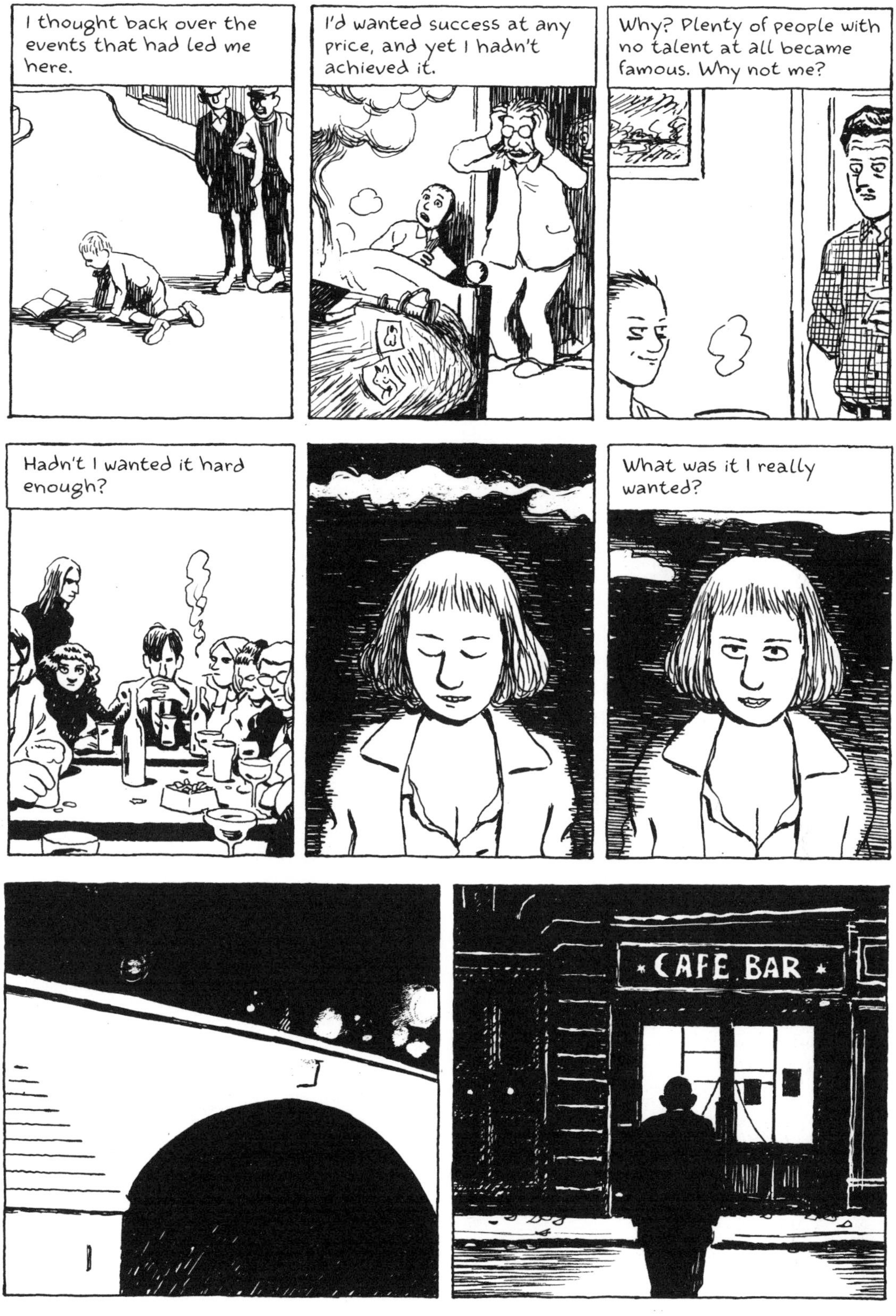
I thought back over the events that had led me here.
I'd wanted success at any price, and yet I hadn't achieved it.
Why? Plenty of people with no talent at all became famous. Why not me?
Hadn't I wanted it hard enough?
What was it I really wanted?
CAFE BAR

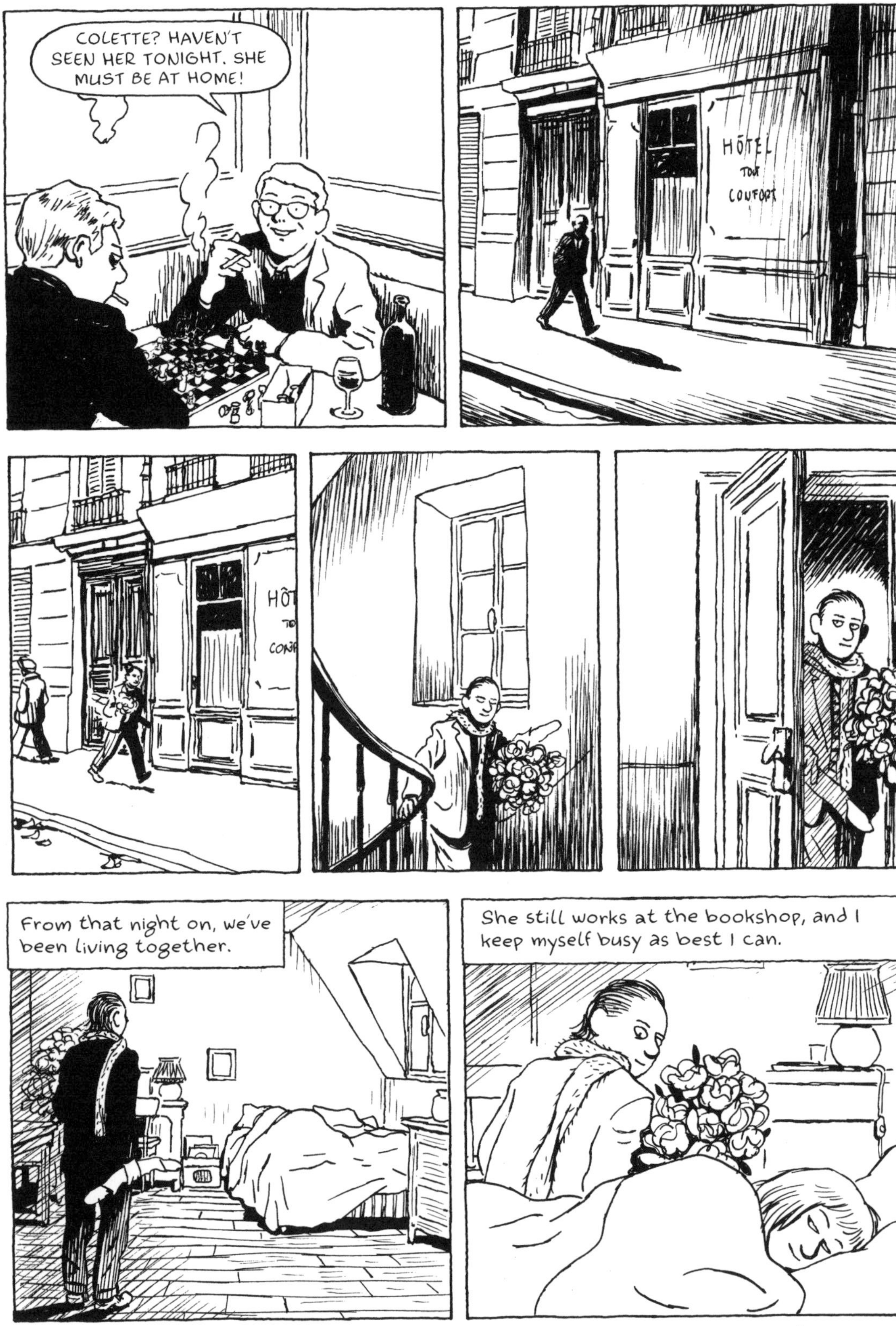
COLETTE? HAVEN'T SEEN HER TONIGHT. SHE MUST BE AT HOME!
HÔTEL TOUT CONFORT
From that night on, we've been living together.
She still works at the bookshop, and I keep myself busy as best I can.

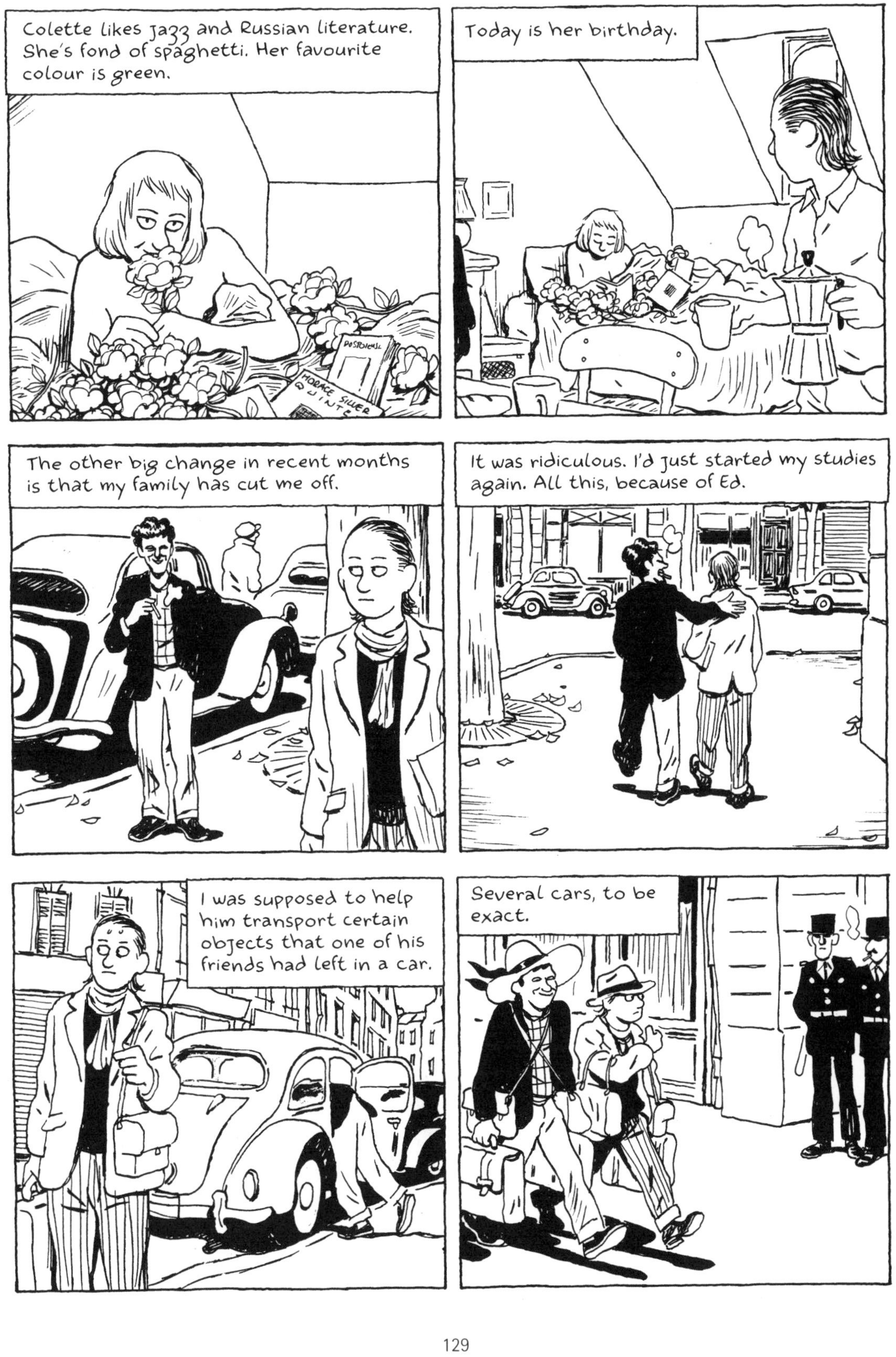
Colette likes Jazz and Russian literature. She's fond of spaghetti. Her favourite colour is green.
Today is her birthday.
The other big change in recent months is that my family has cut me off.
It was ridiculous. I'd just started my studies again. All this, because of Ed.
I was supposed to help him transport certain objects that one of his friends had left in a car.
Several cars, to be exact.

The story wound up in the papers, and the press made a huge deal about it, as usual.

YOUTH GONE WILD

Daniel Brodin and Edmond Hommel, 20, confronted Judge Hoyer at the 12th Correctional Court.

Their clothing (not to mention their comportment) was curious indeed: apple-green velour corduroy trousers and unbelievably thick-soled shoes. And to top it all off, mops of hirsute and perhaps infested hair. Apparently this is the uniform of a certain St.-Germain-des-Près set, essential for "shocking" the bourgeoisie. Every era has had young people who were revolutionary in their mores and ideas: the Incroyables, during the Directoire; the Romantics, during Louis-Philippe; the Fauves and Cubists before 1914; the Surrealists in 1929; the Zazous in 1913; the Existentialists, thanks to Monsieur J.-P. Sartre. But these young people, though they made a great deal of noise and few masterpieces, were not thieves. Brodin and Hommel have perfected the system: not content simply to shock the bourgeoisie, they plunder them. An inspector spotted them "busying"

themselves at cars parked along Boulevard St.-Germain and in the neighbouring streets. At first, their hands were empty; then they were seen emerging with purses, cameras . . . Their hands were free no more, and soon, neither were they, as the inspector brought them all—burglars and burgled goods—back to the precinct.

It is said—almost as a joke—that Judge Royer does not trifle with his clientele. Let's be fair: he knows how to mete out punishments befitting the circumstances. To these two, who had no prior convictions, and who will be able to work once they have understood that the inanity and insanity of their behaviour "shocks" no one, but instead makes everyone suffer, Judge Royer has imposed only a suspended prison sentence of six months and a fine of 12,000 francs.

Outside the courtroom, these two "heroes" were joined by their acolytes: a dozen or so deliberately filthy young men, frantically scratching at their wild hair to "shock" the photographer and the reporter of this minor disturbance.

NEITHER BY PEN NOR SWORD, BUT RATHER, SCALES

Trissotin and Vadius settled their differences themselves, at most demanding Boileau's arbitration. Later—and more cruelly—Voltaire and Jean Fréron argued with epigrams. Those centuries, however litigious (and Racine's The Litigant̲ ̲ ̲ it), were a golden age when one d̲ ̲ ̲ ̲ courts for help with a̲ ̲ ̲ ̲ In our day̲ ̲ ̲ ̲ ̲kinned st̲

HOMMEL

Colette stood bail and everyone was waiting for me outside the hearing.

The old man immediately cut me off. Stopped talking to me. He sent my uncle to tell me.

I DIDN'T KNOW GRANDFATHER READ *DETECTIVE.*

THE WOMAN NEXT DOOR HAS A SUBSCRIPTION.

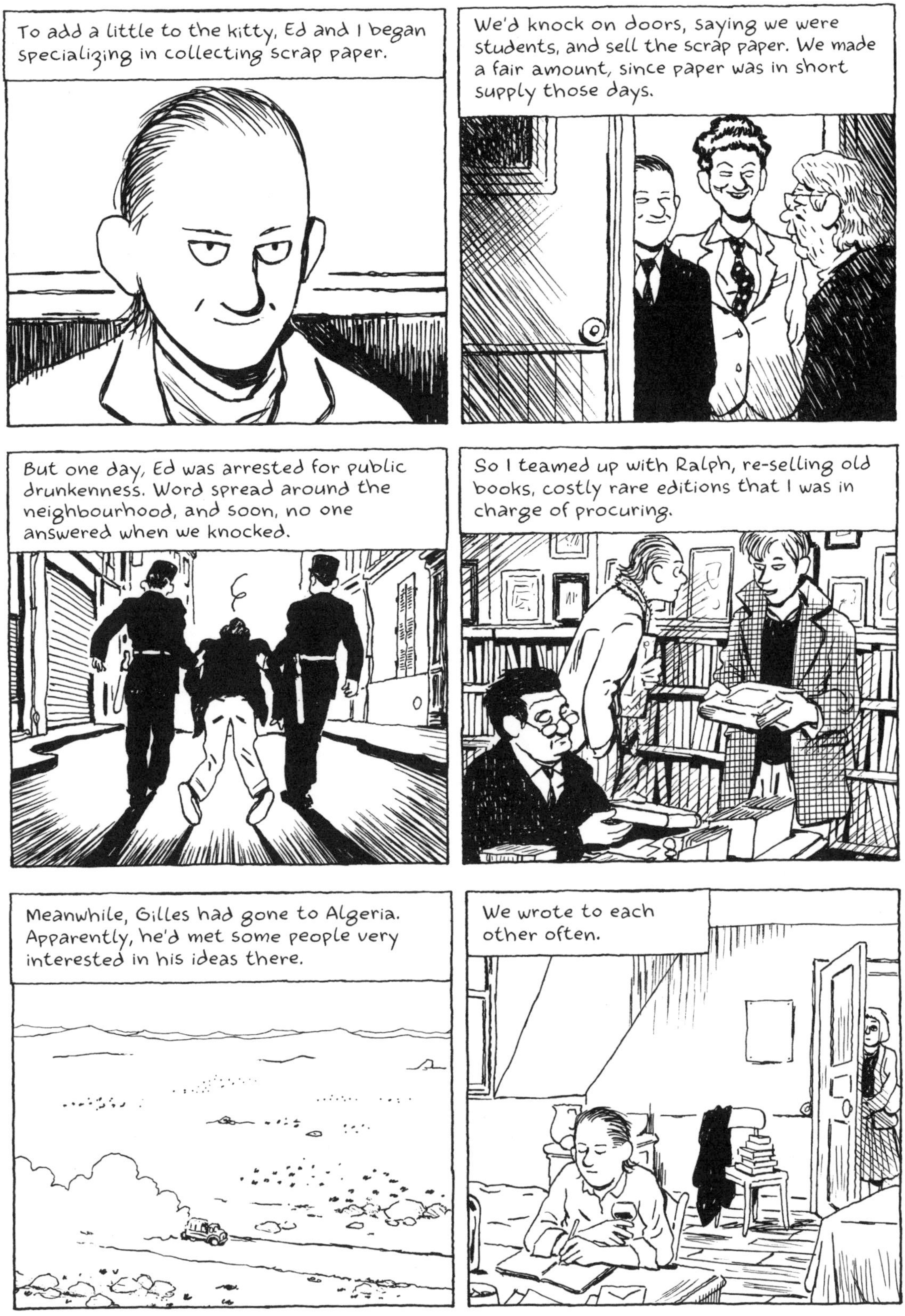
To add a little to the kitty, Ed and I began specializing in collecting scrap paper.
We'd knock on doors, saying we were students, and sell the scrap paper. We made a fair amount, since paper was in short supply those days.
But one day, Ed was arrested for public drunkenness. Word spread around the neighbourhood, and soon, no one answered when we knocked.
So I teamed up with Ralph, re-selling old books, costly rare editions that I was in charge of procuring.
Meanwhile, Gilles had gone to Algeria. Apparently, he'd met some people very interested in his ideas there.
We wrote to each other often.

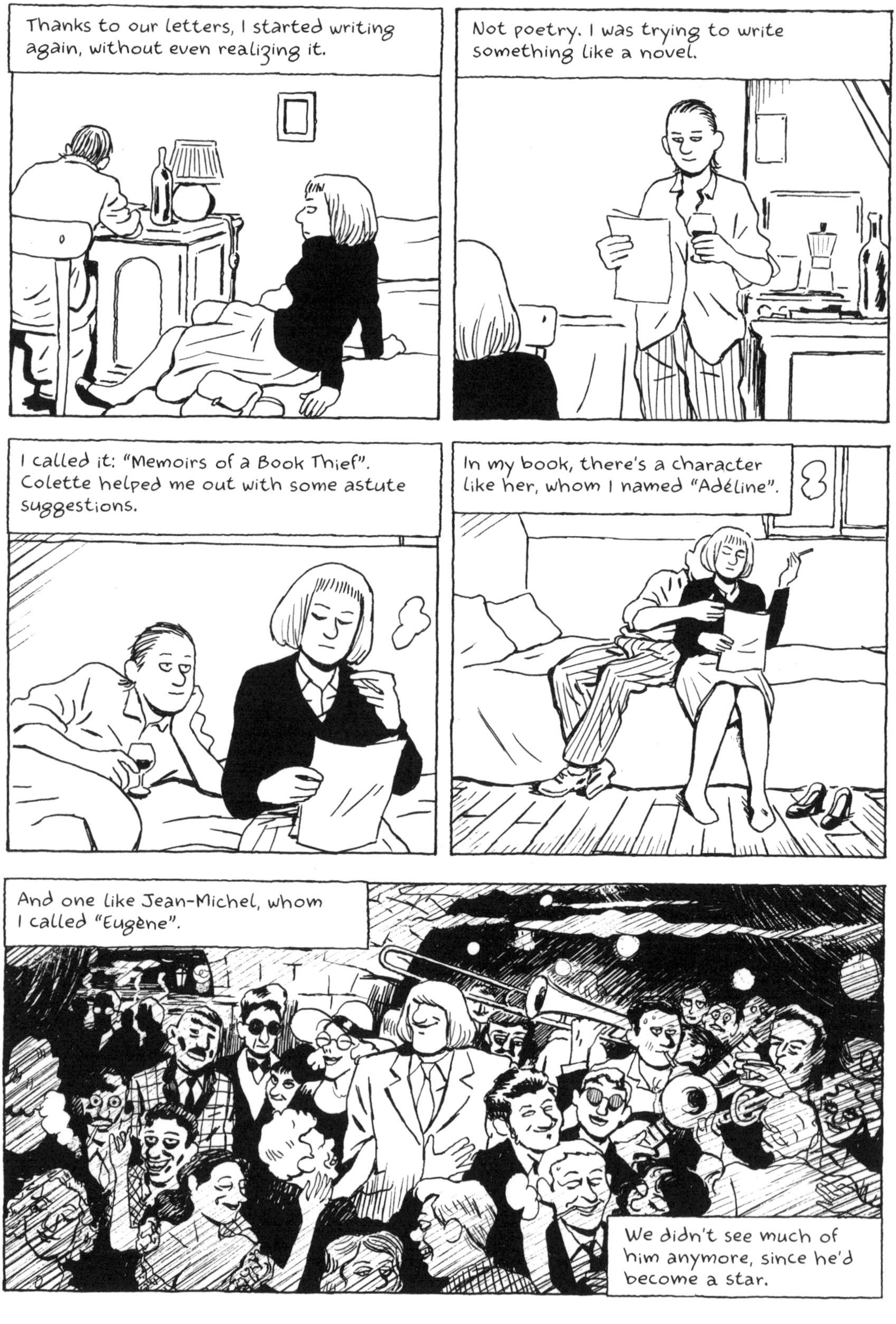
Thanks to our letters, I started writing again, without even realizing it.
Not poetry. I was trying to write something like a novel.
I called it: "Memoirs of a Book Thief". Colette helped me out with some astute suggestions.
In my book, there's a character like her, whom I named "Adéline".
And one like Jean-Michel, whom I called "Eugène".
We didn't see much of him anymore, since he'd become a star.

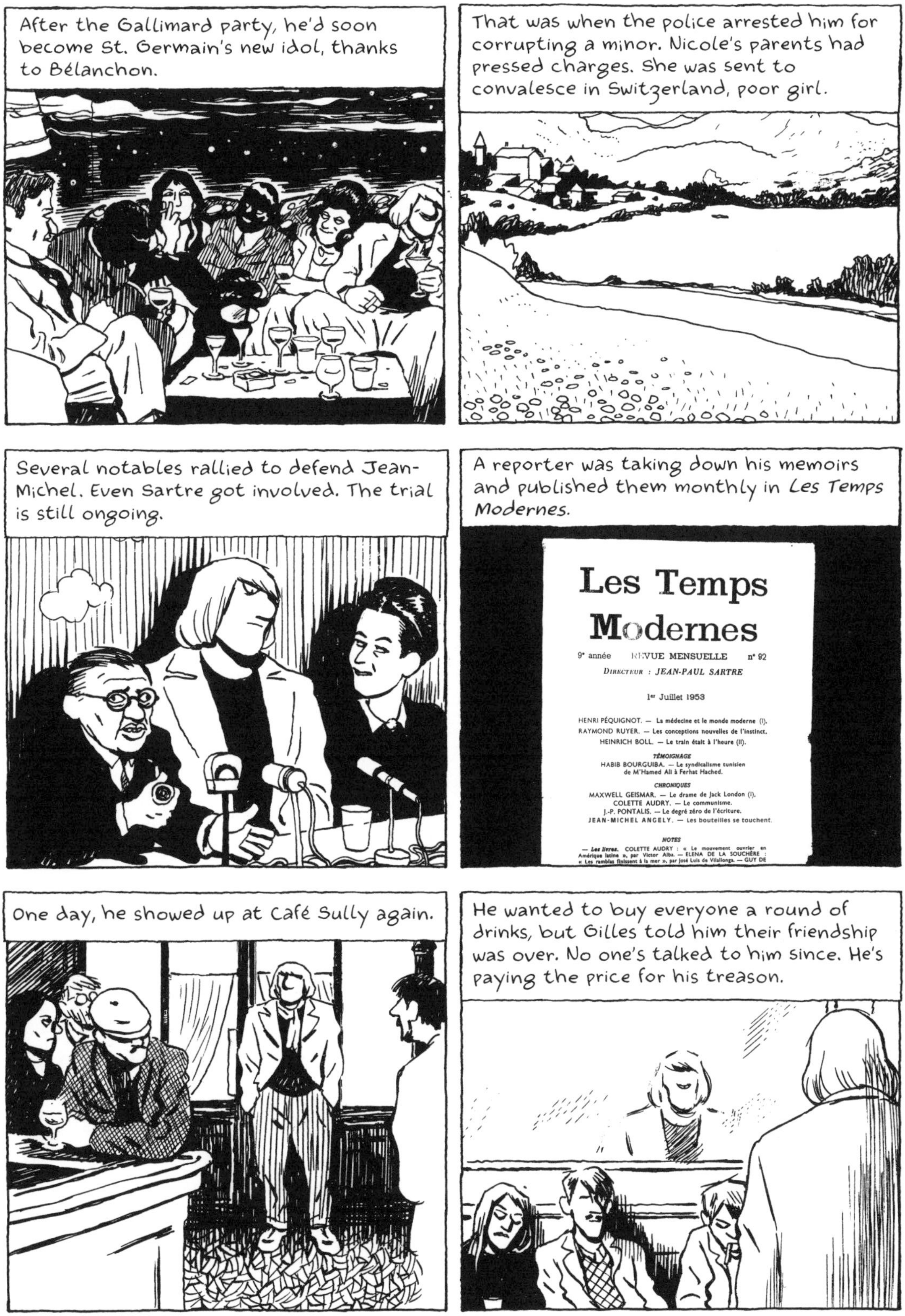
After the Gallimard party, he'd soon become St. Germain's new idol, thanks to Bélanchon.
That was when the police arrested him for corrupting a minor. Nicole's parents had pressed charges. She was sent to convalesce in Switzerland, poor girl.
Several notables rallied to defend Jean-Michel. Even Sartre got involved. The trial is still ongoing.
A reporter was taking down his memoirs and published them monthly in *Les Temps Modernes*.
Les Temps Modernes
9e année REVUE MENSUELLE n° 92
DIRECTEUR : JEAN-PAUL SARTRE
1er Juillet 1953
HENRI PÉQUIGNOT. — La médecine et le monde moderne (I).
RAYMOND RUYER. — Les conceptions nouvelles de l'instinct.
HEINRICH BOLL. — Le train était à l'heure (II).
TÉMOIGNAGE
HABIB BOURGUIBA. — Le syndicalisme tunisien de M'Hamed Ali à Ferhat Hached.
CHRONIQUES
MAXWELL GEISMAR. — Le drame de Jack London (I).
COLETTE AUDRY. — Le communisme.
J.-P. PONTALIS. — Le degré zéro de l'écriture.
JEAN-MICHEL ANGELY. — Les bouteilles se touchent.
NOTES
— Les livres. COLETTE AUDRY : « Le mouvement ouvrier en Amérique latine », par Victor Alba. — ELENA DE LA SOUCHÈRE : « Les ramblas finissent à la mer », par José Luis de Vilallonga. — GUY DE
One day, he showed up at Café Sully again.
He wanted to buy everyone a round of drinks, but Gilles told him their friendship was over. No one's talked to him since. He's paying the price for his treason.

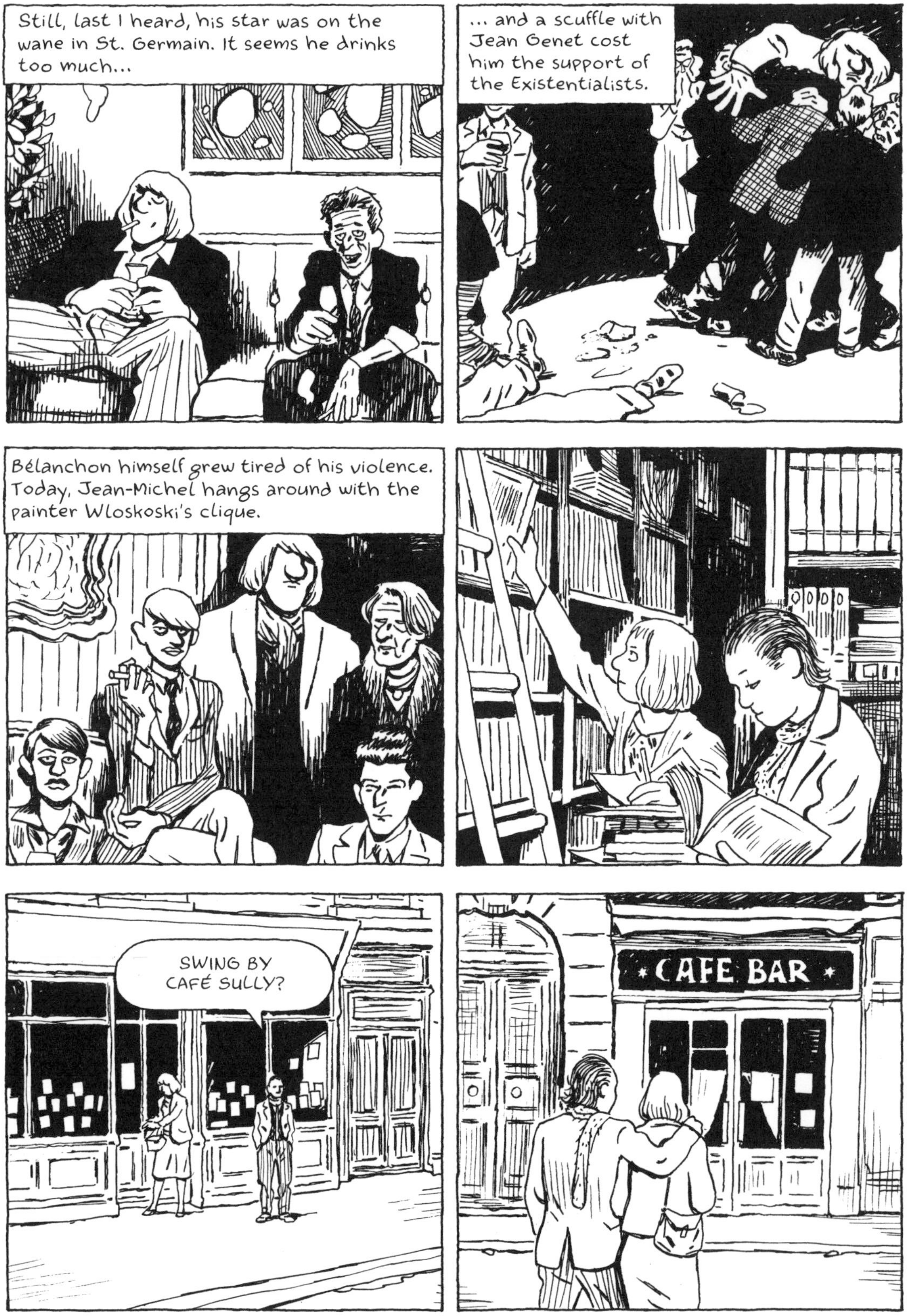
Still, last I heard, his star was on the wane in St. Germain. It seems he drinks too much...
... and a scuffle with Jean Genet cost him the support of the Existentialists.
Bélanchon himself grew tired of his violence. Today, Jean-Michel hangs around with the painter Wloskoski's clique.
SWING BY CAFÉ SULLY?
CAFE BAR

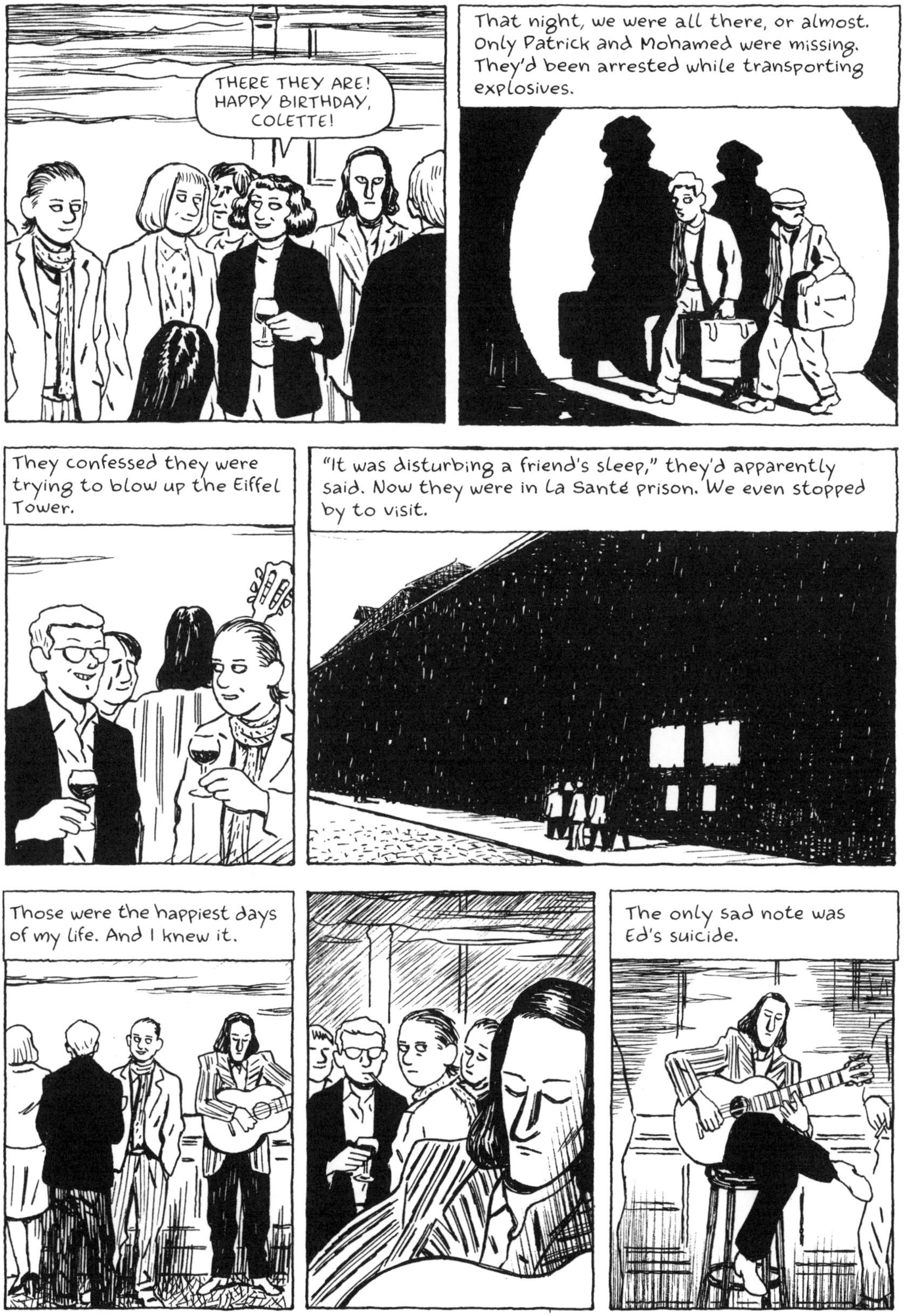
THERE THEY ARE! HAPPY BIRTHDAY, COLETTE!
That night, we were all there, or almost. Only Patrick and Mohamed were missing. They'd been arrested while transporting explosives.
They confessed they were trying to blow up the Eiffel Tower.
"It was disturbing a friend's sleep," they'd apparently said. Now they were in La Santé prison. We even stopped by to visit.
Those were the happiest days of my life. And I knew it.
The only sad note was Ed's suicide.

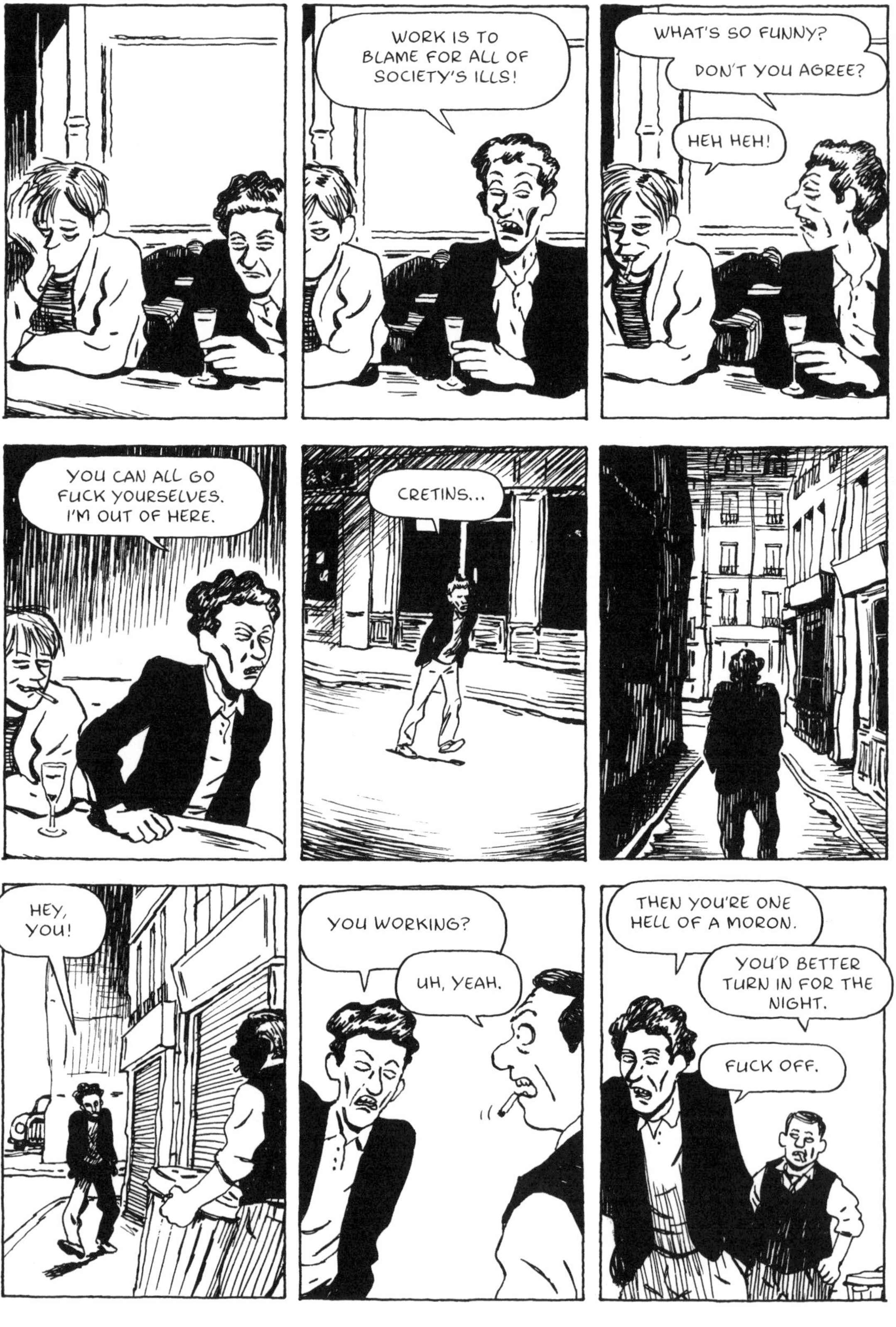
WORK IS TO BLAME FOR ALL OF SOCIETY'S ILLS!
WHAT'S SO FUNNY?
DON'T YOU AGREE?
HEH HEH!
YOU CAN ALL GO FUCK YOURSELVES. I'M OUT OF HERE.
CRETINS...
HEY, YOU!
YOU WORKING?
UH, YEAH.
THEN YOU'RE ONE HELL OF A MORON.
YOU'D BETTER TURN IN FOR THE NIGHT.
FUCK OFF.

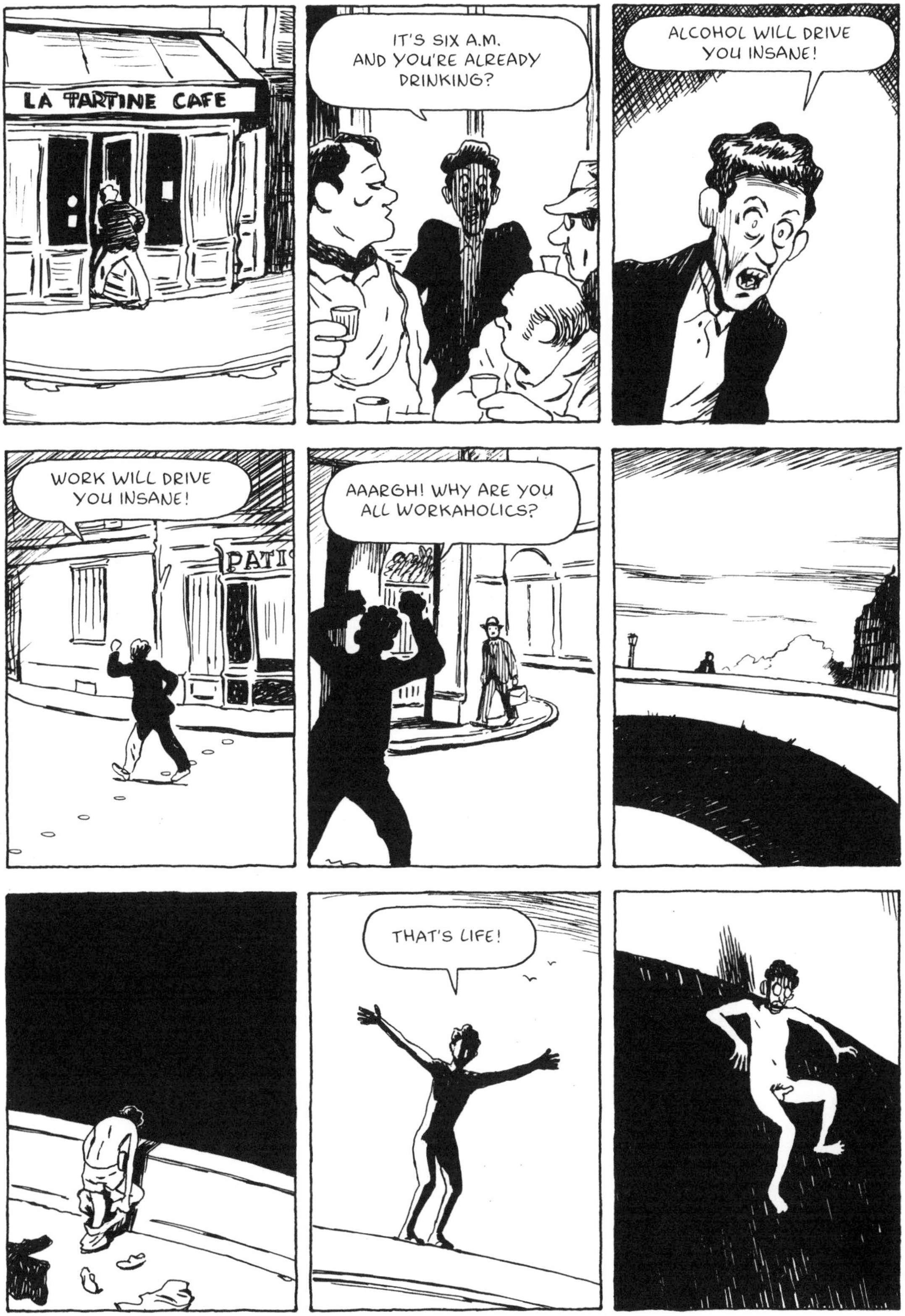
LA TARTINE CAFE
IT'S SIX A.M. AND YOU'RE ALREADY DRINKING?
ALCOHOL WILL DRIVE YOU INSANE!
WORK WILL DRIVE YOU INSANE!
PATI
AAARGH! WHY ARE YOU ALL WORKAHOLICS?
THAT'S LIFE!

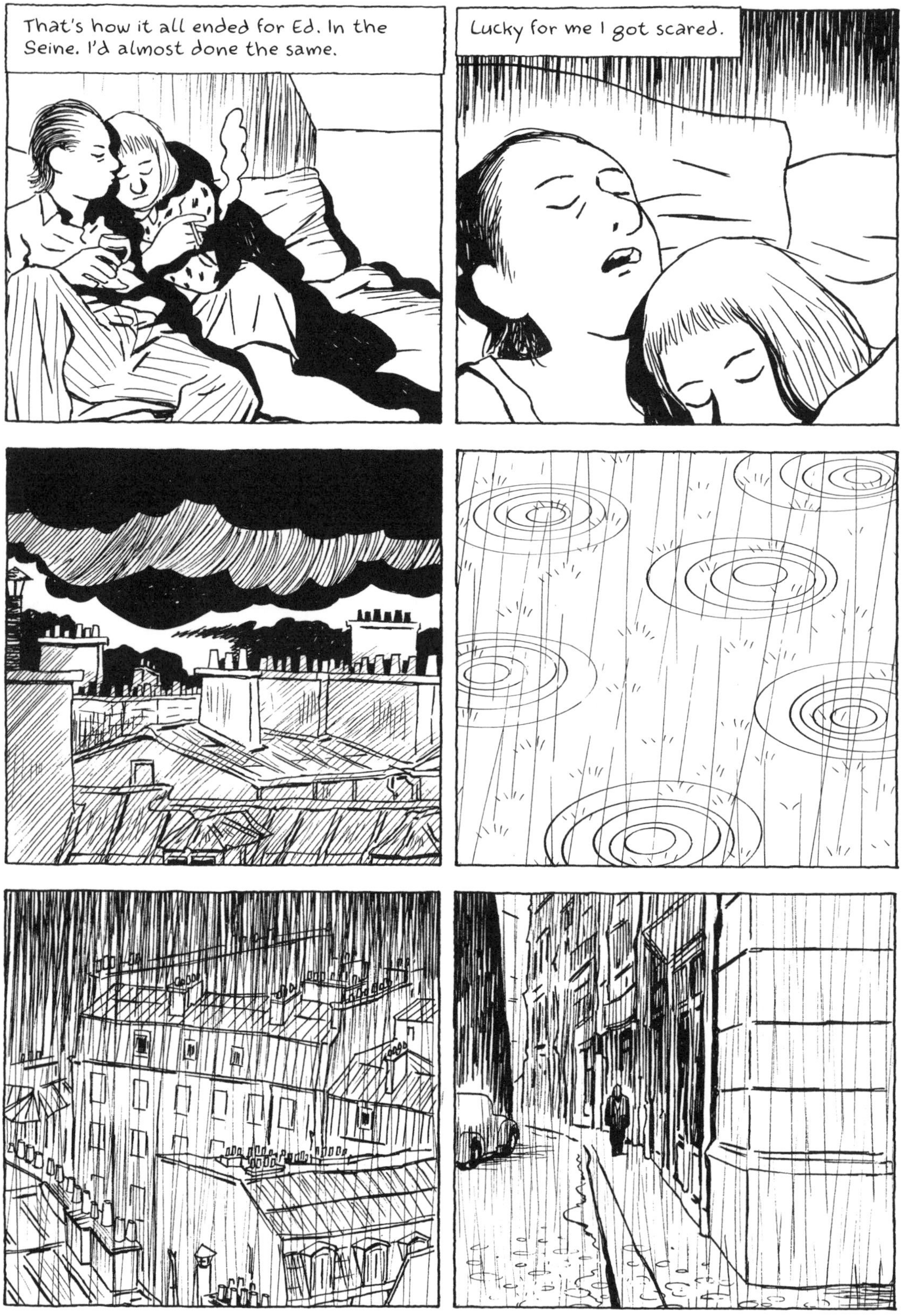
That's how it all ended for Ed. In the Seine. I'd almost done the same.
Lucky for me I got scared.

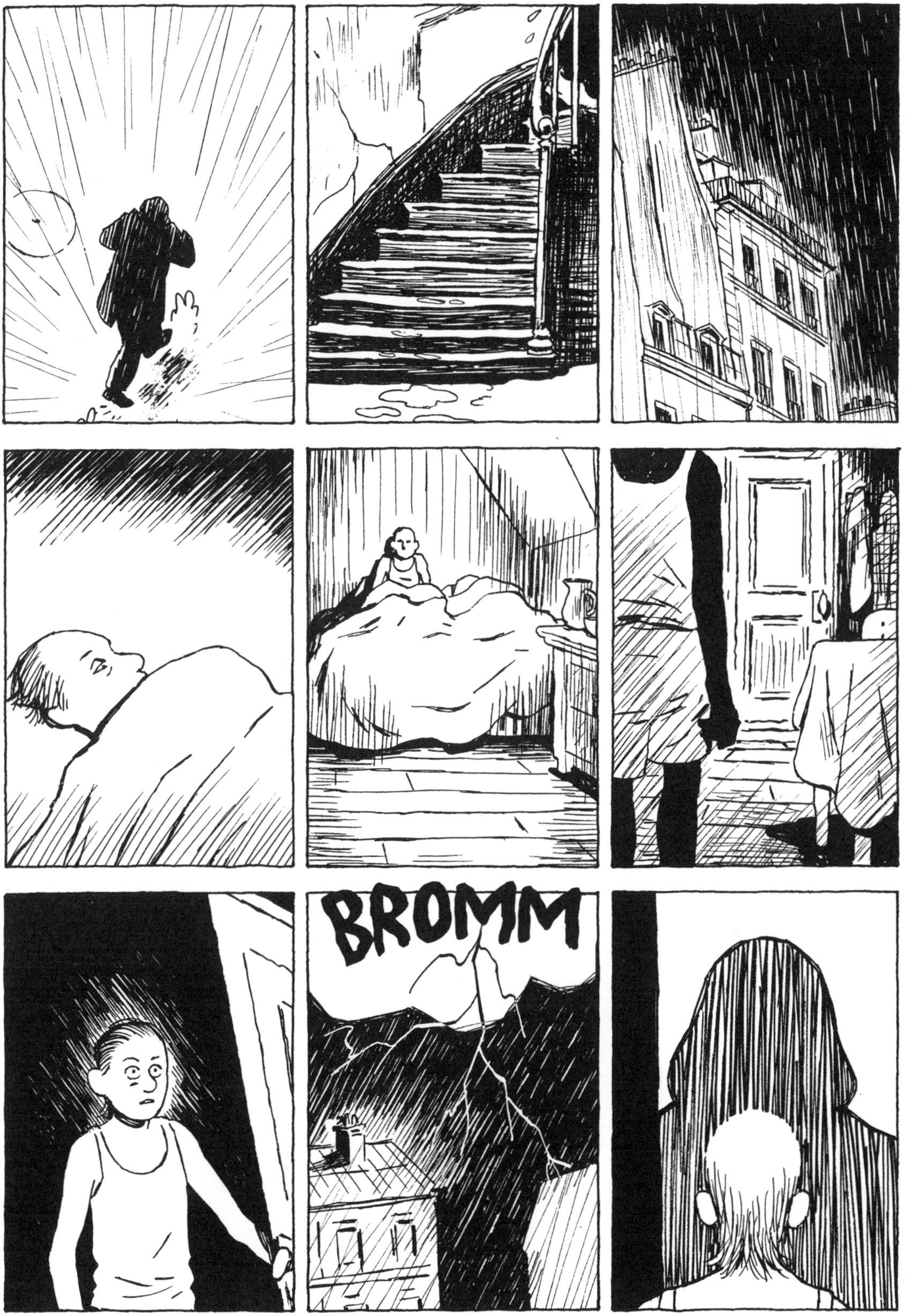
BROMM

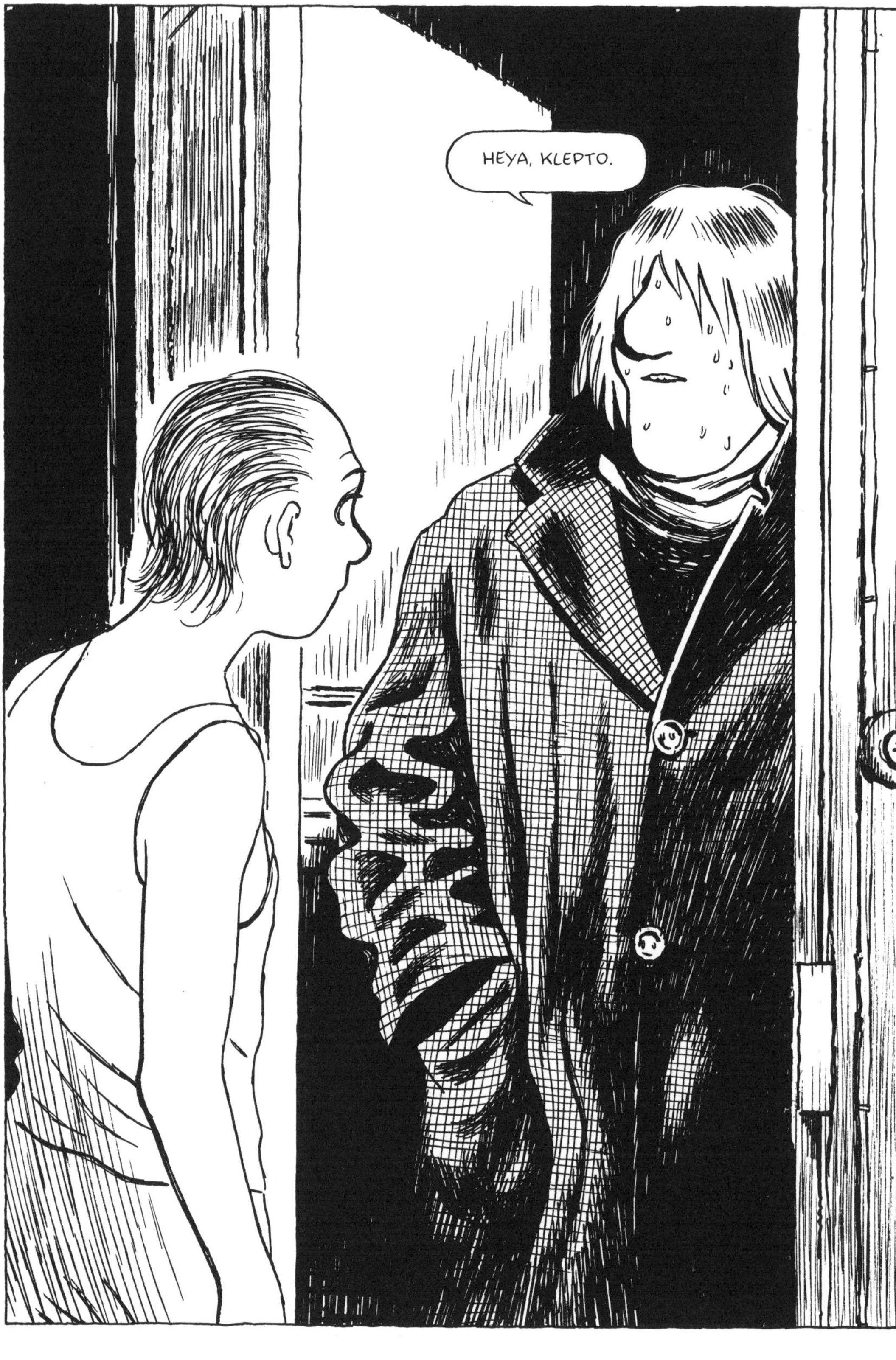
HEYA, KLEPTO.

CHAPTER 6

"YOU'VE EXCELLED YOURSELF, BRODIN!"
François B.

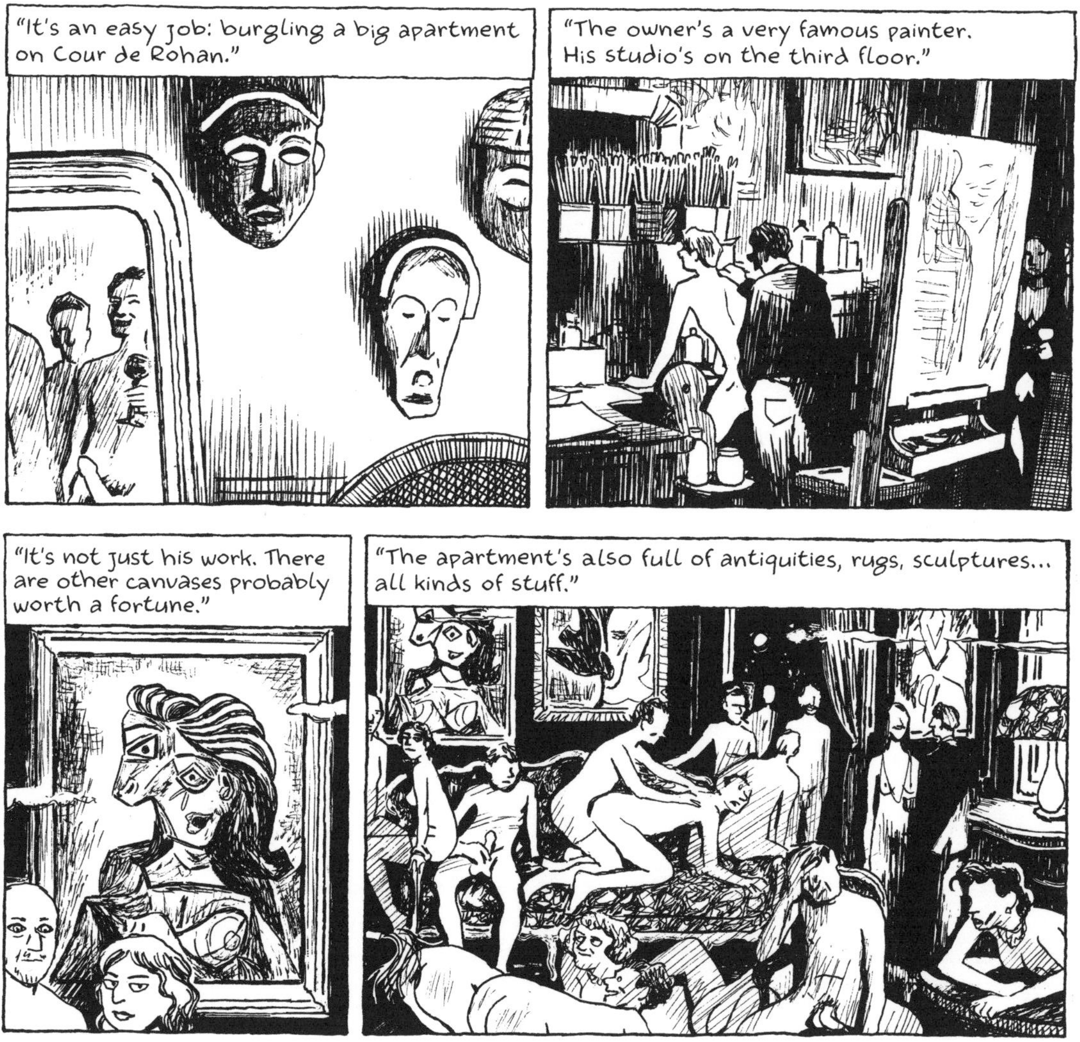
"It's an easy job: burgling a big apartment on Cour de Rohan."
"The owner's a very famous painter. His studio's on the third floor."
"It's not just his work. There are other canvases probably worth a fortune."
"The apartment's also full of antiquities, rugs, sculptures... all kinds of stuff."

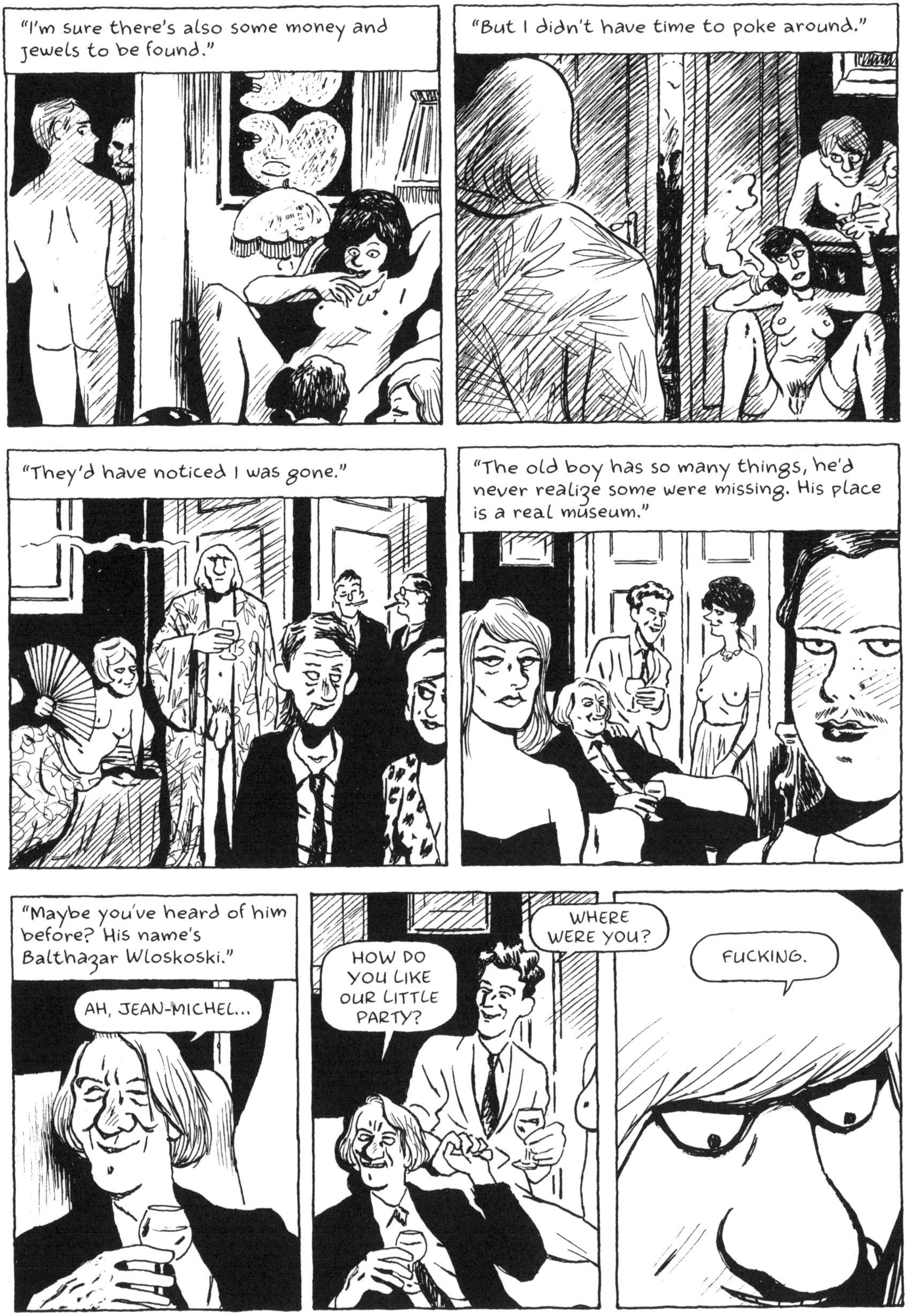
"I'm sure there's also some money and jewels to be found."
"But I didn't have time to poke around."
"They'd have noticed I was gone."
"The old boy has so many things, he'd never realize some were missing. His place is a real museum."
"Maybe you've heard of him before? His name's Balthazar Wloskoski."
AH, JEAN-MICHEL...
WHERE WERE YOU?
HOW DO YOU LIKE OUR LITTLE PARTY?
FUCKING.

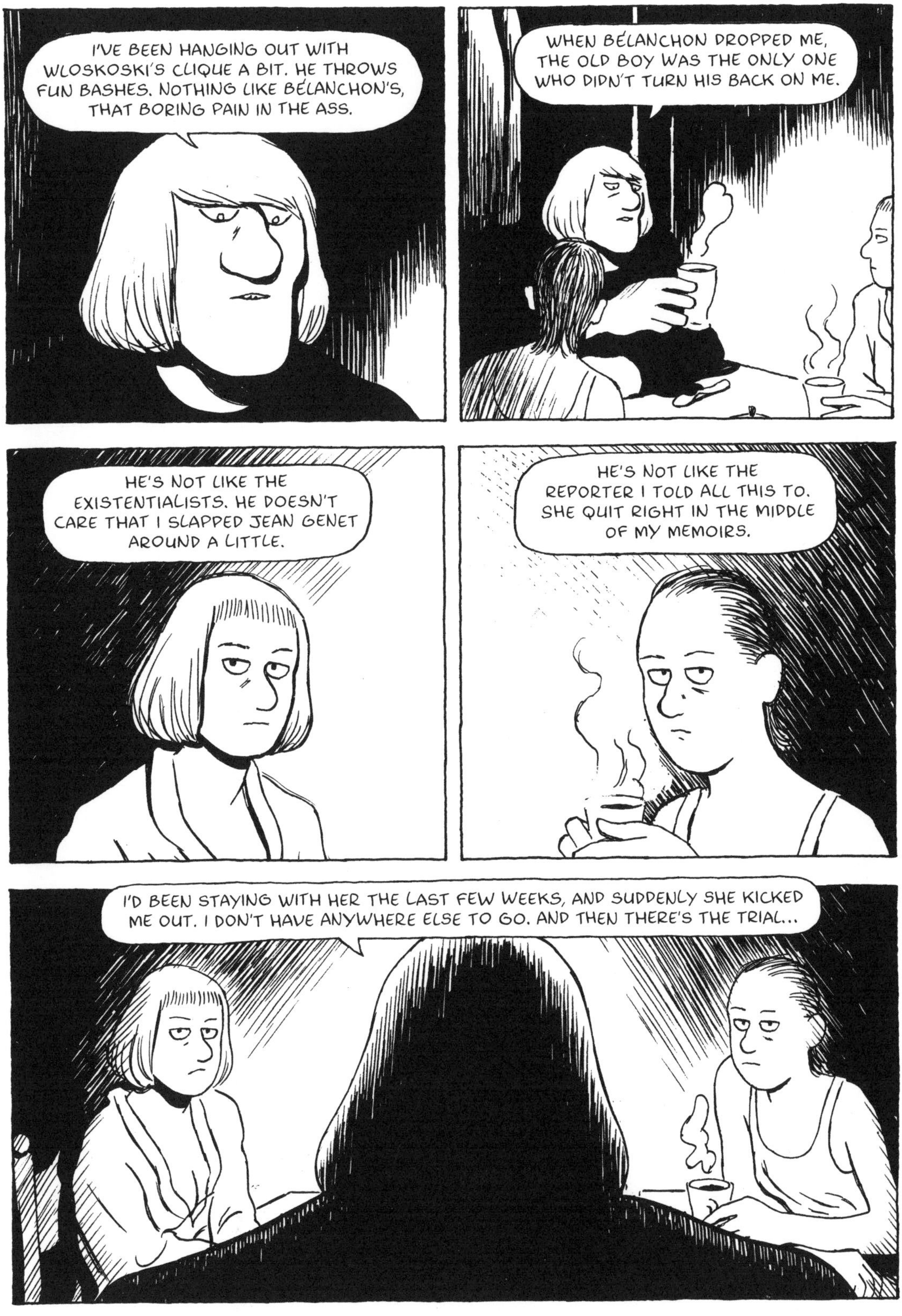
I'VE BEEN HANGING OUT WITH WLOSKOSKI'S CLIQUE A BIT. HE THROWS FUN BASHES. NOTHING LIKE BÉLANCHON'S, THAT BORING PAIN IN THE ASS.
WHEN BÉLANCHON DROPPED ME, THE OLD BOY WAS THE ONLY ONE WHO DIDN'T TURN HIS BACK ON ME.
HE'S NOT LIKE THE EXISTENTIALISTS. HE DOESN'T CARE THAT I SLAPPED JEAN GENET AROUND A LITTLE.
HE'S NOT LIKE THE REPORTER I TOLD ALL THIS TO. SHE QUIT RIGHT IN THE MIDDLE OF MY MEMOIRS.
I'D BEEN STAYING WITH HER THE LAST FEW WEEKS, AND SUDDENLY SHE KICKED ME OUT. I DON'T HAVE ANYWHERE ELSE TO GO. AND THEN THERE'S THE TRIAL...

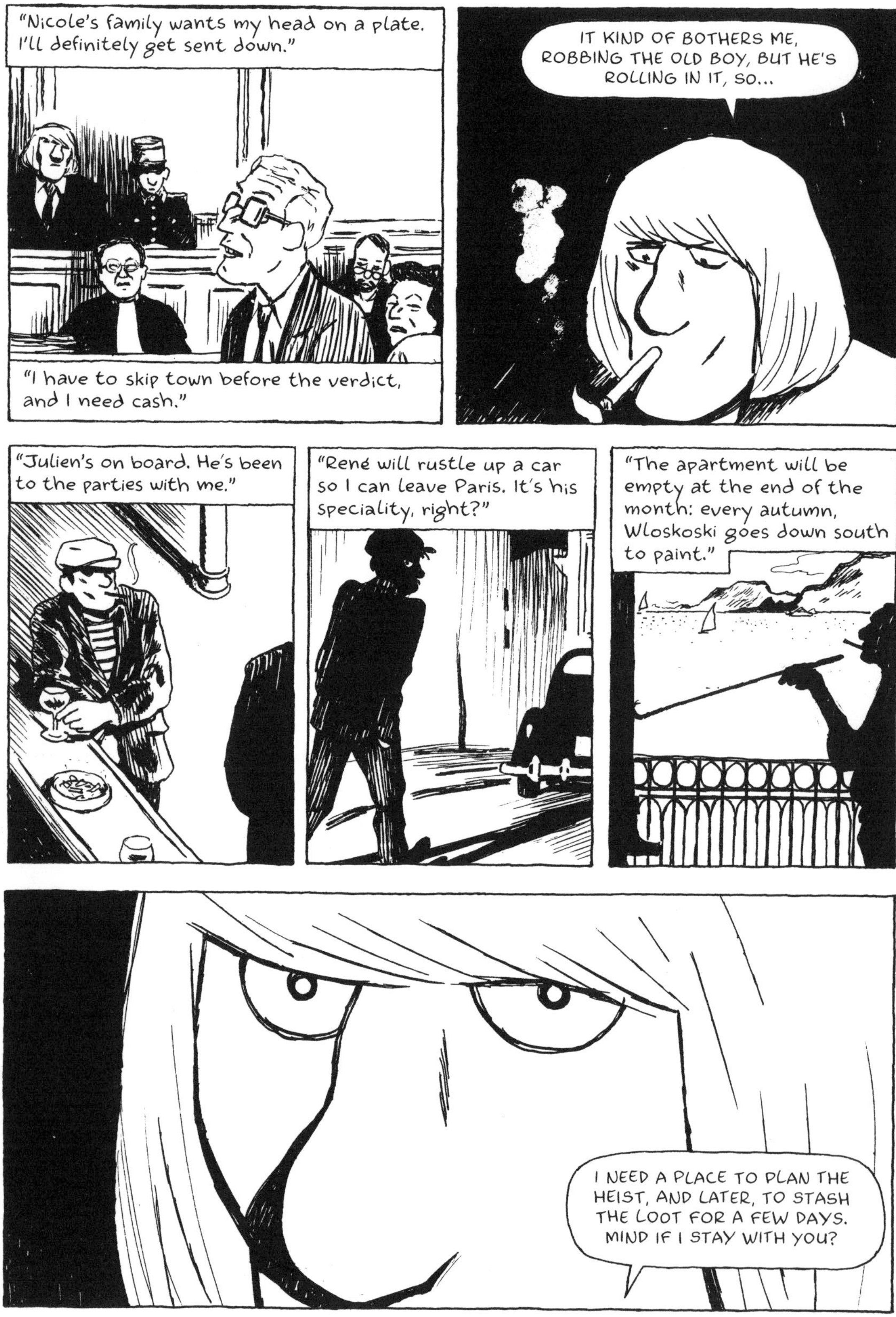
"Nicole's family wants my head on a plate. I'll definitely get sent down."
"I have to skip town before the verdict, and I need cash."
IT KIND OF BOTHERS ME, ROBBING THE OLD BOY, BUT HE'S ROLLING IN IT, SO...
"Julien's on board. He's been to the parties with me."
"René will rustle up a car so I can leave Paris. It's his speciality, right?"
"The apartment will be empty at the end of the month: every autumn, Wloskoski goes down south to paint."
I NEED A PLACE TO PLAN THE HEIST, AND LATER, TO STASH THE LOOT FOR A FEW DAYS. MIND IF I STAY WITH YOU?

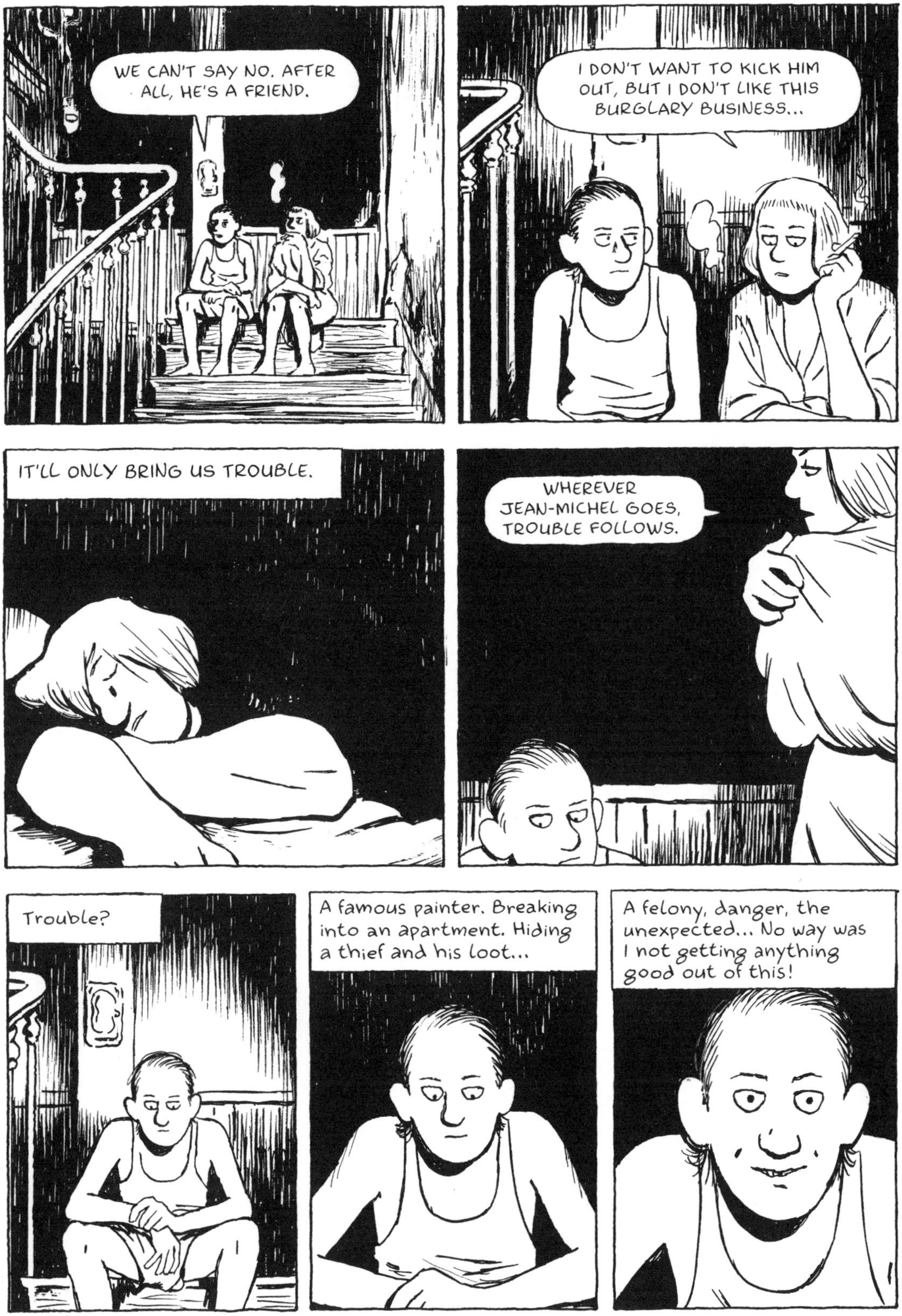
WE CAN'T SAY NO. AFTER ALL, HE'S A FRIEND.
I DON'T WANT TO KICK HIM OUT, BUT I DON'T LIKE THIS BURGLARY BUSINESS...
IT'LL ONLY BRING US TROUBLE.
WHEREVER JEAN-MICHEL GOES, TROUBLE FOLLOWS.
Trouble?
A famous painter. Breaking into an apartment. Hiding a thief and his loot...
A felony, danger, the unexpected... No way was I not getting anything good out of this!

Pages, that's what I'd get! Pages for my novel!

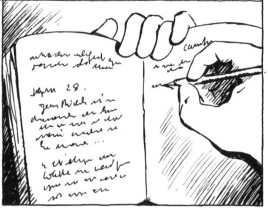

But I needed more details...

HE LIVES UP THERE.

"That's his window."

"At night, the entrance to the building is gated. No way to get in there."

SEE THAT DOOR, THOUGH? ON THE TOP FLOOR, THERE'S A TINY WINDOW LEADING UP TO THE ROOF.

WE'LL COME OVER THE ROOF TO REACH THAT WINDOW OVER THE SALON.

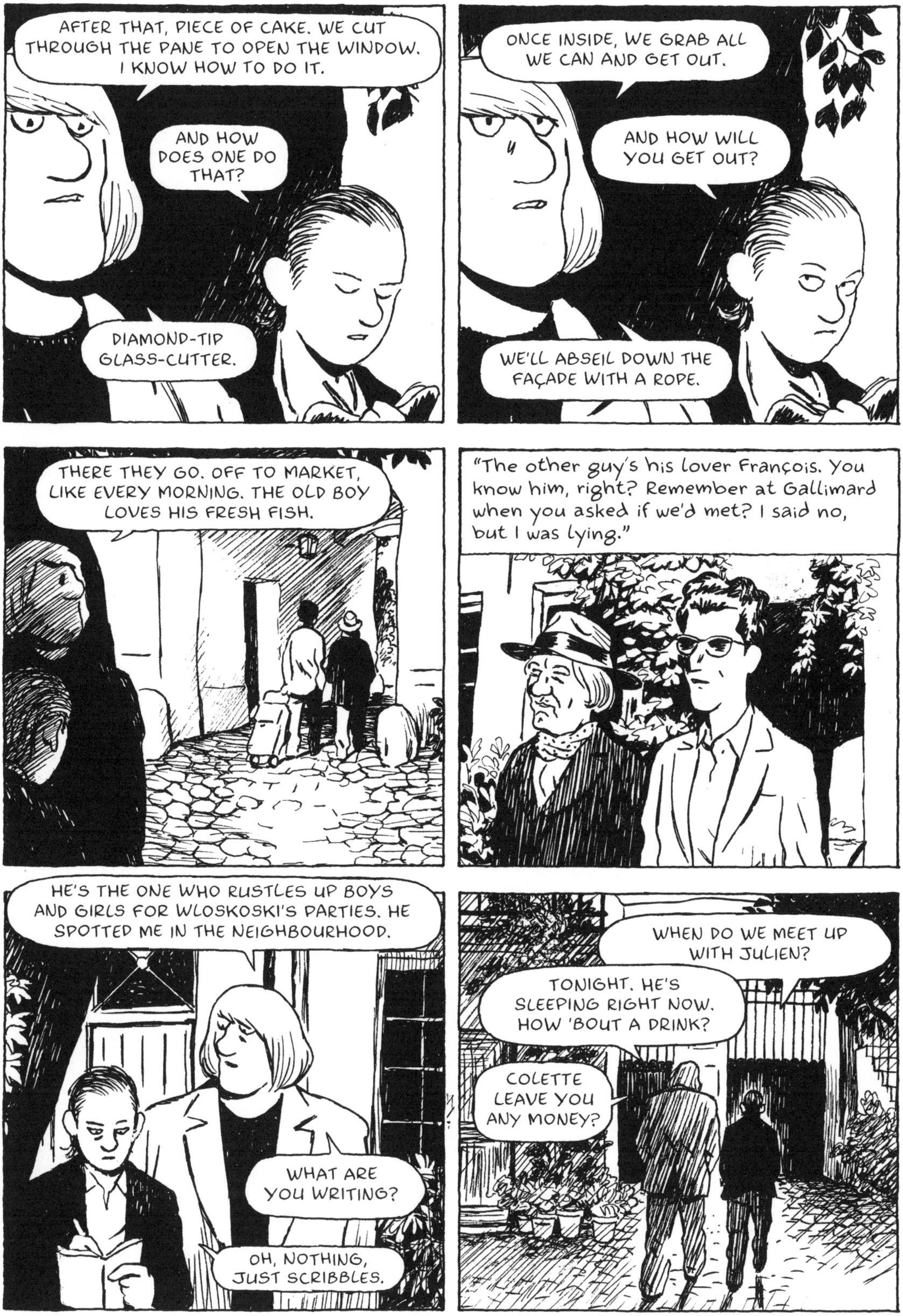
AFTER THAT, PIECE OF CAKE. WE CUT THROUGH THE PANE TO OPEN THE WINDOW. I KNOW HOW TO DO IT.
AND HOW DOES ONE DO THAT?
DIAMOND-TIP GLASS-CUTTER.
ONCE INSIDE, WE GRAB ALL WE CAN AND GET OUT.
AND HOW WILL YOU GET OUT?
WE'LL ABSEIL DOWN THE FAÇADE WITH A ROPE.
THERE THEY GO. OFF TO MARKET, LIKE EVERY MORNING. THE OLD BOY LOVES HIS FRESH FISH.
"The other guy's his lover François. You know him, right? Remember at Gallimard when you asked if we'd met? I said no, but I was lying."
HE'S THE ONE WHO RUSTLES UP BOYS AND GIRLS FOR WLOSKOSKI'S PARTIES. HE SPOTTED ME IN THE NEIGHBOURHOOD.
WHAT ARE YOU WRITING?
OH, NOTHING, JUST SCRIBBLES.
WHEN DO WE MEET UP WITH JULIEN?
TONIGHT. HE'S SLEEPING RIGHT NOW. HOW 'BOUT A DRINK?
COLETTE LEAVE YOU ANY MONEY?

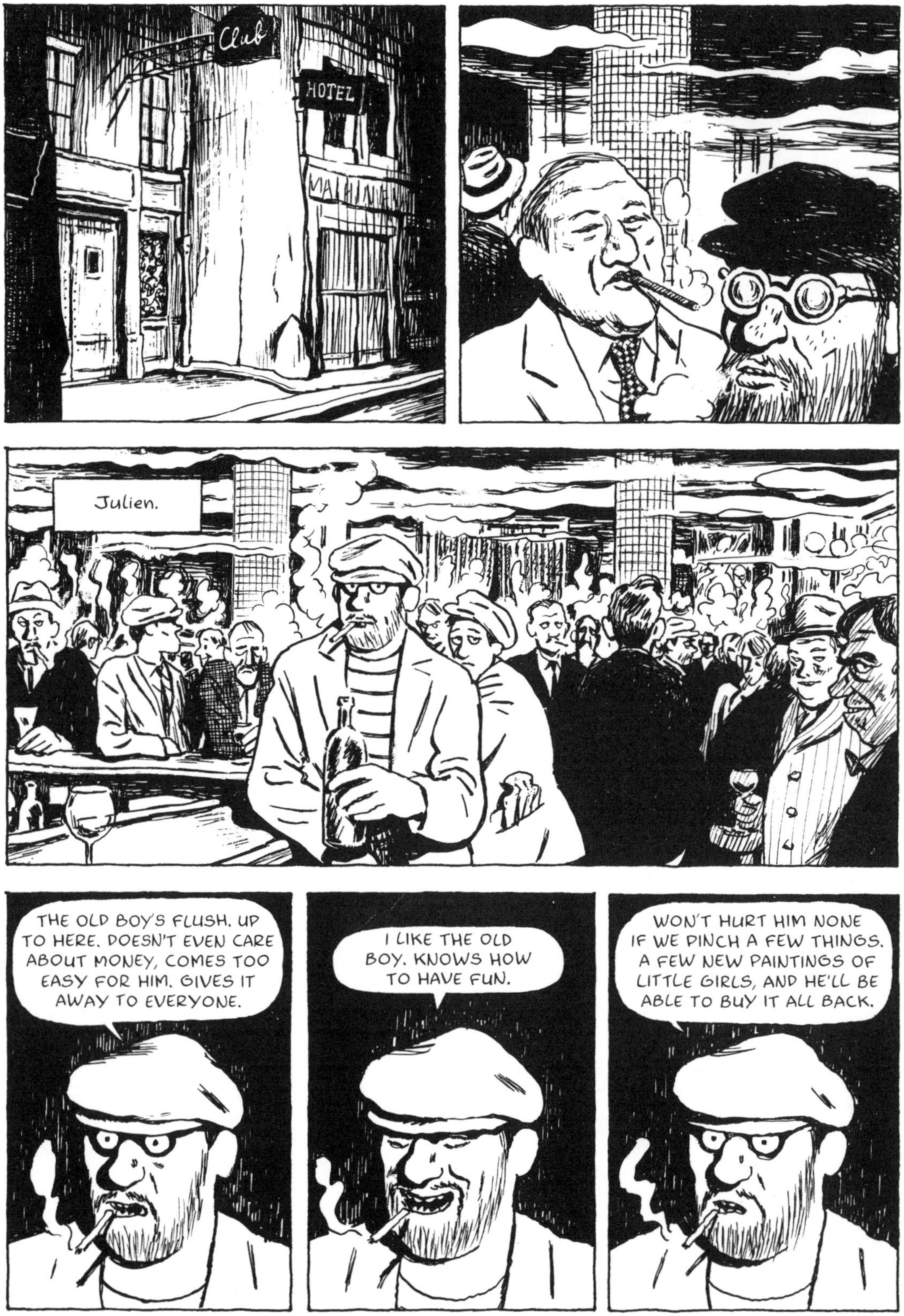
Club
HOTEL
Julien.
THE OLD BOY'S FLUSH. UP TO HERE. DOESN'T EVEN CARE ABOUT MONEY, COMES TOO EASY FOR HIM. GIVES IT AWAY TO EVERYONE.
I LIKE THE OLD BOY. KNOWS HOW TO HAVE FUN.
WON'T HURT HIM NONE IF WE PINCH A FEW THINGS. A FEW NEW PAINTINGS OF LITTLE GIRLS, AND HE'LL BE ABLE TO BUY IT ALL BACK.

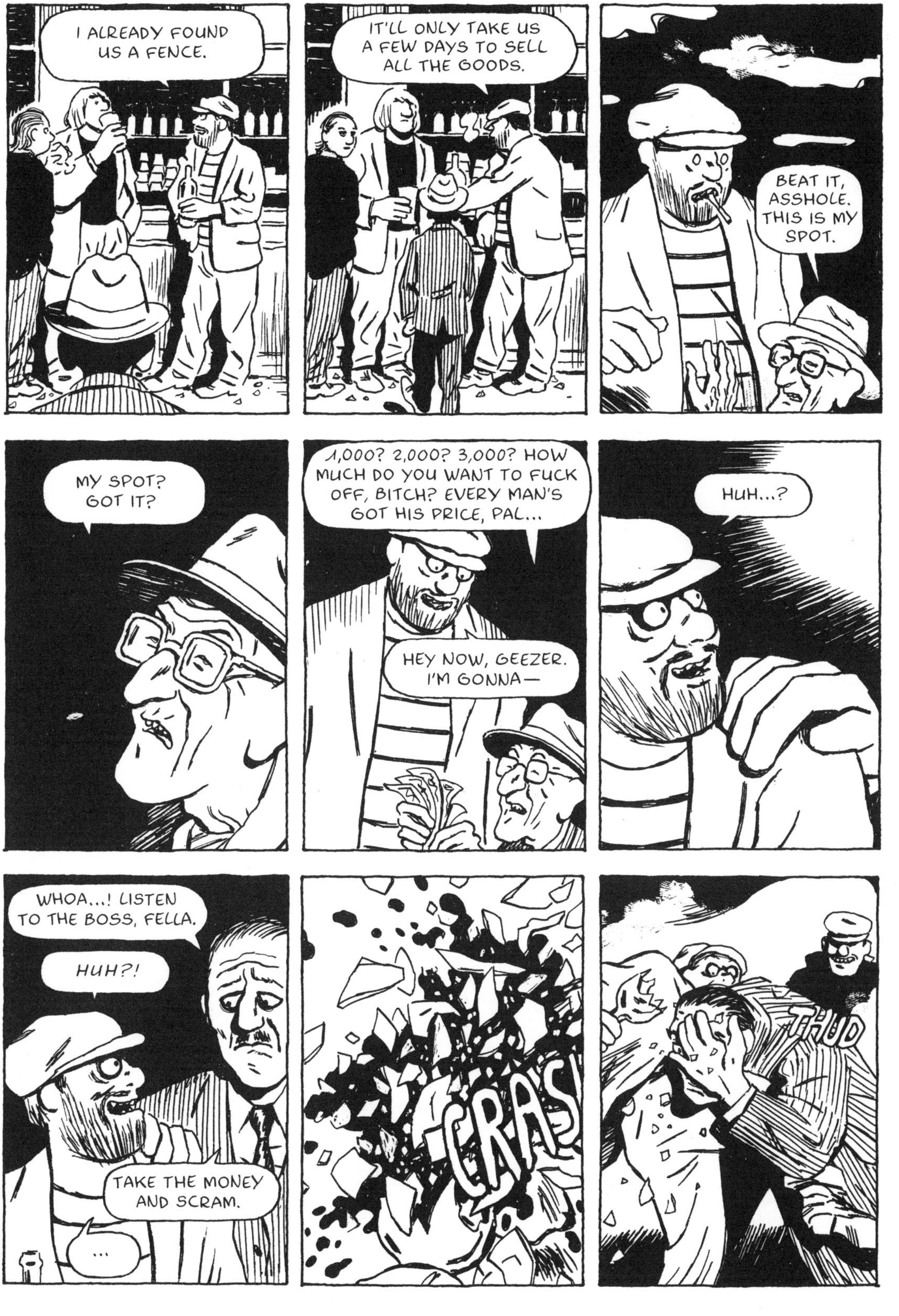

I ALREADY FOUND US A FENCE.
IT'LL ONLY TAKE US A FEW DAYS TO SELL ALL THE GOODS.
BEAT IT, ASSHOLE. THIS IS MY SPOT.
MY SPOT? GOT IT?
1,000? 2,000? 3,000? HOW MUCH DO YOU WANT TO FUCK OFF, BITCH? EVERY MAN'S GOT HIS PRICE, PAL...
HEY NOW, GEEZER. I'M GONNA—
HUH...?
WHOA...! LISTEN TO THE BOSS, FELLA.
HUH?!
TAKE THE MONEY AND SCRAM.
...
CRASH
THUD

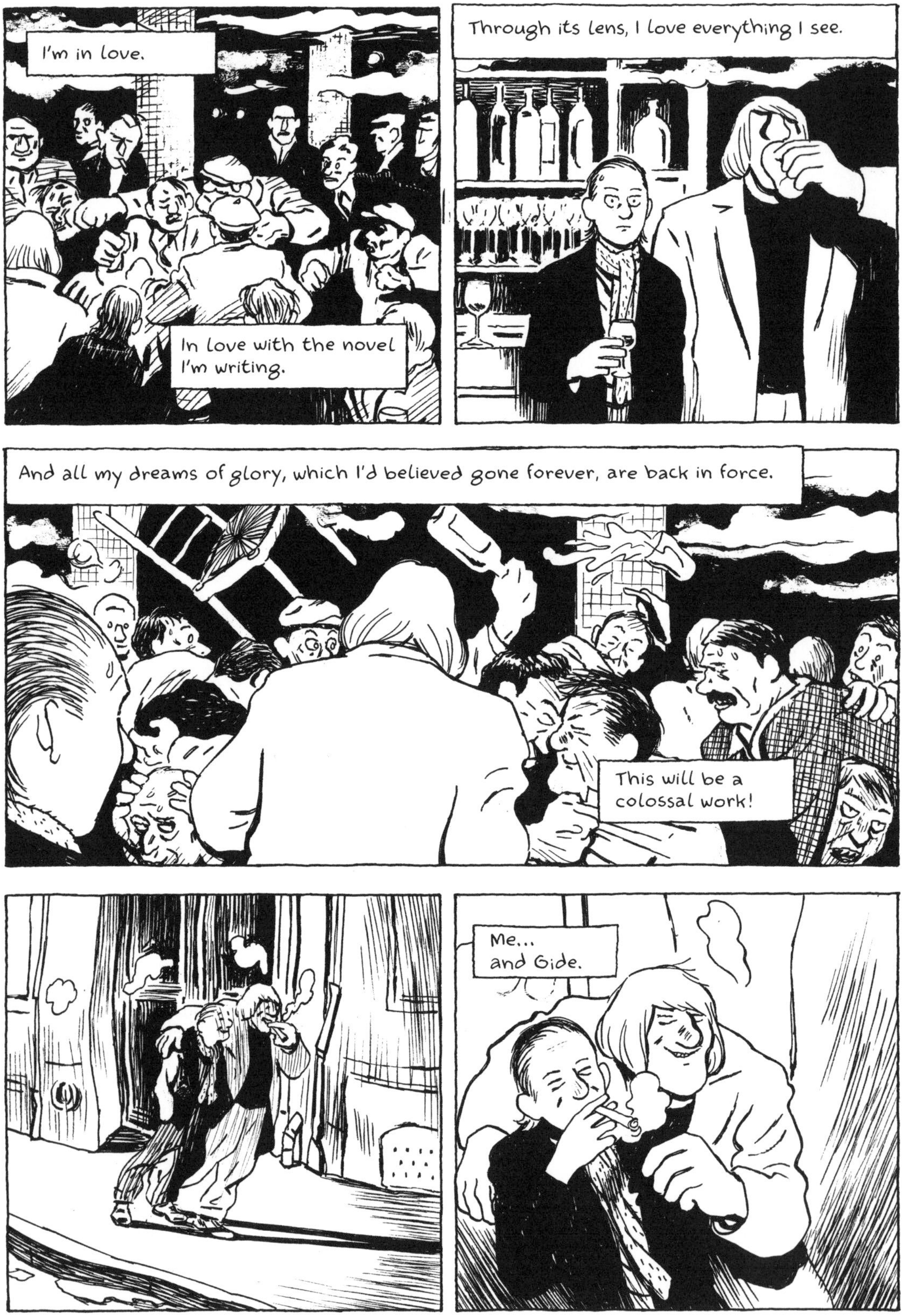
I'm in love.
In love with the novel I'm writing.
Through its lens, I love everything I see.
And all my dreams of glory, which I'd believed gone forever, are back in force.
This will be a colossal work!
Me... and Gide.

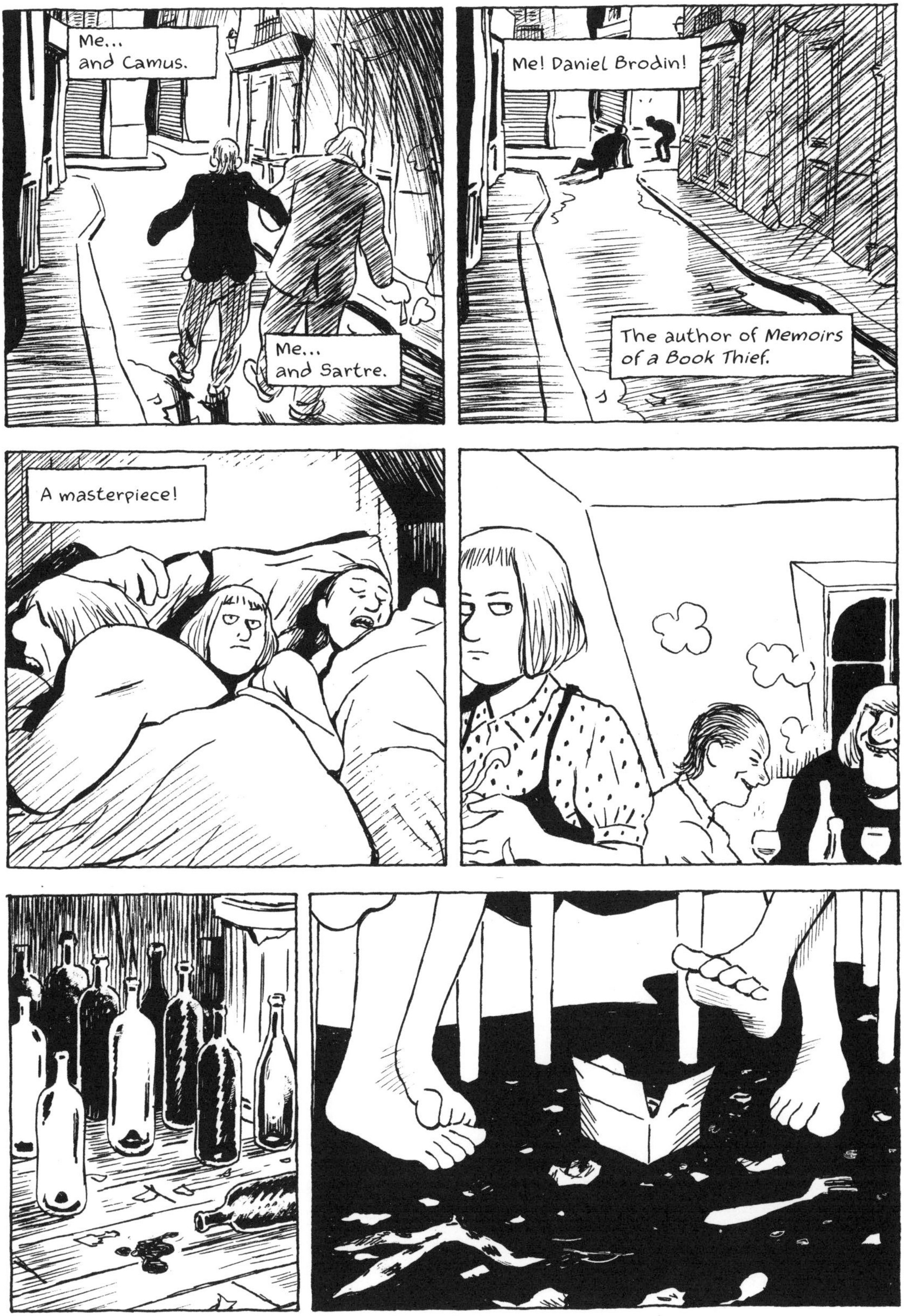
Me...
and Camus.
Me...
and Sartre.
Me! Daniel Brodin!
The author of *Memoirs of a Book Thief*.
A masterpiece!

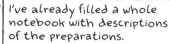
18 September. Just a few more days till the heist.

I've already filled a whole notebook with descriptions of the preparations.

I couldn't make up my mind about the end. Would the burglary go as planned, or would it turn out a fiasco?

And the character based on Colette? What would become of her? Would she offer help or keep her distance?

In the novel, my alter ego was the one committing the burglary. But in real life, I'd stay quietly at home, out of harm's way. No real risk: such was the narrator's privilege.

YOU GOT ANOTHER LETTER FROM GILLES.

WHEN ALL THIS IS OVER, WHY DON'T YOU AND I LEAVE TOWN TOO?

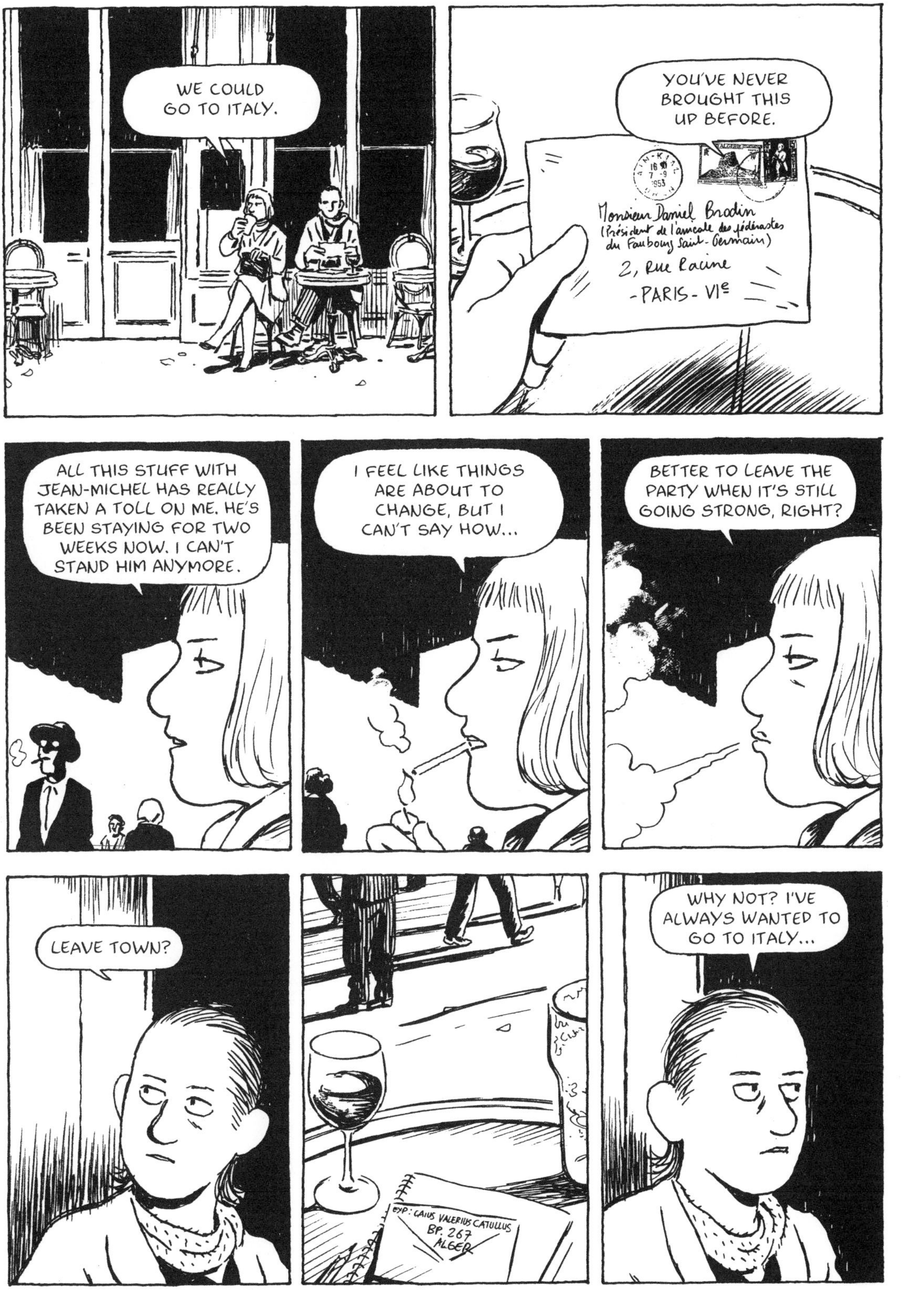
WE COULD GO TO ITALY.
YOU'VE NEVER BROUGHT THIS UP BEFORE.
Monsieur Daniel Brodin
(Président de l'amicale des pédérastes du Faubourg Saint-Germain)
2, Rue Racine
-PARIS- VIe
ALL THIS STUFF WITH JEAN-MICHEL HAS REALLY TAKEN A TOLL ON ME. HE'S BEEN STAYING FOR TWO WEEKS NOW. I CAN'T STAND HIM ANYMORE.
I FEEL LIKE THINGS ARE ABOUT TO CHANGE, BUT I CAN'T SAY HOW...
BETTER TO LEAVE THE PARTY WHEN IT'S STILL GOING STRONG, RIGHT?
LEAVE TOWN?
EXP: CAIUS VALERIUS CATULLUS
BP. 267
ALGER
WHY NOT? I'VE ALWAYS WANTED TO GO TO ITALY...

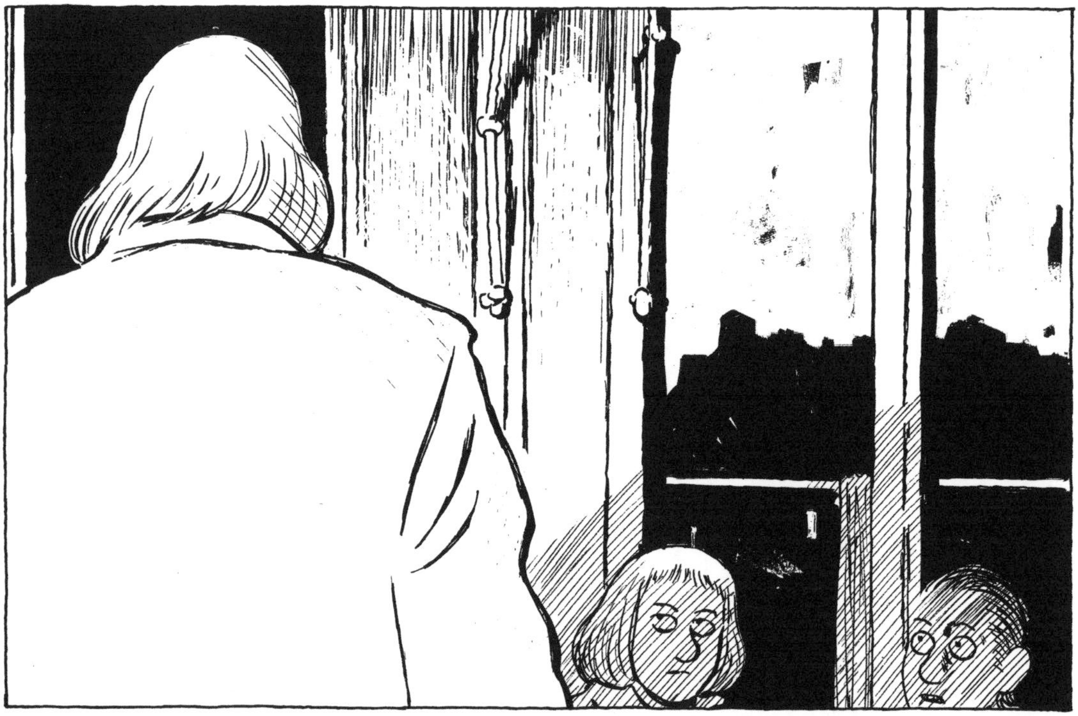

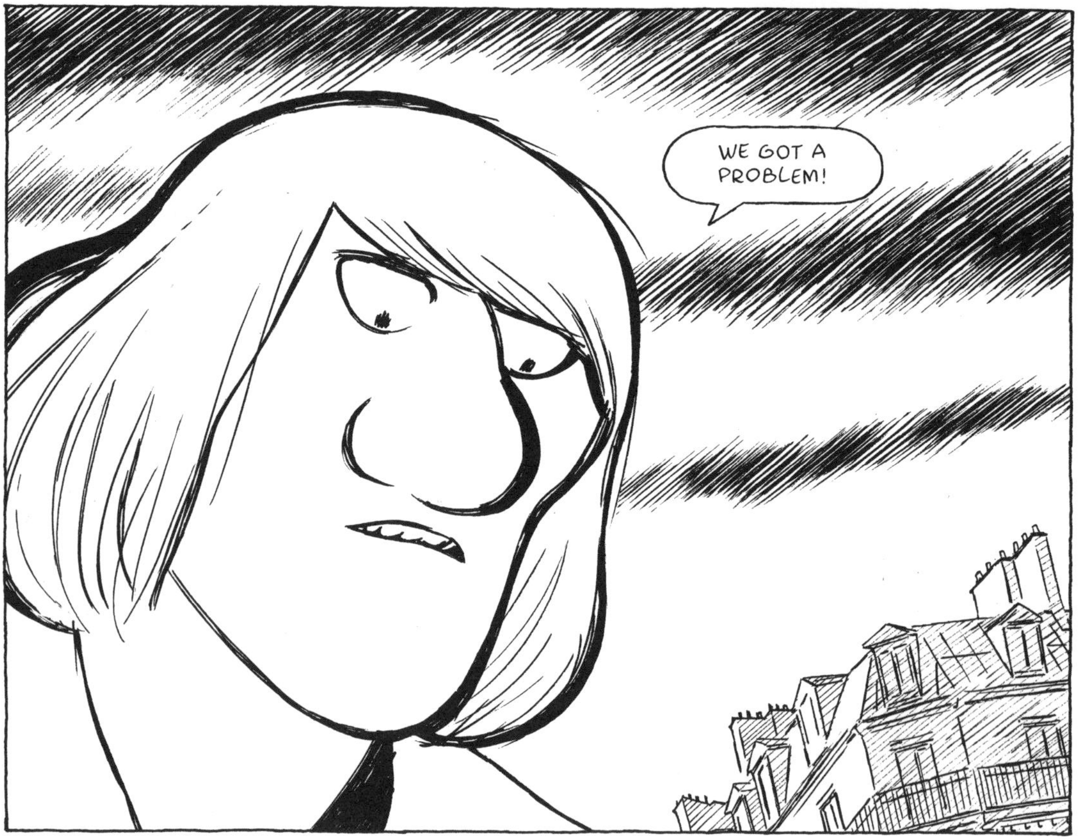
WE GOT A PROBLEM!

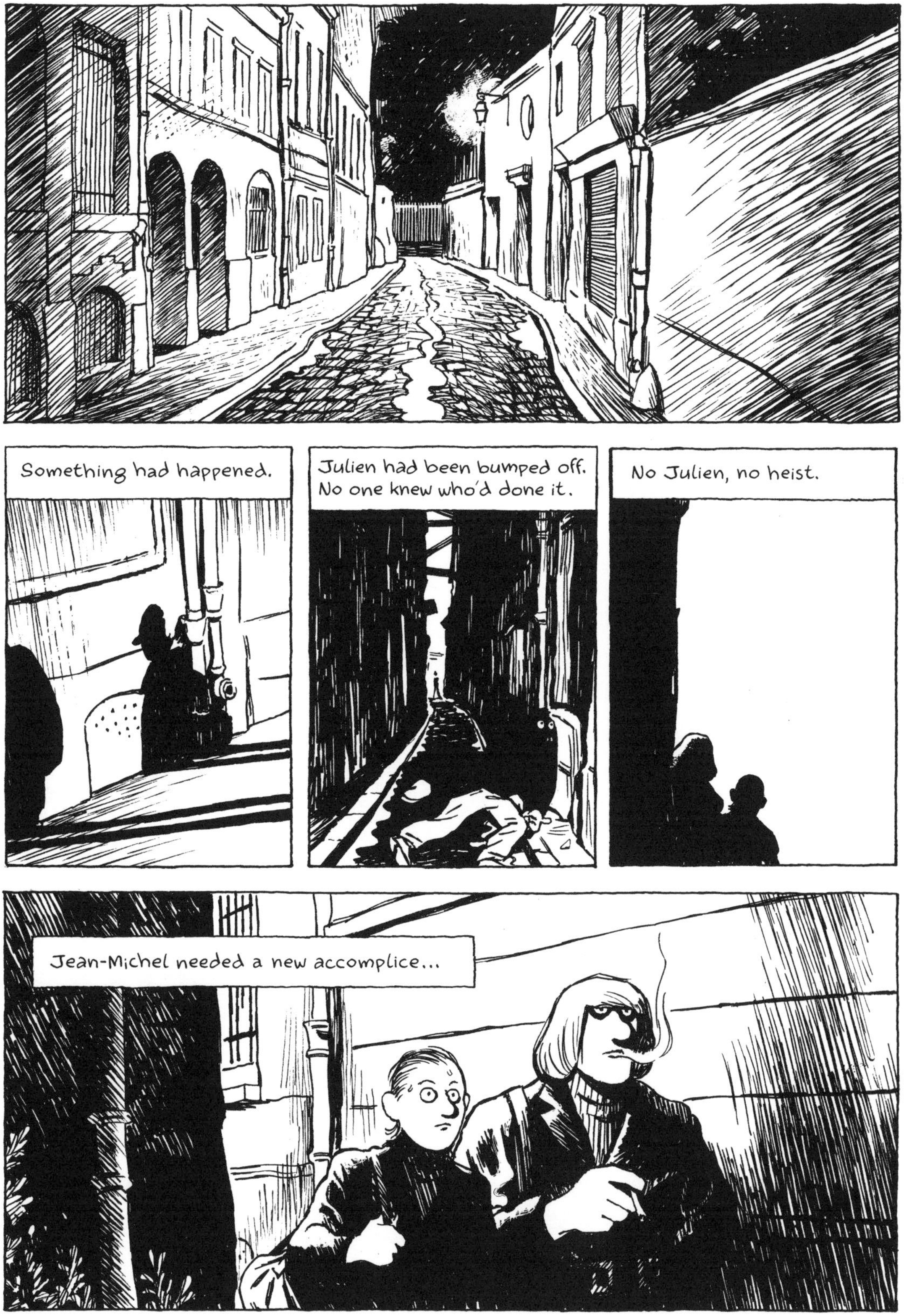
Something had happened.
Julien had been bumped off. No one knew who'd done it.
No Julien, no heist.
Jean-Michel needed a new accomplice...

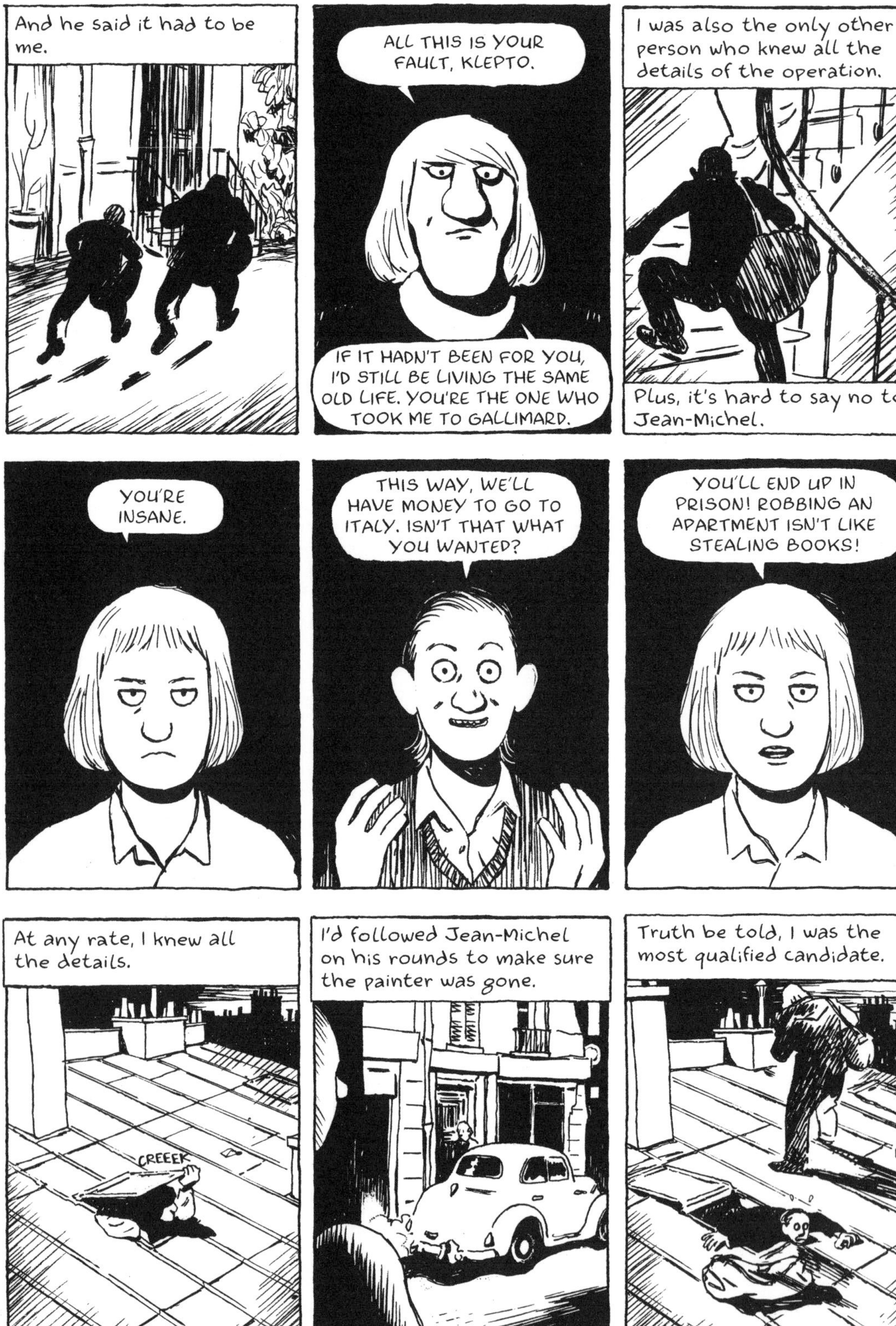
And he said it had to be me.
ALL THIS IS YOUR FAULT, KLEPTO.
IF IT HADN'T BEEN FOR YOU, I'D STILL BE LIVING THE SAME OLD LIFE. YOU'RE THE ONE WHO TOOK ME TO GALLIMARD.
I was also the only other person who knew all the details of the operation.
Plus, it's hard to say no to Jean-Michel.
YOU'RE INSANE.
THIS WAY, WE'LL HAVE MONEY TO GO TO ITALY. ISN'T THAT WHAT YOU WANTED?
YOU'LL END UP IN PRISON! ROBBING AN APARTMENT ISN'T LIKE STEALING BOOKS!
At any rate, I knew all the details.
CREEEK
I'd followed Jean-Michel on his rounds to make sure the painter was gone.
Truth be told, I was the most qualified candidate.

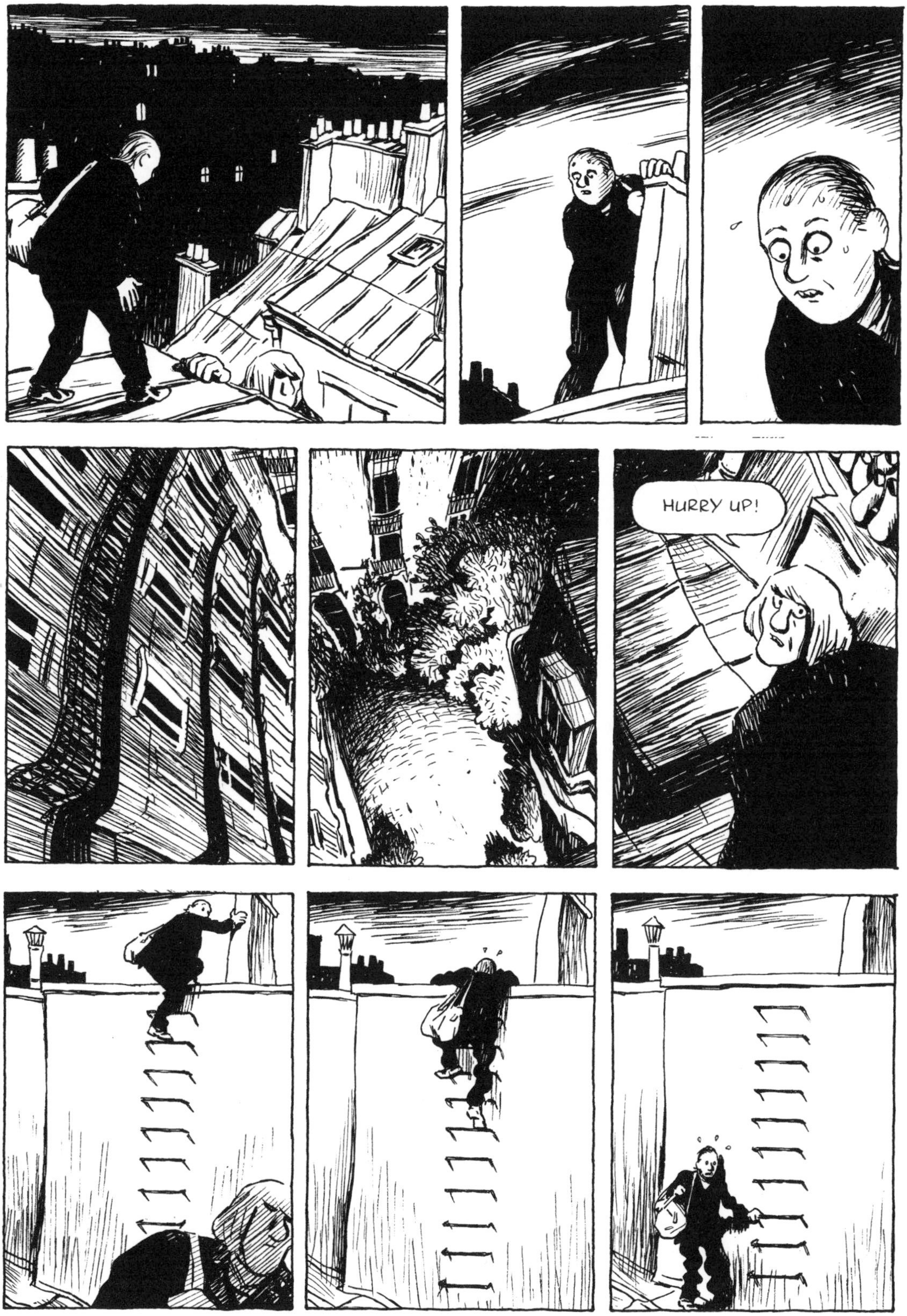
HURRY UP!

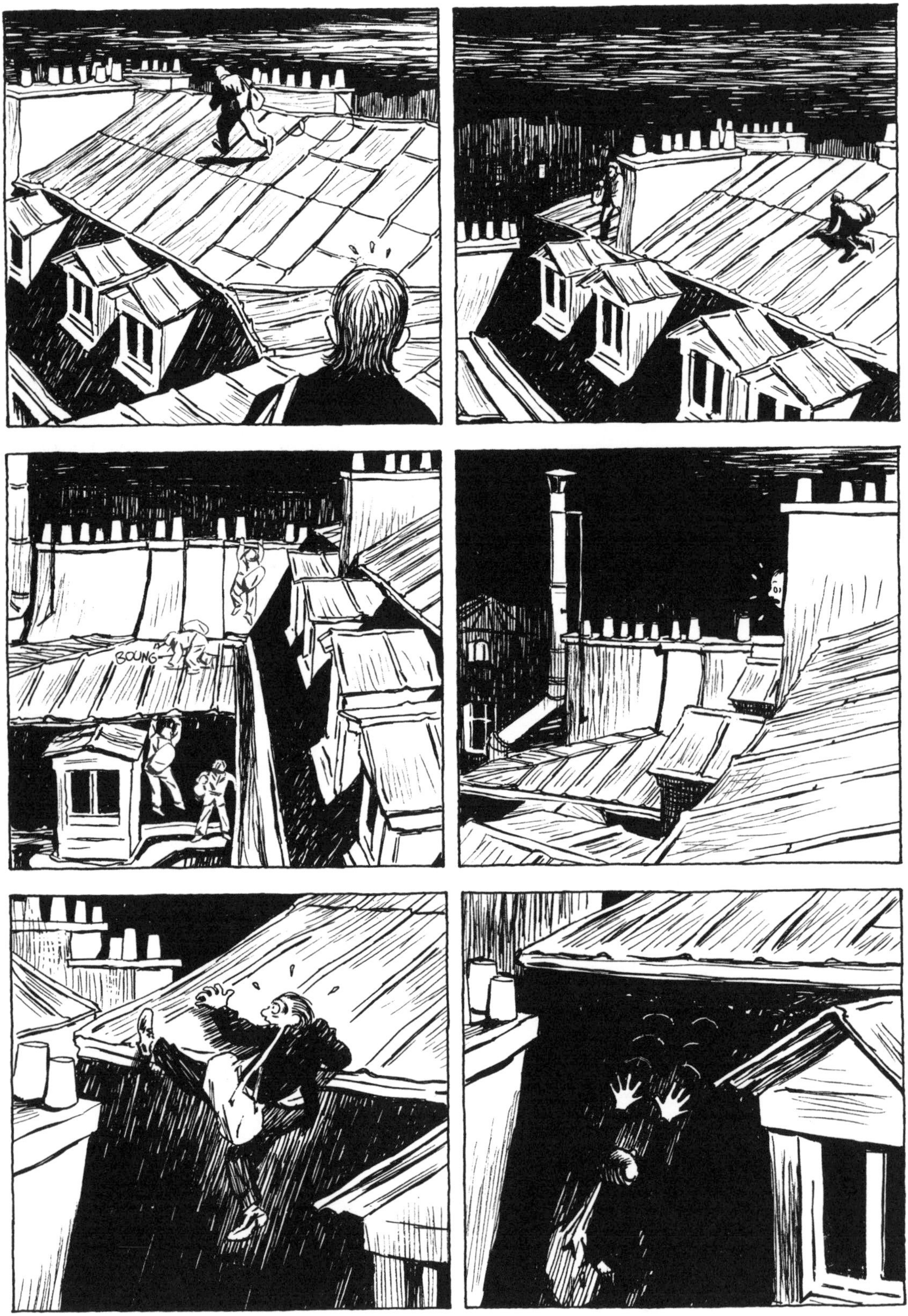
BOUNG

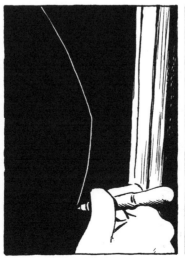

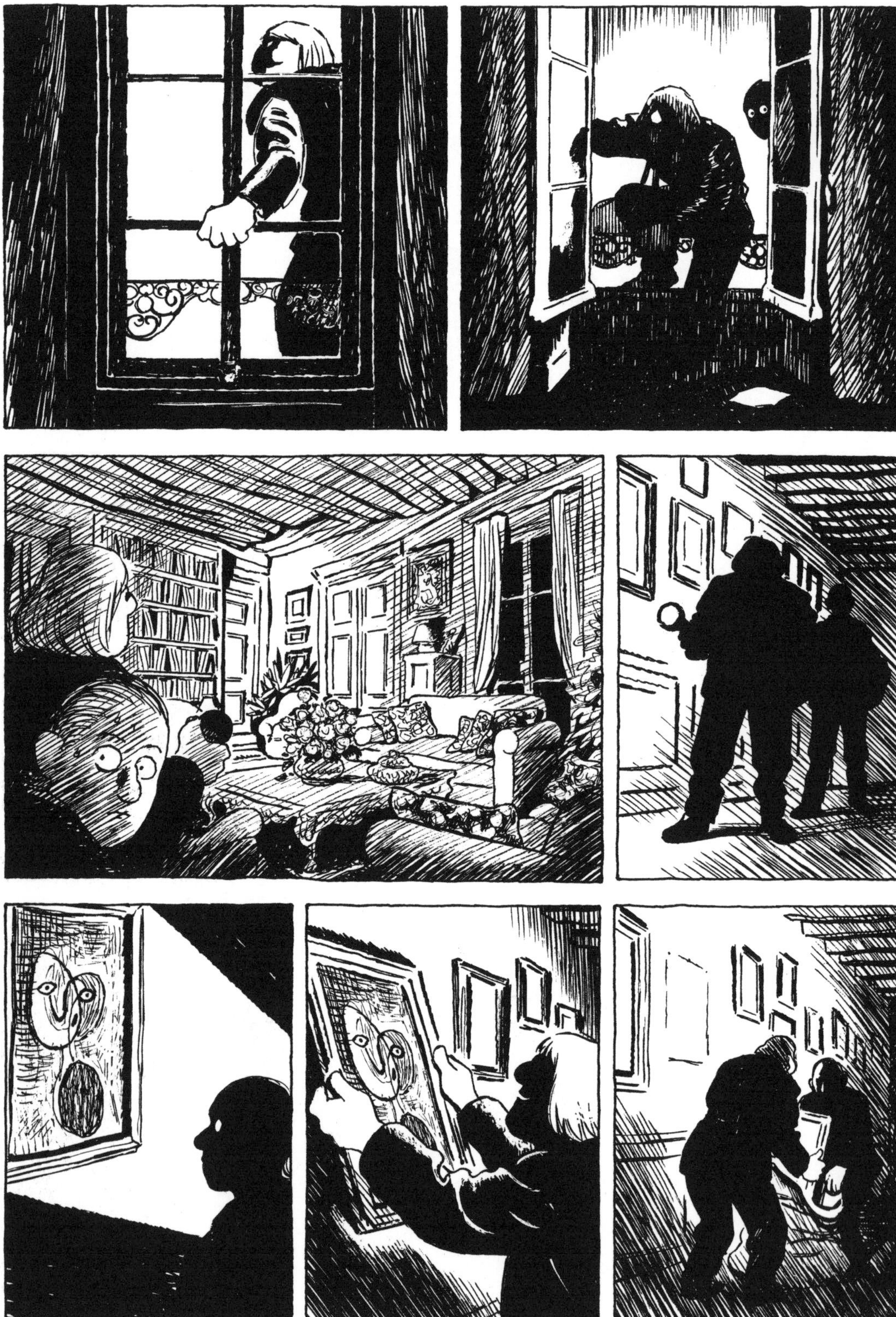

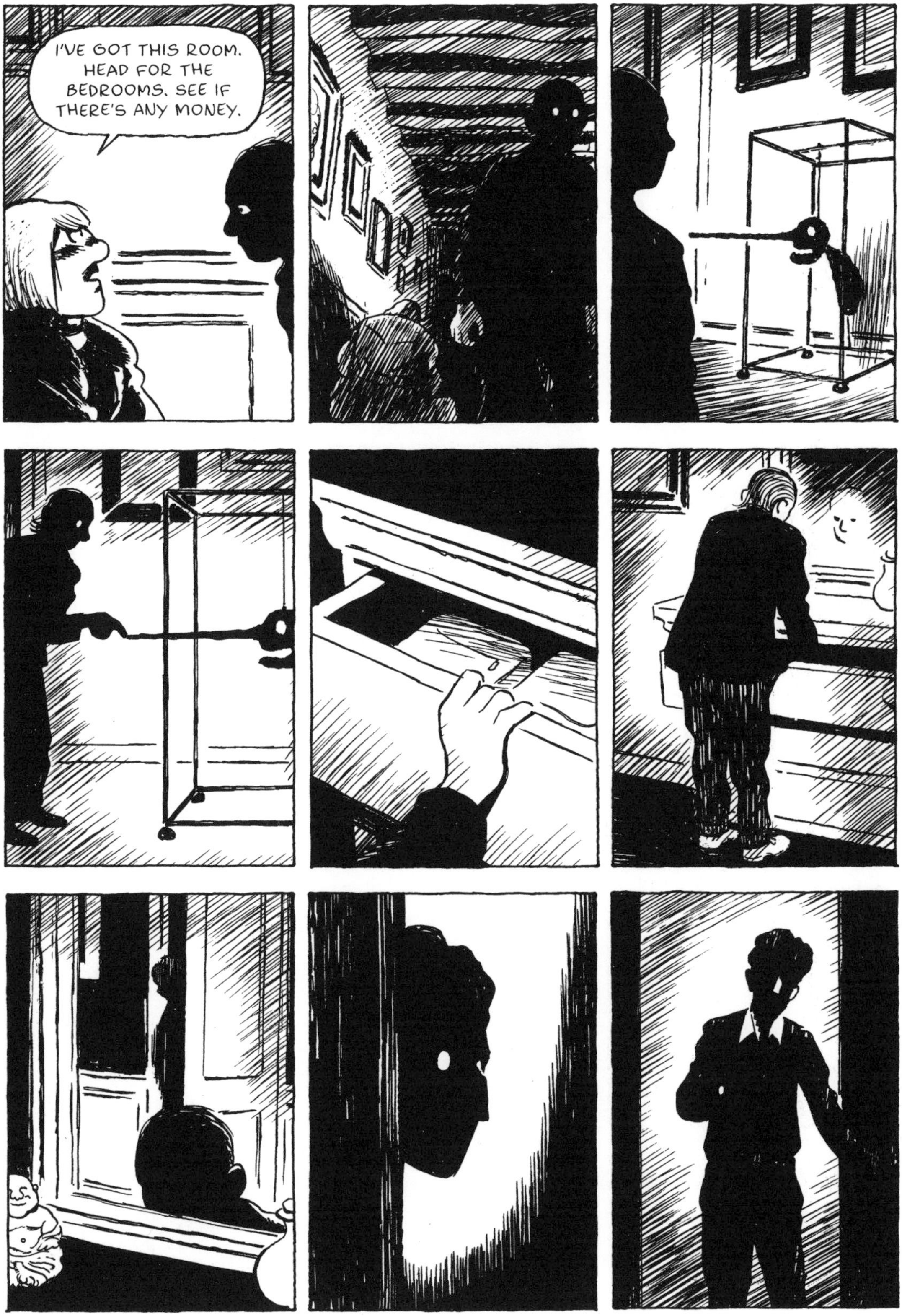
I'VE GOT THIS ROOM. HEAD FOR THE BEDROOMS. SEE IF THERE'S ANY MONEY.

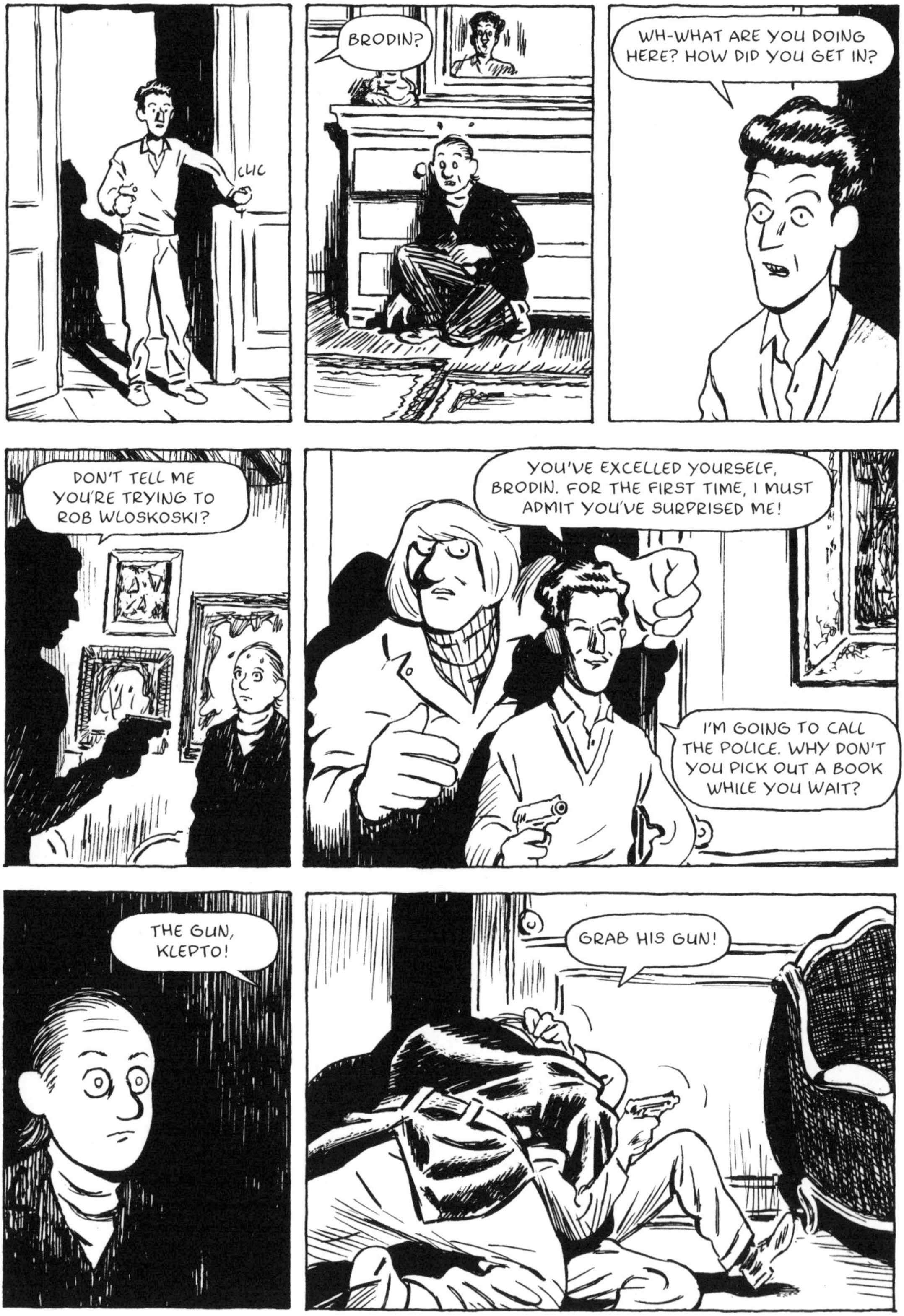
CLIC
BRODIN?
WH-WHAT ARE YOU DOING HERE? HOW DID YOU GET IN?
DON'T TELL ME YOU'RE TRYING TO ROB WLOSKOSKI?
YOU'VE EXCELLED YOURSELF, BRODIN. FOR THE FIRST TIME, I MUST ADMIT YOU'VE SURPRISED ME!
I'M GOING TO CALL THE POLICE. WHY DON'T YOU PICK OUT A BOOK WHILE YOU WAIT?
THE GUN, KLEPTO!
GRAB HIS GUN!

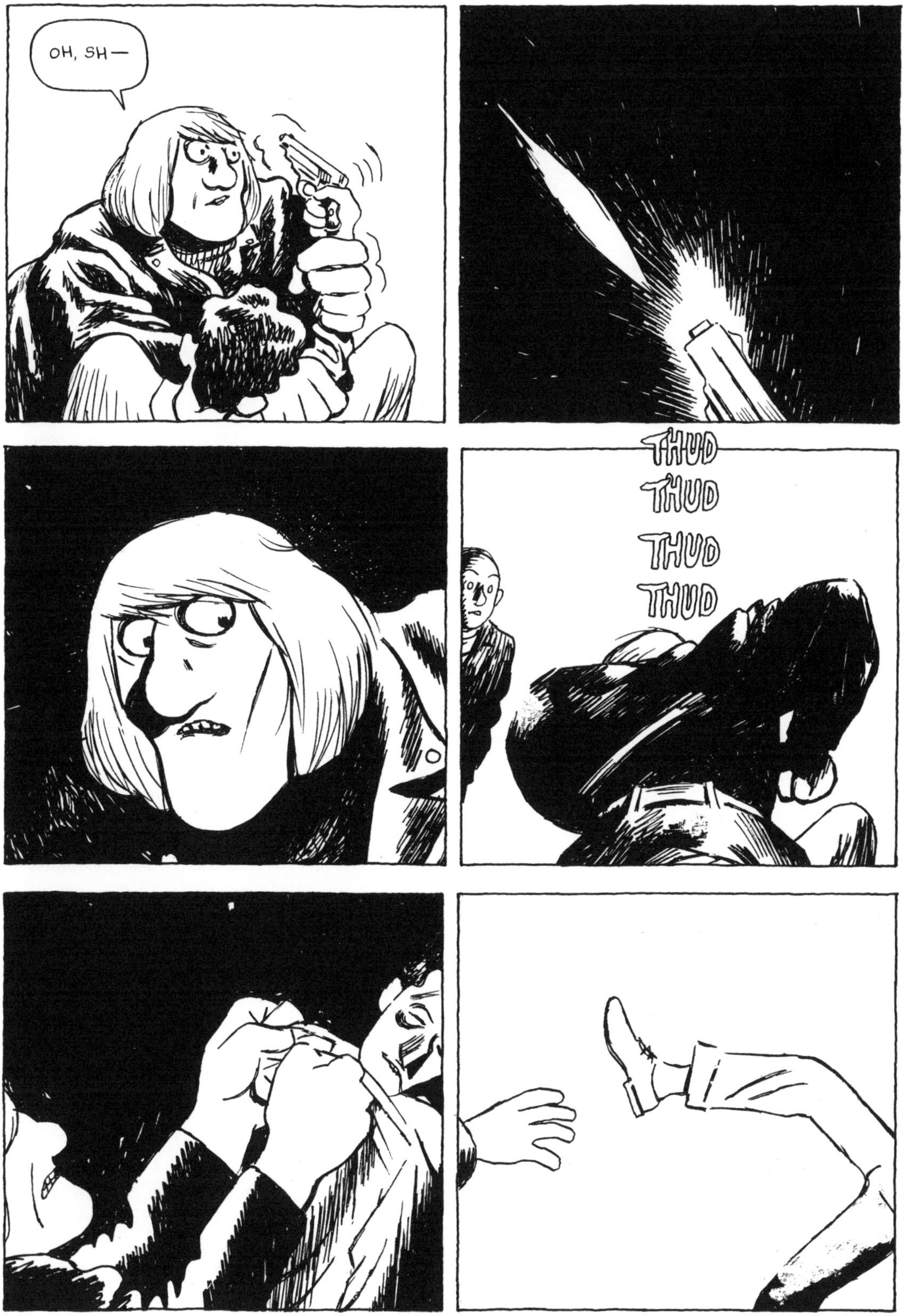
OH, SH—
THUD
THUD
THUD
THUD

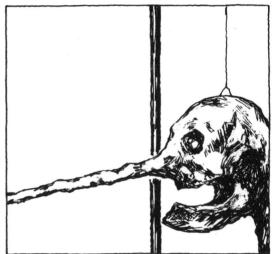

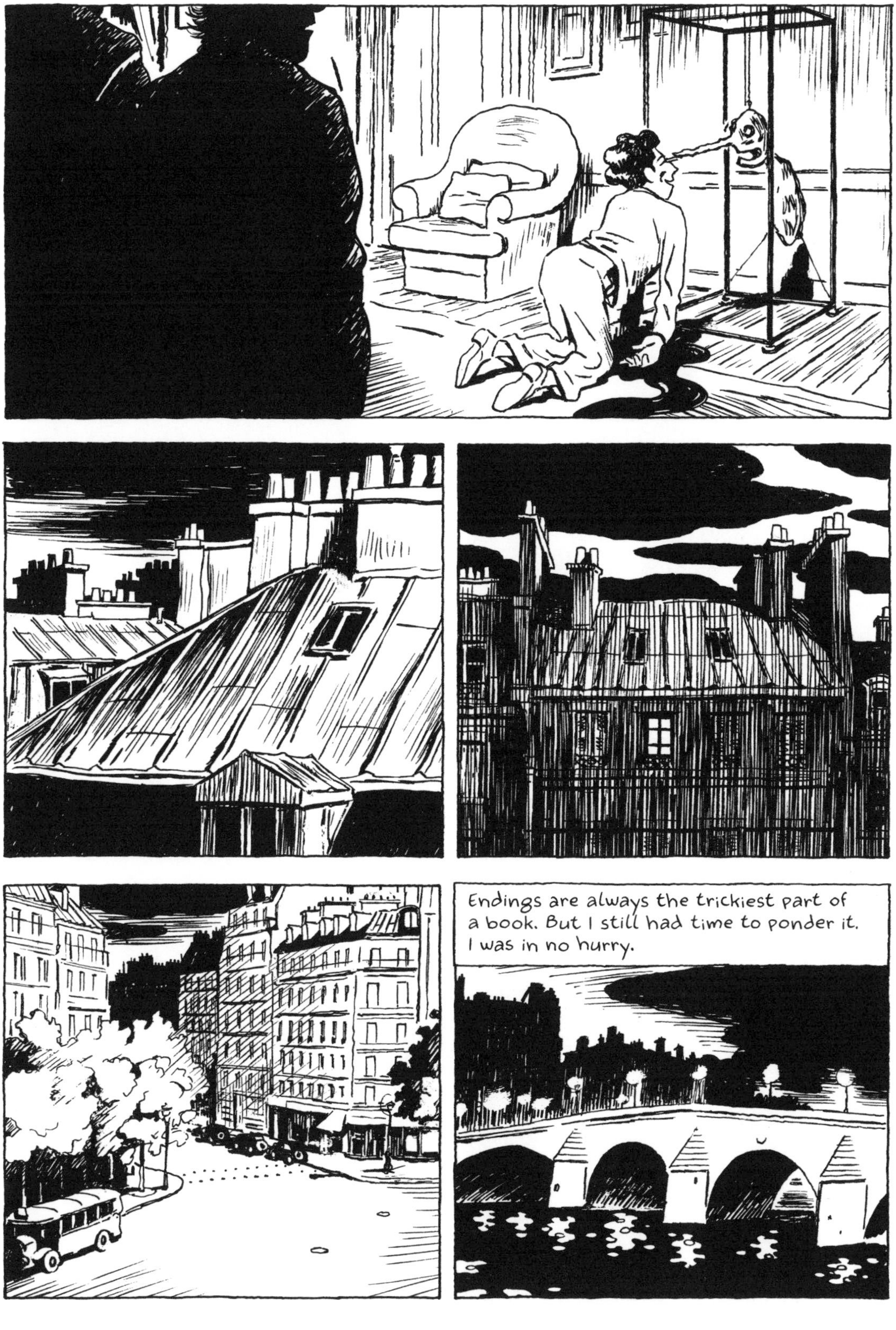
Endings are always the trickiest part of a book. But I still had time to ponder it. I was in no hurry.

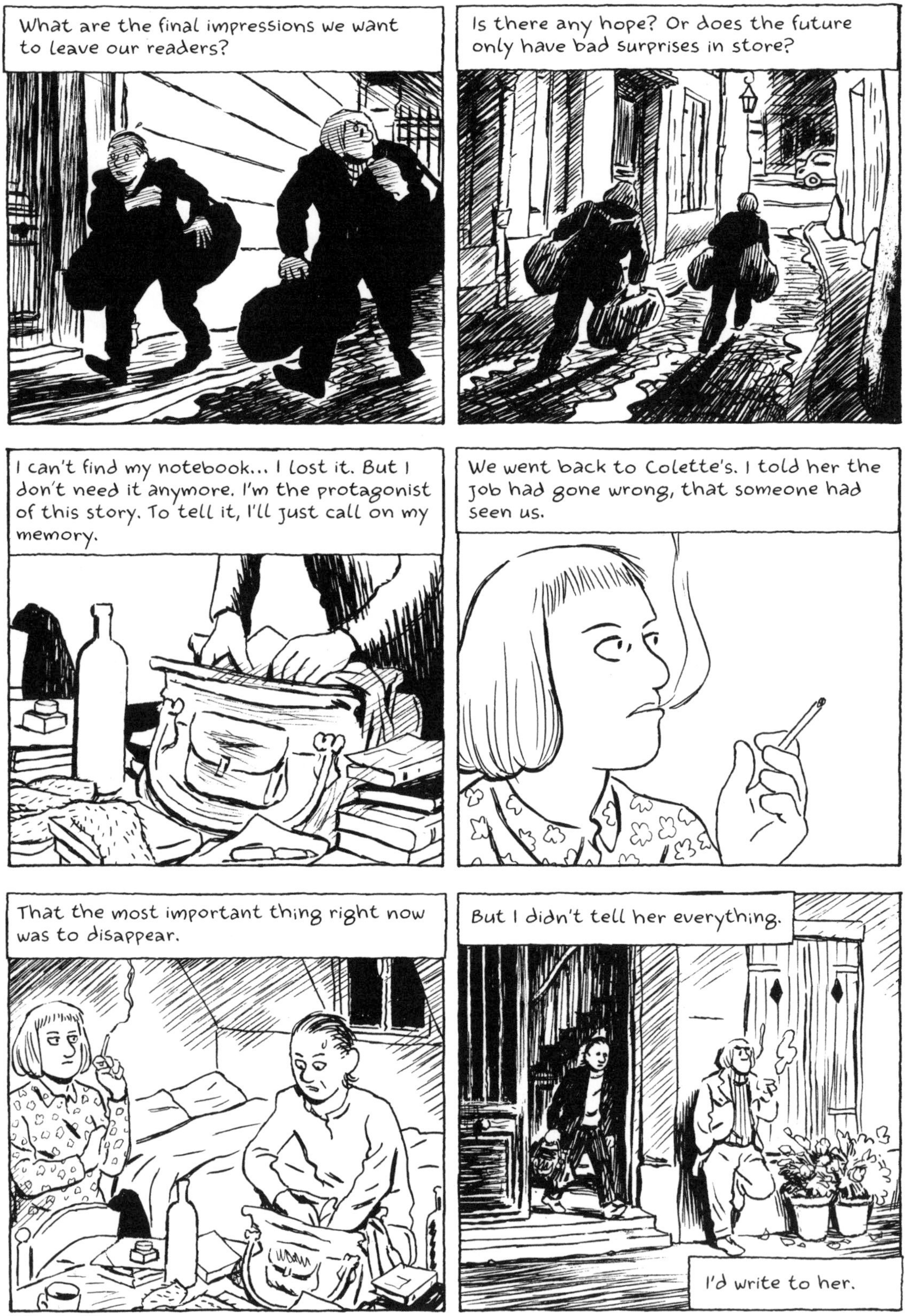
What are the final impressions we want to leave our readers?
Is there any hope? Or does the future only have bad surprises in store?
I can't find my notebook... I lost it. But I don't need it anymore. I'm the protagonist of this story. To tell it, I'll just call on my memory.
We went back to Colette's. I told her the job had gone wrong, that someone had seen us.
That the most important thing right now was to disappear.
But I didn't tell her everything.
I'd write to her.

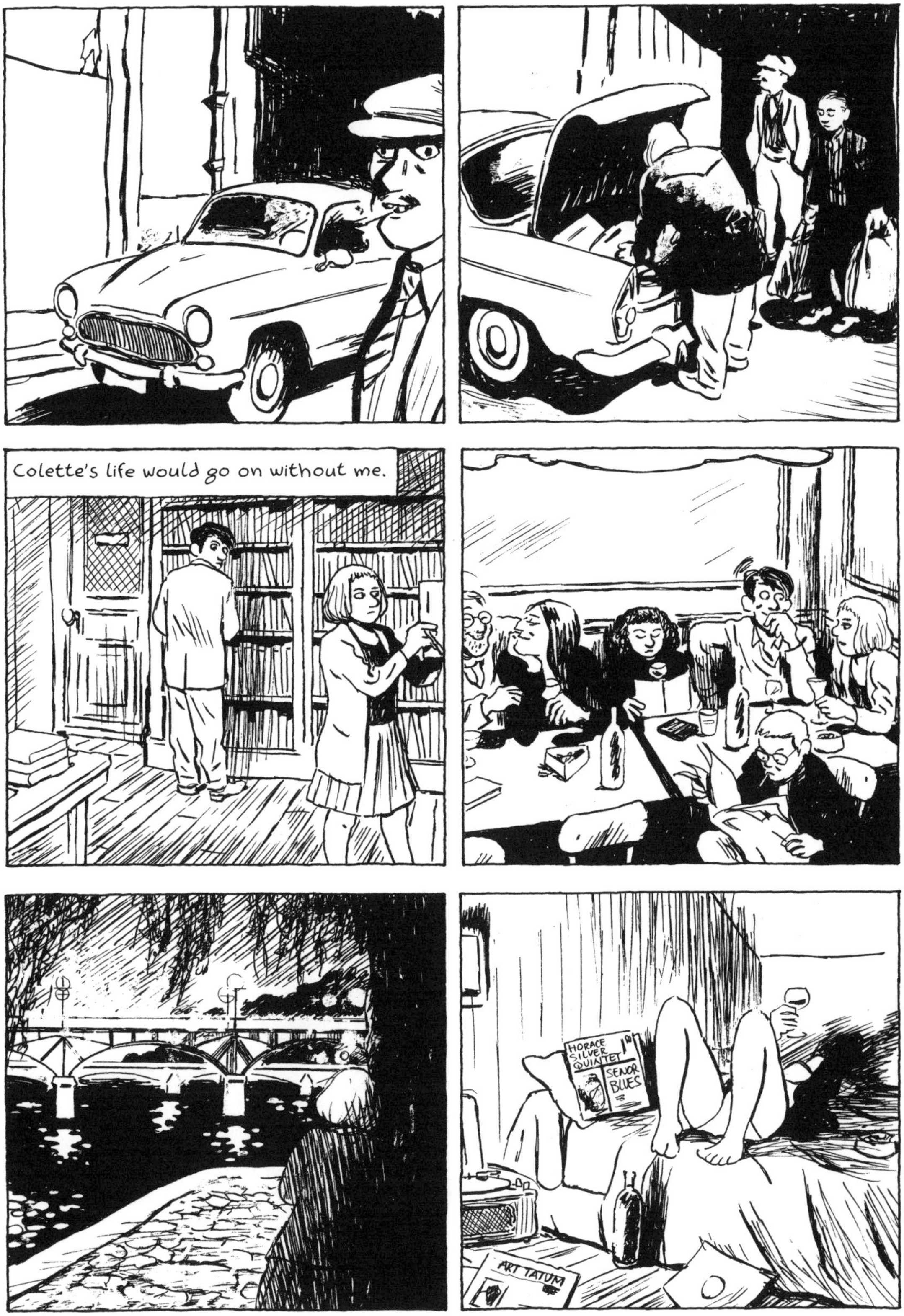
Colette's life would go on without me.
HORACE SILVER QUINTET
SEÑOR BLUES
ART TATUM

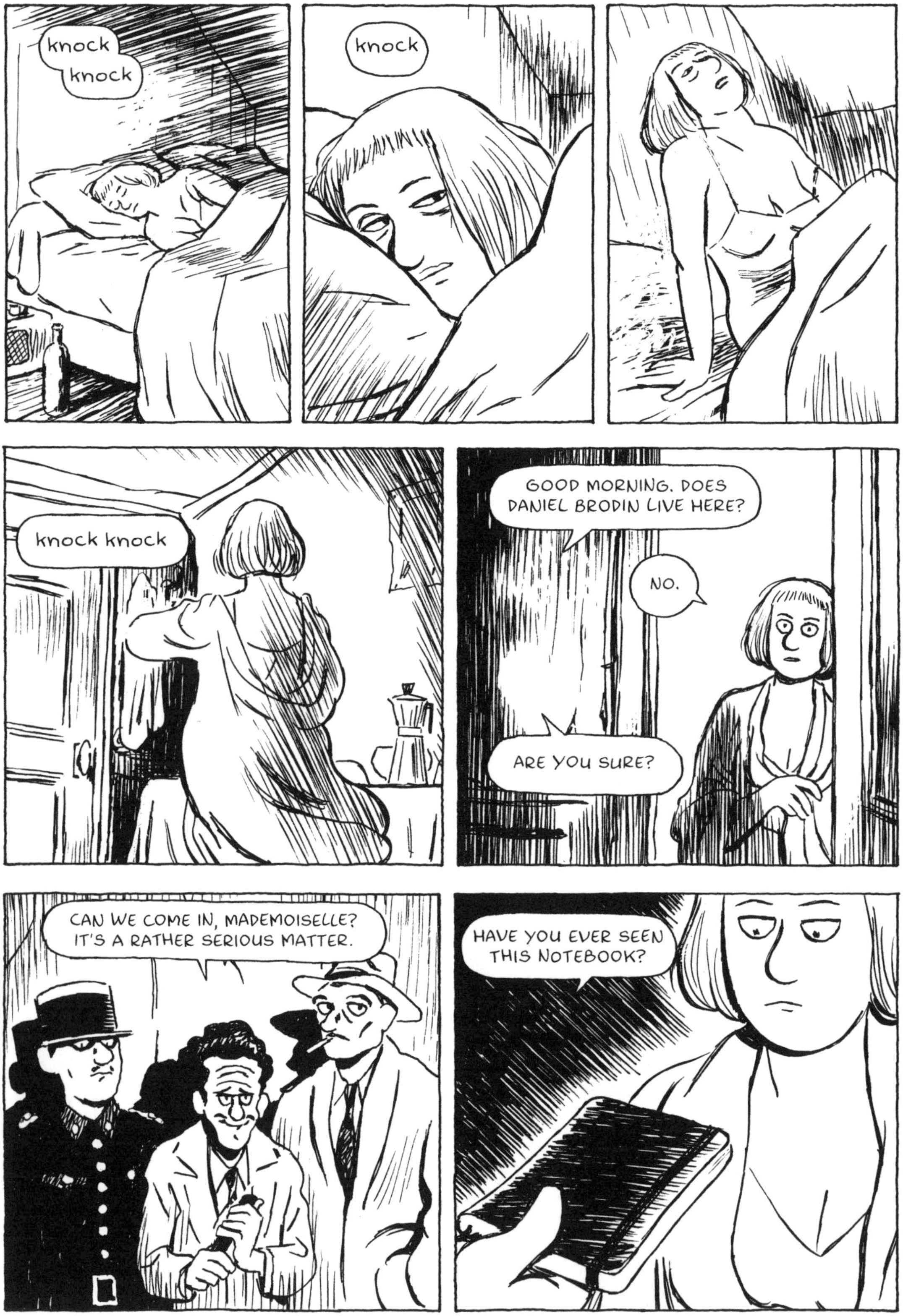
knock
knock
knock
knock knock
GOOD MORNING. DOES DANIEL BRODIN LIVE HERE?
NO.
ARE YOU SURE?
CAN WE COME IN, MADEMOISELLE? IT'S A RATHER SERIOUS MATTER.
HAVE YOU EVER SEEN THIS NOTEBOOK?

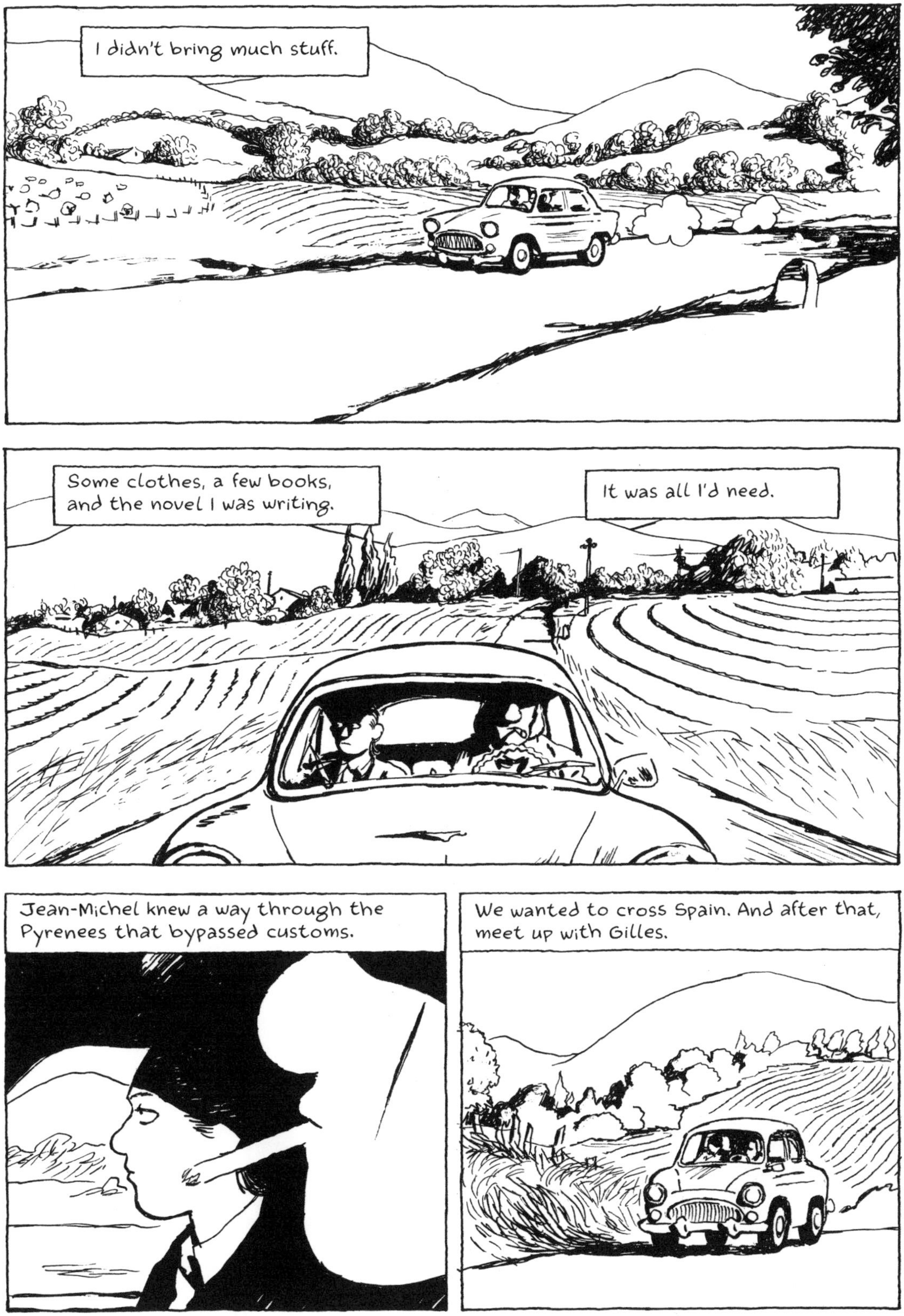
I didn't bring much stuff.
Some clothes, a few books, and the novel I was writing.
It was all I'd need.
Jean-Michel knew a way through the Pyrenees that bypassed customs.
We wanted to cross Spain. And after that, meet up with Gilles.

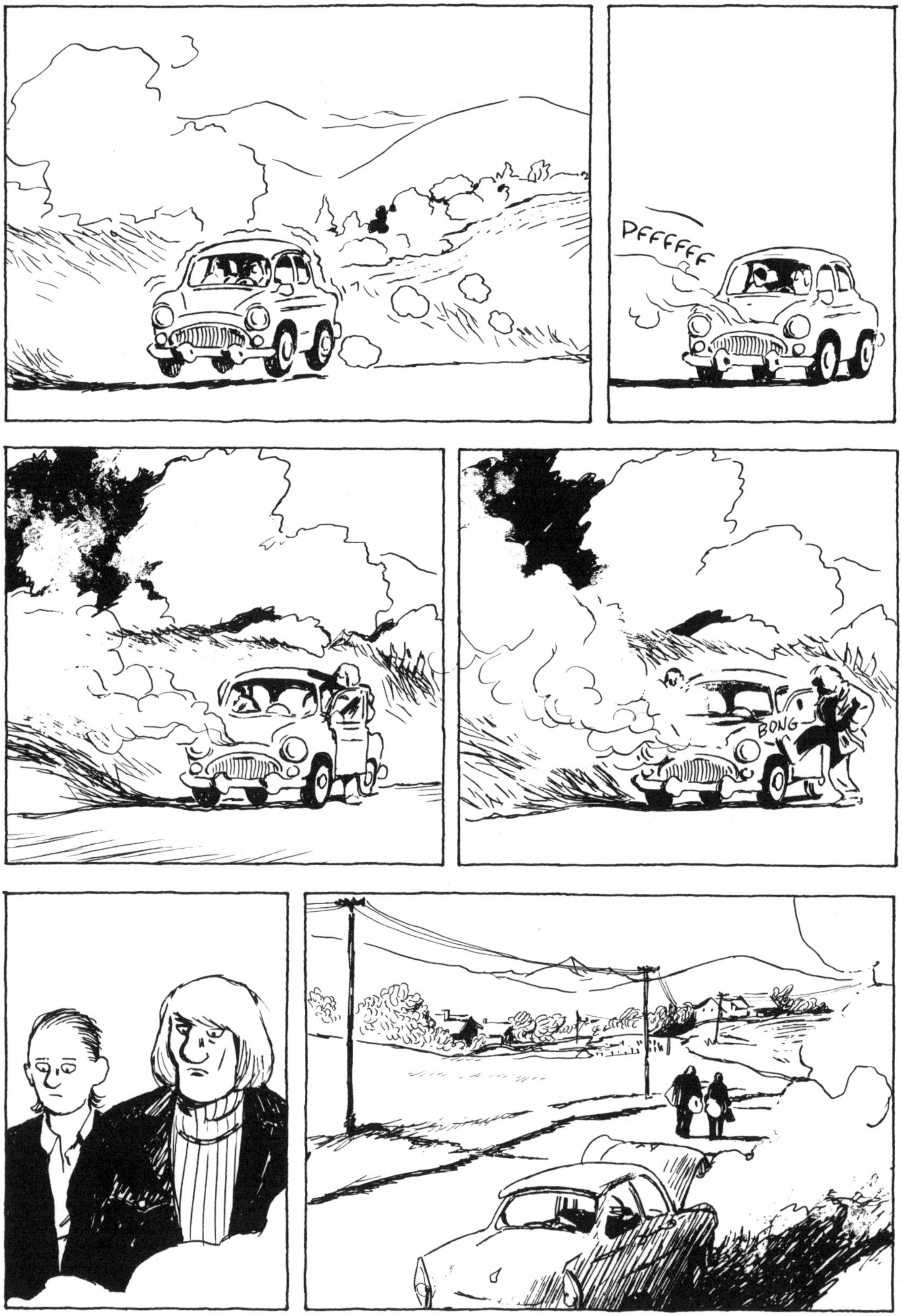
PFFFFFF
BONG

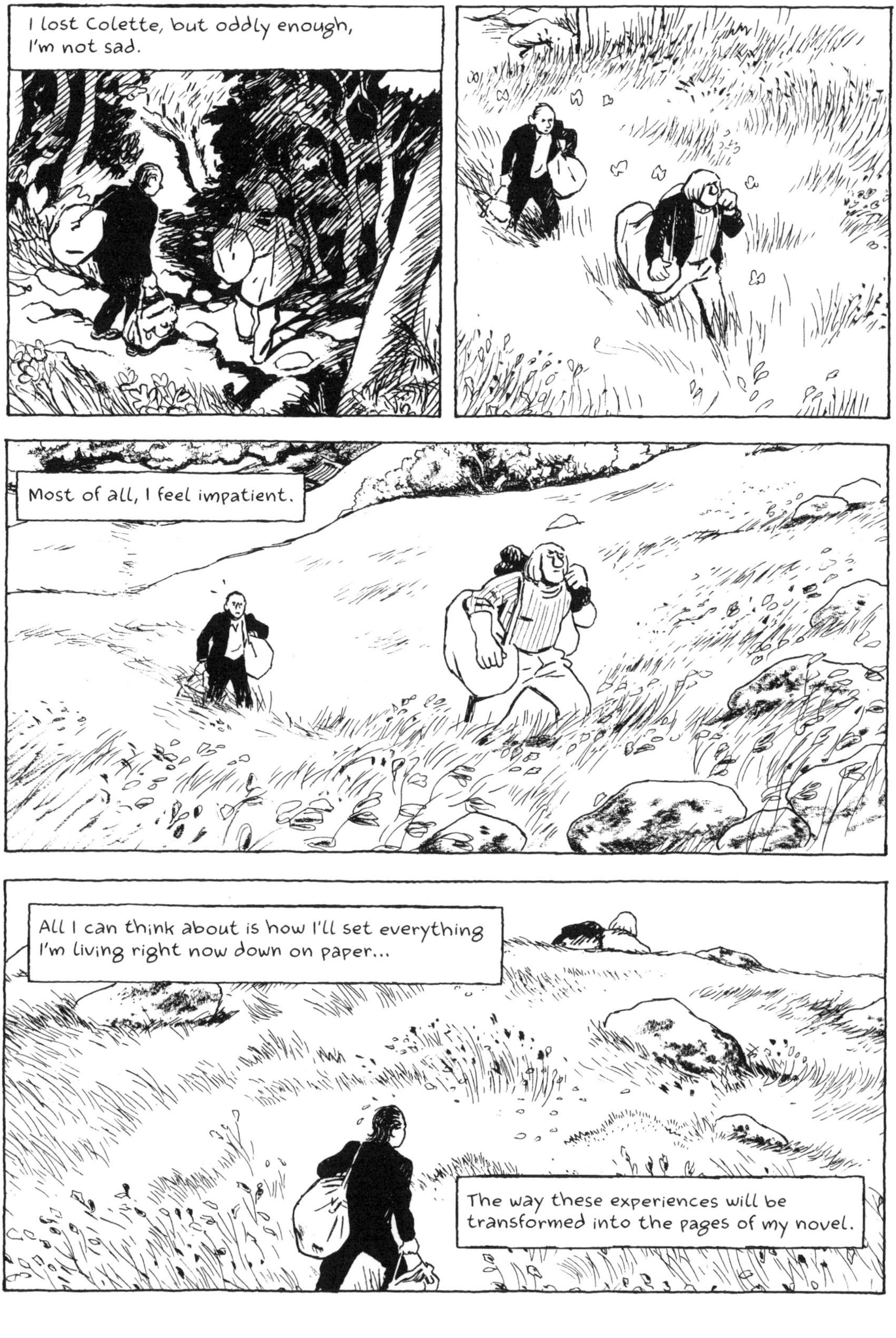
I lost Colette, but oddly enough, I'm not sad.
Most of all, I feel impatient.
All I can think about is how I'll set everything I'm living right now down on paper...
The way these experiences will be transformed into the pages of my novel.

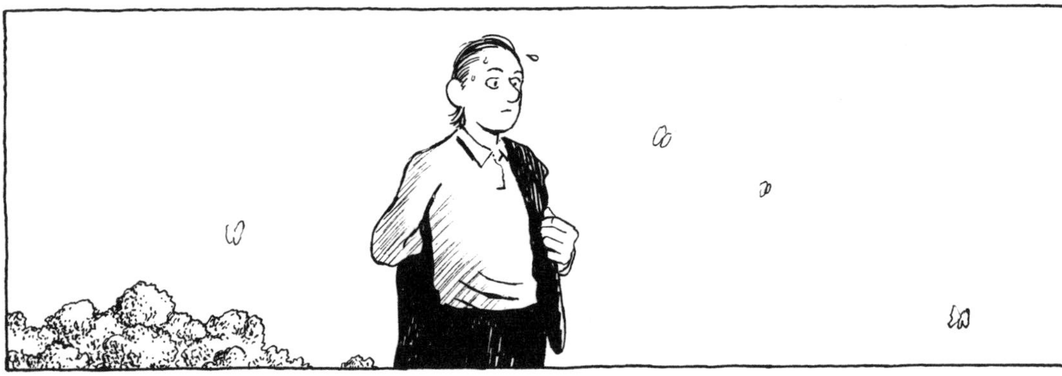

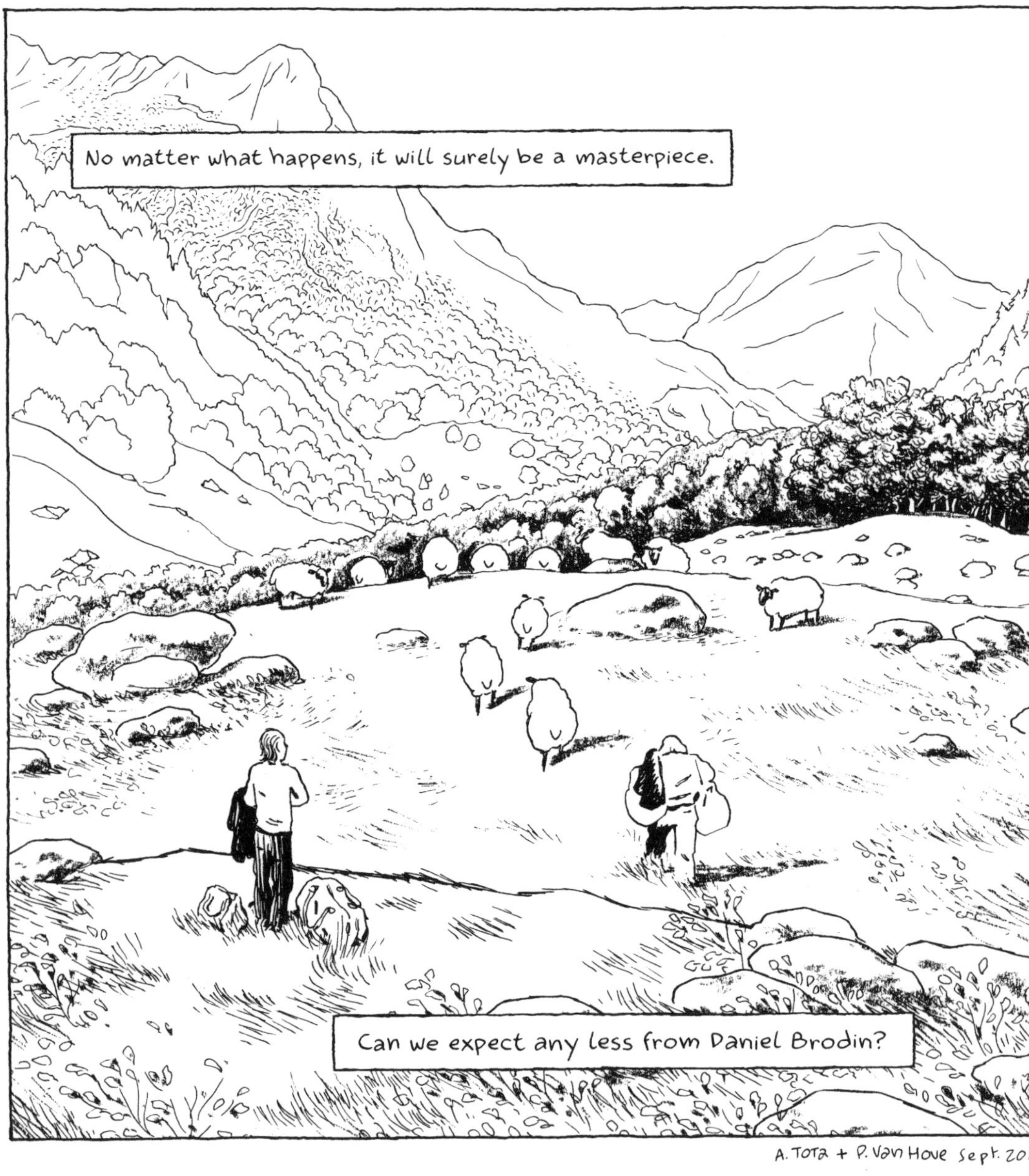
No matter what happens, it will surely be a masterpiece.
Can we expect any less from Daniel Brodin?

A. Tota + P. Van Hove Sept. 2014

With thanks to Claude; to Volker; to Igort; to *Professeur Cyclope*; to our
friends at Gatto Giallo, and Les Dents de la Poule; and to Nicolas Hubesch,
Ed van der Elsken, Jean-Michel Mension, Leonardo Rizzi;
and to drinkers everywhere.
Thanks, too, to Yoan Minet for the typeface.

The authors